Teaching Movement & Dance

Other Movement and Dance Materials by Phyllis S. Weikart

BOOKS

Teaching Movement & Dance: Intermediate Folk Dance

Round the Circle: Key Experiences in Movement for Children

Movement Plus Music: Activities for Children Ages 3–7

Movement Plus Rhymes, Songs, & Singing Games

RECORDS AND CASSETTES

Rhythmically Moving 1–9

Changing Directions 1–4

Rhythmically Walking

VIDEOTAPES

Folk Dances Illustrated 1–3

Fitness Over Fifty

Note: The *Rhythmically Moving 1–9* series of records/cassettes contains the music for the movement activities presented in *Round the Circle, Teaching Movement & Dance: A Sequential Approach to Rhythmic Movement,* and *Movement Plus Music: Activities for Children Ages 3–7.* The *Changing Directions 1–4* series of records/cassettes contains the music for the folk dances described in *Teaching Movement & Dance: Intermediate Folk Dance*.

THE HIGH/SCOPE® PRESS

A division of the High/Scope® Educational Research Foundation
Ypsilanti, Michigan

P H Y L L I S   S.   W E I K A R T

Teaching Movement & Dance

Third Edition, Revised and Expanded

A SEQUENTIAL APPROACH TO RHYTHMIC MOVEMENT

THE HIGH/SCOPE PRESS

Published by
THE HIGH/SCOPE® PRESS

A division of the
High/Scope® Educational Research Foundation
600 North River Street
Ypsilanti, Michigan 48198
(313) 485-2000

First Edition 1982. Third Edition 1989.

Library of Congress Cataloging in Publication Data: LC 89-11196

ISBN 0-929816-03-X
Printed in the United States of America

10   9   8   7   6   5

To my family

Contents

Tables and Figures

Preface

It has been a distinct pleasure to have had the opportunity to work with persons of all ages, from preschool children to senior citizens, during my three decades as a teacher of movement and international folk dance. I have learned a great deal about people and about the teaching/learning cycle through these hands-on experiences. Helping students succeed and to feel good throughout the learning phase, has always been an important goal for me. When a student has difficulty with a task I want to know *why.* The questions I ask myself are, Is the task too difficult for the age and skill level of the student? Have I presented the task in a simple enough manner? Is the student attending to the task and trying to be successful — if not, why not? These and similar questions have guided my teaching and research over the years. At first, I attempted to answer these questions by simplifying and modifying tasks without really looking at the skill development of the student. I discovered, however, after numerous trials and errors, that unless beginners mastered the basic skills involved in rhythmic movement activities, they would not succeed, regardless of how clearly I might present the task and no matter how motivated they might be to do well.

The ability to perform rhythmic movement activities, including dance, is an important yet undervalued skill in our society. Most of us can recall occasions when rhythmic movement activities were important to us. The difficult teen years in high school are made more pleasurable if the student is comfortable on the dance floor or with other rhythmic movement activities. Students I have taught in the University of Michigan's folk dance classes and in the High/Scope summer program for teens report feeling better about themselves when they improve their rhythmic movement and dance ability. The data I have collected informally over the past ten years support the notion that attainment of rhythmic competency and comfort with movement helps students master physical skills found in sport and games, enhances students' music skills, including pitch matching, and helps students develop reading, language, and math skills.

There are a number of skills associated with rhythmic movement and life-long learning that may not develop without our assistance. These include aural and visual decoding (the attending skills), kinesthetic awareness (the understanding of what one is doing in movement), comfort with movement, awareness of body, language, space, and time in movement, balance, basic timing (beat awareness and beat competency — walking to the steady beat), and beat coordination producing overall coordination of the body and a healthy self-concept. Because many children are not as active today and because many of them have not had enough hours of "natural play" with other children in cross-age situations, their physical development may lag behind their chronological age. I see teens every summer who have the motor-skill development of six- and seven-year-olds. Yet beat competency — the ability to walk to the steady beat — is the basis for any rhythmic movement activity.

I wrote this book, now in its third edition, for all teachers of rhythmic movement activities who share my desire to assure success for their students — child or adult. Music and physical education teachers, dance teachers, preschool and elementary classroom teachers, teachers of special populations, curriculum coordinators and supervisors, persons working with older adults, and parents, will find this book useful.

I certainly do not have all the answers, and my teaching model will not guarantee universal success, but I believe we are getting much closer to solving the problems students have with movement activities. For example, we now know that if we only describe or demonstrate or offer hands-on guidance at any single point in the presentation (SEPARATE), if we break down the task into subtasks (SIMPLIFY), and if we actively engage the student in the teaching/learning cycle (FACILITATE), more students will succeed in movement activities.

I wish to express sincere thanks to all the people who have helped me over the years as I wrote and revised the information contained in this book:

• The students of all ages who have worked with me through all my trials and errors.

• The dedicated educators who have become certified and those who have become Endorsed Trainers in my Rhythmic Movement and Folk Dance Curriculum. These individuals are part of a national network committed to helping children and adults attain success academically, artistically, musically, and physically.

• My friends and colleagues who have listened patiently to my ideas, reacted, advised, reviewed chapters, and tried out the teaching sequences for this revision, with special appreciation to Gloria Abrams, to Carolyn Tower, and to my Endorsed Trainers.

• The "tiny teachers" in the first and second grades and their music teacher, Sue Lawson, with whom I had the pleasure of working for two years and from whom I learned so much.

• The many folk dance teachers in this country from whom I have had the pleasure and privilege to learn. These include Fred Berk, Sunni Bloland, Dick Crum, Andor Czompo, Eliahu Gamliel, Rickey Holden, Athan Karras, Martin Keonig, Atanas Kilarovsky, Judith and Kalman Magyar, Yves Moreau, Moshe Itzchak-Halevy, Michael and Maryann Herman, Bora Ozkok, Ken Spear, and Ron Wixman.

In addition, I am most grateful to the many professionals at the High/Scope Foundation who have offered assistance in the development of the key experiences in movement, which have been integrated into the High/Scope Curriculum. Deepest appreciation also is extended to the staff of the High/Scope Press who have contributed their time and talents unselfishly to the production of this book. Special thanks go to my editors, Polly Neill and Lynn Spencer, for their expertise, their patience, and their excellent advice. I also extend thanks to Carol Ofiara who patiently typed and re-typed this manuscript and to Linda Eckel for her excellent design.

Most especially, I thank my husband, David, daughters Cindy, Cathy, Jenny, and Gretchen, and sons-in-law Dale and Vince for their encouragement, support, and understanding over the years and for the joy I have experienced dancing with them. For my grandson, Brian, I hope all my rocking and tactile stimulation in beat will help produce a rhythmically competent young man.

Teaching Movement & Dance

INTRODUCTION
Rhythmic Movement: Keys to Success

Rhythmic movement performed to music is one of the most exciting and unifying experiences we can provide for children and adults. This book is for concerned teachers who want their students of all ages to become more comfortable with and proficient in all types of rhythmic movement activities. Children and adults who succeed in such activities are more likely to join in and enjoy dance, musical activities, and sports. They learn to appreciate the meter and rhyme of spoken language; and they have little fear of "looking silly" or of failing to perform adequately in front of others.

Opportunities for successful rhythmic movement experiences abound: in elementary classrooms, in music and physical education classes, in competitive athletics, in dance, and in exercise and recreation programs for people of all ages. These types of activities are important for the broad development of children and for the long-term well-being of adults (including senior citizens and special-needs populations).

The Elements of Rhythmic Movement

The teaching methods and activities described in the following chapters show teachers how to help beginners succeed in rhythmic movement activities, and just as important, how to assure that beginners enjoy themselves and feel comfortable throughout the process. You will learn how to lead beginners through a step-by-step, easy-to-follow sequence of movement experiences, culminating in enjoyable beginning folk dances. The book also presents the theory behind the learning process for achieving rhythmic movement competency, thus giving you an in-depth understanding of *why* as well as *how* to teach movement and dance to all age groups.

The simplest rhythmic movement activities are those in which the student performs to his or her *own* beat, not to a beat created by another person or group. Thus, we would ask a class of beginners to "MARCH 8 steps, JUMP 8 times, and then HOP 4 times on each leg," but in giving the signal to begin, we would not establish a group beat. Instead, the students would perform the rhythmic movement to their own beat. This type of rhythmic movement is evident in sports activities as well. For example, swimmers move their arms and legs in a coordinated pattern of strokes and kicks to their own beat.

Next in order of rhythmic movement difficulty are those activities in which an individual moves to an externally produced beat, either alone or in a group. For example, students who march, jump, and hop to a teacher's drum beat, or persons who perform exercise warm-ups together are performing fairly difficult rhythmic movements because they must move to an externally produced beat. Dancing in a group to music is another example of an activity requiring persons to match their movements to an external beat.

The most difficult rhythmic movement activities are those in which participants move to an external beat they themselves produce — doing two things at once. Participating in a marching band is an excellent example of this type of activity. Singing while moving, speaking while moving, and singing while playing a hand-held or barred instrument like a xylophone are additional examples of the most difficult rhythmic movement activities.

Clearly, "rhythmic movement" describes a variety of activities that can occur in many different learning situations. In music programs, the term refers to musical activities that integrate various movement sequences; in physical education, to movement activities that use music, such as free exercise in gymnastics, figure skating, synchronized swimming, or activities that require integrated movements of the upper and lower body with or without a common beat, such as exercise warm-ups; and in the classroom, to language-based activities that involve movement, such as writing. Of course, rhythmic movement also describes all types of dance activities. In this sense, the term replaces the word "dance" when it denotes too narrow a concept or when you may want to use a less threatening term in working

with persons for whom "dance" has negative connotations. "Rhythmic movement" also can be used in place of "creative movement" if you think a particular group would be put off by "creative."

In summary, rhythmic movement requires that a person be able to use space and time effectively. The **ability to feel and indicate the beat (beat awareness)** and the **ability to walk to the beat (beat competency)** create **basic timing** ability. Beginners have to use their **basic timing** ability and build **beat coordination** skill to achieve **rhythmic competency.**

You can use the teaching progression presented in Chapter 4 to help beginners attain a basic level of rhythmic competency. Again, individuals who are rhythmically competent possess **basic timing,** which means they can (1) accurately "feel" and express beat (beat awareness) and (2) match that beat by walking to it (beat competency). Persons who possess rhythmic competency can also move with others to a common beat (**beat coordination**). You can use the other teaching progression, presented in Chapter 3, to help your students develop **comfort with movement.** In following the teaching progression, you will enable each of your students to move their bodies in a relaxed manner to their own beat and tempo. Four ways to move are specified: **nonlocomotor movement, locomotor movement, integrated movement,** and **movement with objects.** Beginners who have achieved comfort with movement and rhythmic competency are able to perform rhythmic movement.

The teaching progressions for attaining comfort with movement and rhythmic competency should be presented concurrently.

The Four-Step Language Process

Students must become actively involved in the rhythmic movement learning process so that they eventually can master movement sequences and function without a visual model. I use a **Four-Step Language Process** to encourage active learning.

The Four-Step Language Process, described in Chapter 2, is a necessary part of the teaching progression leading to the development of rhythmic competency. It therefore appears throughout the book in conjunction with suggestions for introducing rhythmic experiences ranging from simple coordination sequences to organized dance. The Four-Step Language Process, however, requires individuals to organize movement to an external beat and is therefore not part of the beginning movement experiences presented in Chapter 3. (Later in the chapter, however, the language process is used to introduce *integrated movement.*) Language is used in yet another way in beginning movement experiences — guiding the problem-solving activities presented to promote the students' aural and visual discrimination and their understanding of movement concepts. We should ask our students to use language to identify, describe, plan, and recall their movement experiences.

Working With Beginners of Any Age

I originally developed the teaching progressions leading to rhythmic competency and comfort with movement to help elementary-school children attain a level of rhythmic movement that would allow them to succeed in art, music, and physical education programs and in classroom movement activities. But the audience for these progressions has expanded to include all age groups (preschool to senior citizens) and all ability levels, including the special-needs population.

Preschoolers are not participating in as many hours of natural play activities as in previous years. Therefore, they are entering school with inadequate motor development, and this seems to be affecting their early academic ability. In *Round the Circle: Key Experiences in Movement for Children,* I address these inadequacies and offer suggestions for providing appropriate movement experiences for young children. I present eight **key experiences in movement** and suggest activities that children should have experienced by the time they enter first grade. The key experiences in movement are designed to help young children develop aural, visual, and tactile/kinesthetic decoding abilities; comfort with movement; space awareness; basic timing (including beat awareness and beat competency); beat coordination; problem-solving skills; and creative movement and language ability. These fundamental abilities are critical elements in young children's mental and physical development.

Moreover, although many older children and adults, including senior citizens, are attracted to such rhythmic activities as exercise to music, aerobic dance, and ballroom dance, they often lack the rhythmic competency and comfort with movement needed to succeed. So, I designed the activities presented in *Teaching Movement and Dance* for older children (first grade and above) and for adults using the same eight key experiences I developed for younger children, and I added another key experience involving integrated movement (see Table 4). It is important to

note that although the key experiences are very similar between the two books, the activities presented in this book are appropriate for the *older* student.

Whatever their ages, beginners need to develop certain basic skills to be successful with more complicated rhythmic activities. Working with early-elementary-aged children is easiest because children of this age are less resistant to movement activities and have not experienced repeated failures. By age eight or nine, however, children who have experienced repeated failures may be difficult students, and so may be adults who have had similar negative experiences. In such situations, teachers often must contend with students who have low self-esteem, who exhibit a pattern of misbehavior to cover up their perceived failures, and who balk at trying out movement activities for fear of repeating past failures. Such students are tense, insecure, and fall into the "I don't want to do it" syndrome. Because these attitudes are apparent in all age groups, my teaching techniques for dealing with reluctant students suit all ages.

Why do people experience failure so often in rhythmic movement activities — whether adult or child? We can all identify family members, friends, casual acquaintances and strangers who refuse to participate in rhythmic movement activities such as dance and athletics. Think of all the people you have seen standing on the edge of a dance floor watching others enjoy the music, movement, and fellowship of dancing.

Perhaps the answer to this question lies in the activities children experience in their earliest years. Some parents are not aware of the importance of providing appropriate, developmentally sequenced rhythmic activities for infants (for example, patting or stroking babies to the steady beat of music, rocking babies, bouncing babies on the knee to a beat, or playing "pat-a-cake" with them using a steady beat). Many preschool teachers are not aware of the importance of offering developmentally appropriate activities that reinforce the concept of beat and promote comfortable movement. In addition, significant changes have occurred over the last two decades in children's play activities. Television viewing consumes children's valuable play time as well as time that parents or older siblings could spend

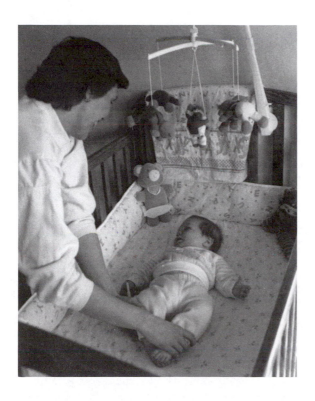

2) are too difficult for children of this age, and the children fail repeatedly when they try to do them.

The Rhythmic Competency Analysis Test and the Beat Coordination Screening Test

To test some of my assumptions, I developed the **Rhythmic Competency Analysis Test**. Initially, the test was used to determine the number of students in a group of first through third graders who could feel (identify) an underlying beat in a musical selection and the number who could walk to that same beat. Three tasks were developed to determine at what level the breakdown in a young child's rhythmic ability occurs: (1) feeling the beat; (2) organizing and repeating two non-locomotor motions to the beat; and (3) walking to the beat. The test was administered to 464 children in grades 1 – 3 over a two-month period.

Table 1 presents the findings. Results show that 61 percent (60 percent male, 63 percent female) of the first graders could accurately identify the underlying beat of the music (Task 1); 43 percent (37 percent male, 49 percent female) could coordinate two nonlocomotor motions to the beat (Task 2); but only 34 percent (26 percent male, 43 percent female) could walk to that same beat (Task 3). Test results for second graders indicate that 59 percent (57 percent male, 61 percent female) could identify the beat (Task 1); 55 percent (55 percent male, 56 percent female) could do Task 2; but only 37 percent (41 percent male, 33 percent female) could walk to the beat (Task 3). With third graders, 74 percent (72 percent male, 76 percent female) could identify the underlying beat (Task 1); 70 percent (67 percent male, 73 percent female) could do Task 2; but only 51 percent (45 percent male, 58 percent female) could walk to the beat (Task 3). When another musical selection with a different tempo was played for grades 1 – 3, the results were the same. These findings suggest two things. First, if walking to the beat of

playing with or reading to them. Passive forms of play, such as computer games, often take the place of more vigorous physical activity, such as jumping rope, swinging, using the teeter-totter, playing hop scotch, or playing language-based rhythmic games (for example, "one potato, two potato"). And finally, many of the movement activities designed by early childhood educators (grades K –

TABLE 1

**Results of Rhythmic Competency Analysis Test
Administered to Children in Grades 1 – 3**

GRADE	NUMBER	TASK 1[a]			TASK 2[b]			TASK 3[c]		
		Total %	M %	F %	Total %	M %	F %	Total %	M %	F %
1	186	61	60	63	43	37	49	34	26	43
2	165	59	57	61	55	55	56	37	41	33
3	113	74	72	76	70	67	73	51	45	58

[a]Task 1: Child identifies underlying steady beat and matches that beat by patting the top of the head with both hands.
[b]Task 2: Child identifies underlying steady beat and matches that beat by patting the top of the head and then the tops of the shoulders with both hands (one pat to each body part in a double coordinated motion).
[c]Task 3: Child walks to the underlying steady beat.

the music is one of the simplest rhythmic movement tasks, then many of the most common movement activities occurring in the early elementary grades are too difficult for children to perform successfully. Second, boys appear to have more difficulty with rhythmic movement tasks than girls do.

Does beat competency increase as youngsters mature? To answer this question, a modified form of the Rhythmic Competency Analysis Test was administered to 301 students in grades 4 – 6, and to 90 teens in two High/Scope summer workshops for gifted and talented teens (aged 13 to 18). The results of this test, shown in Table 2, point to differences in male/female success rates. (The modification omitted Task 2, which involved organizing and repeating two nonlocomotor motions to the beat. It seemed unnecessary to include this task because I already had enough evidence to support my contention that the younger children would experience lower rates of success as the coordination tasks became more difficult. In addition, I did not think this activity was suitable for the older children because "touching the head, touching the shoulders" might seem to them to be something only younger children would normally do.)

TABLE 2

**Results of Modified*
Rhythmic Competency Analysis Test
Administered to Children in Grades 4 – 6
and to Teenagers**

GRADE	NUMBER	TASK 1[a]			TASK 3[b]		
		Total %	M %	F %	Total %	M %	F %
4	78	73	64	82	73	59	88
5	119	84	78	90	78	69	87
6	104	81	77	86	76	72	80
Teens #1[c]	45	96	92	100	71	62	81
Teens #2[d]	45	97	94	100	75	66	85

* Task 2 was eliminated for this age group.
[a]Task 1: Child identifies underlying steady beat and matches that beat by patting the legs with both hands.
[b]Task 3: Child walks to the underlying beat.
[c]Participants in four-week camp program, May.
[d]Participants in seven-week camp program, June – August.

I plotted the results of the Rhythmic Competency Analysis Test for all age groups to illustrate the overall performance pattern (see Figure 1). Results show that the children tested in the early elementary grades had not experienced sufficient opportunities to identify a beat or to match the beat with simple body coordinations. Fewer than two thirds of the first and second graders tested could feel the beat (Task 1); of those who could identify the beat, only about half could walk to it (Task 3). Third graders showed a slight improvement; boys and girls were about even in their ability to identify the beat and walk to it, but girls were slightly ahead. In the fourth and fifth grades, the girls moved well ahead of the boys on Task 3, and girls outperformed boys by approximately 20 percentage points in the teen sample as well. Although more than 90 percent of male teens could identify the beat (Task 1), only 62 percent (group 1 males) and 66 percent (group 2 males) could walk to the beat (Task 3). In contrast, all the teen girls could identify the beat (Task 1), and over 80 percent could walk to the music (Task 3). Why do girls consistently outperform boys in these activities? A major factor is certainly that girls have more experience with rhythmic movement activities than boys. By fourth grade, girls have participated in many activities that use beat — jumping rope, current dance fads, hand-jive — whereas boys have not engaged as much in such activities.

Since the Rhythmic Competency Analysis Test is not a practical test for most classroom situations because it can only be administered to one student at a time, I developed the easy-to-administer Beat Coordination Screening Test. (A complete

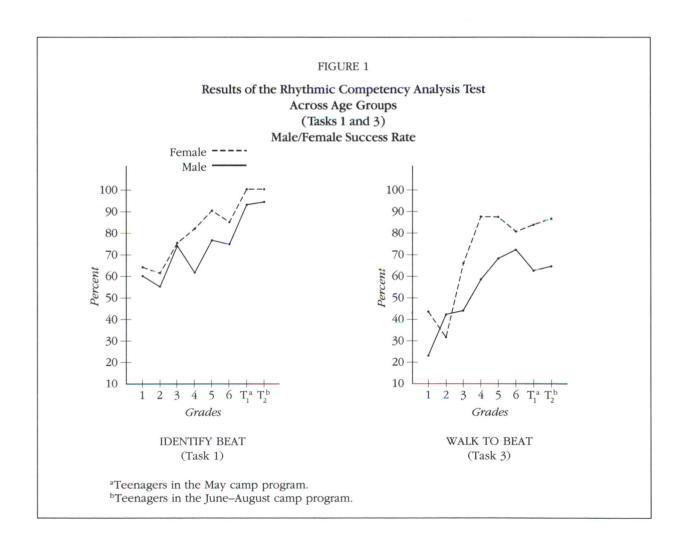

FIGURE 1

**Results of the Rhythmic Competency Analysis Test
Across Age Groups
(Tasks 1 and 3)
Male/Female Success Rate**

Female - - - - -
Male ———

IDENTIFY BEAT
(Task 1)

WALK TO BEAT
(Task 3)

[a]Teenagers in the May camp program.
[b]Teenagers in the June–August camp program.

description of this test appears in Appendix B.) This test allows teachers to quickly and simply gauge an individual's ability to be successful with beat coordination activities. (To assess the test's accuracy, I administered it to the same sample of 301 students in grades 4 – 6 and the 90 teens mentioned earlier, before I gave them the Rhythmic Competency Analysis Test. In 95 percent of the cases, those who had difficulty with the Beat Coordination Screening Test could not walk to the beat of the music.) Experienced teachers who present rhythmic activities to their classes, or who teach music, physical education, or dance, can use the Beat Coordination Screening Test to quickly assess a student's or group's beat coordination ability level.

Can teaching make a difference? To test the assumption that teaching progressions providing an ordered series of experiences help youngsters succeed in rhythmic movement activities, I arranged for students in a combined first and second grade class to be given the Rhythmic Competency Analysis Test as part of their regular music class. When I first tested the class in early October, I found that only 55 percent of the students could identify the underlying beat in a musical selection by tapping the top of their heads with both hands, and only 22 percent could walk to the same piece of music. Three months later (January), after the class had followed these teaching progressions, I retested them: Every child could identify the underlying beat, and 77 percent of the students in the class could walk to the beat. By May, every child in the class could walk to the beat of several musical selections. Figure 2 illustrates these findings. This pattern of success was repeated in another first-grade classroom in which the teacher presented the sequenced tasks daily to students during short activity sessions.

In a related experiment, I asked one of the original groups of teens who had taken the Rhythmic Competency Analysis Test (see Table 2) to take part in a sequence of movement experiences consisting of 20 minutes of beat coordination tasks that were divided into five 4-minute blocks of "follow-the-leader" experiences and about 12 hours of beginning folk dance activities. I conducted the activities for the teens during three weeks of our four-week High/Scope summer

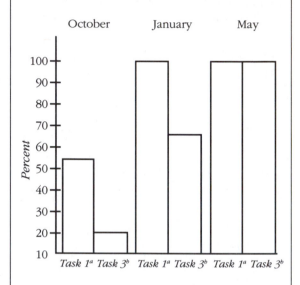

FIGURE 2

Results of Rhythmic Competency Analysis Test for Combined First and Second Grade Class (23 Children)

[a]Task 1: Child identifies underlying steady beat and matches that beat by patting the top of the head with both hands.

[b]Task 3: Child walks to the underlying beat.

workshop session. As illustrated in Figure 3, the pretest results of the modified Rhythmic Competency Analysis Test show that all the girls could identify the underlying beat (Task 1), and 81 percent of the girls could walk to the underlying beat (Task 3). Of the boys, 92 percent could identify the beat, but only 62 percent could successfully walk to it. The results of a posttest, administered at the end of the three weeks (see Figure 3), show that 95 percent of the boys and 92 percent of the girls could walk successfully to the music. (Please note that the music used for the pretest and posttest was not heard by any of the tested groups outside of the testing sessions.)

Eight years later. As I continued to work with teens each summer in the High/Scope workshop, I began to notice that fewer and fewer of them could walk to the beat. Therefore, eight years after the initial teen data were collected, I tested an-

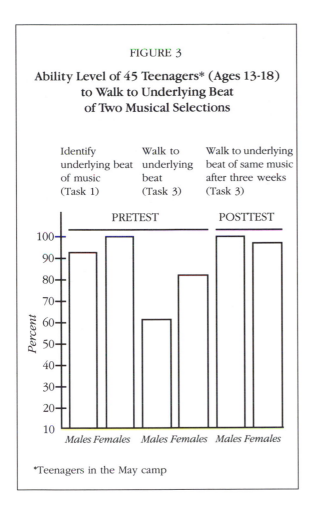

FIGURE 3

Ability Level of 45 Teenagers* (Ages 13-18) to Walk to Underlying Beat of Two Musical Selections

Identify underlying beat of music (Task 1) · Walk to underlying beat (Task 3) · Walk to underlying beat of same music after three weeks (Task 3)

PRETEST · POSTTEST

Males Females · Males Females · Males Females

*Teenagers in the May camp

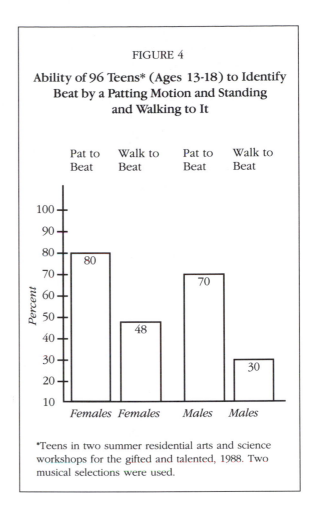

FIGURE 4

Ability of 96 Teens* (Ages 13-18) to Identify Beat by a Patting Motion and Standing and Walking to It

Pat to Beat · Walk to Beat · Pat to Beat · Walk to Beat

Females · Females · Males · Males

*Teens in two summer residential arts and science workshops for the gifted and talented, 1988. Two musical selections were used.

other group of teens; also, I altered the original Rhythmic Competency Analysis Test to create more steps of increasing difficulty. (Appendix A contains a complete copy of the revised test.) The results of the test confirmed my suspicions (see Figure 4). Each teen was asked to pat their legs with both hands, then to alternate the pat, to walk their feet while seated, to walk standing in one spot, to walk forward, and to walk backward. Of the girls tested, 80 percent could express the beat with the alternating pat (for both musical selections used for the test), but only 48 percent could walk to the beat while standing. Of the boys tested, 70 percent could pat the beat of both musical selections, and 30 percent could walk to the beat.

These additional findings also show that 85 percent of those teens who could not walk to the beat also could not visually decode an integrated

4-beat movement sequence, which was presented as many times as the subject wished to see it before trying to duplicate it. Preliminary information from a verbally presented test suggests that this group also could not accurately repeat a series of four words that were spoken once at a medium tempo.

These data suggest again that boys have more difficulty performing rhythmic movements than girls. However, my observations lead me to believe that the differences are not as great now as they were eight years ago, because, today, girls do not appear to be experiencing as many of the rhythmic activities as they did then. These male/female differences also appear to be declining in the adult populations I have been assessing informally over the past few years. **My observations and findings lead me to believe that less than half of the adults in the United States possess rhyth-**

mic competency, which means that many people are not able to enjoy a number of popular rhythmic movement activities.

The suggestion from all the findings is that beat coordination may not develop naturally as individuals mature. Nevertheless, it appears that most children and adults who lack the skills necessary to successfully engage in rhythmic movement activities can succeed if they experience a sequence of interrelated and increasingly complex beat coordination activities. Since I found the learning experiences available to foster these skills to be inadequate, I designed the teaching progressions and methods described in the following chapters to fill the gap.

How to Use This Book

This book is divided into two parts. The first part (Chapters 1 through 6) presents my approach to teaching rhythmic movement and folk dance to beginners. The approach relies on **nine key experiences in movement,** eight of which are described for the younger child in the first book in this series, **Round the Circle: Key Experiences in Movement for Children.** The ninth key experience involves **integrated movement** and is introduced in this book because it is most suitable for older beginners (second grade to adult). Table 3 illustrates how these key experiences relate to

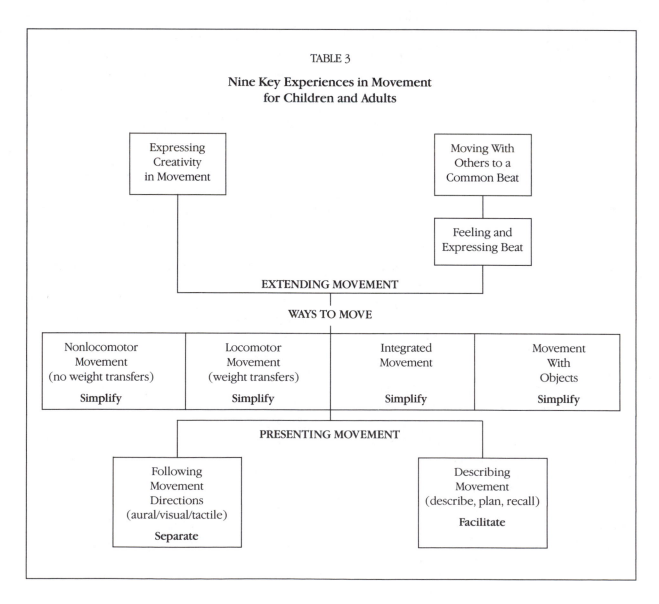

TABLE 3

**Nine Key Experiences in Movement
for Children and Adults**

- Expressing Creativity in Movement
- Moving With Others to a Common Beat
- Feeling and Expressing Beat

EXTENDING MOVEMENT

WAYS TO MOVE

Nonlocomotor Movement (no weight transfers)	Locomotor Movement (weight transfers)	Integrated Movement	Movement With Objects
Simplify	**Simplify**	**Simplify**	**Simplify**

PRESENTING MOVEMENT

- Following Movement Directions (aural/visual/tactile)
  Separate
- Describing Movement (describe, plan, recall)
  Facilitate

the information presented in the following chapters.

Chapter 1, The Teaching Model, explains the basic plan to follow in teaching all movement activities regardless of curriculum. Chapter 2, Presenting Movement and Dance Activities, discusses the two key experiences in movement a child or adult must fully understand to do a movement activity successfully. The first key experience is Following Movement Directions — being able to follow spoken directions, to imitate accurately, or to understand a movement through a teacher's hands-on guidance. The second key experience is Describing Movement — being able to identify and talk about a movement being performed, to plan the movement before it occurs, or to recall the movement after doing it and associate the movement with a descriptive word, SAY & DO. The next four key experiences in movement are presented in Chapter 3, Ways to Move: A Teaching Progression Leading to Comfort With Movement. These four key experiences involve four major

types of movement: **nonlocomotor movement, locomotor movement, integrated movement, and moving with objects**. Chapter 4, Extending Movement Activities, contains a section on **creative movement** in which the seventh key experience, Expressing Creativity in Movement, is presented. Most of the chapter, however, is devoted to a description of **rhythmic competency** that includes a review of the last two key experiences, Feeling and Expressing Beat and Moving With Others to a Common Beat. The teaching progression for beat coordination is also presented in Chapter 4. Chapter 5 contains the rationale for focusing on international folk dance and offers suggestions for presenting introductory folk dances. Chapter 6 describes how teachers can successfully present folk dance to beginners. Part Two of this book contains complete descriptions of 119 folk dances. These dances are appropriate for beginners from age six to adulthood (including senior citizens and special-needs populations).

Part One

A Sequential Approach to Rhythmic Movement

The Teaching Model: 1
Separate, Simplify, Facilitate

The ease with which children or adults grasp movement activities is often the result of the way teachers present the activity. Before presenting movement activities, we should consider whether the activity is developmentally appropriate for the age group being taught by asking ourselves if we have accurately assessed the skill level of the group. Does the group possess the prerequisite experiences and/or coordination needed to be successful? Have we planned our presentations so that *all* the students will experience at least partial success? (They still may need more experience or practice to be completely successful.) Are the stu-

dents attending to and engaged in the learning process, or are their thoughts elsewhere?

The Teaching Model described here will help teachers from any discipline present activities to both children and adults. Teachers in physical education and dance, music, classroom, special education, and recreation are using the model successfully. Persons I have trained in my workshops and institutes report that their students (both children and adults) do better when the model is followed. Several parents also have reported using the model successfully to increase their children's skill in movement activities.

The Teaching Model can be used to present all types of movement-based activities. Physical education activities, of course, have a movement base. Music activities, too, involve movement — consider the movements involved in fingering an instrument, holding and manipulating an instrument such as the maracas, or playing an instrument by using mallets. In art, using paint brushes, drawing pencils, scissors, clay and sculpture materials requires some type of movement. Tasks using movement in the elementary curriculum include writing with a pen or pencil, manipulating concrete objects in math activities, and reading aloud. For children to experience success, teachers should be consistent in their approach to presenting learning experiences that involve movement.

The Teaching Model has three major components:

● **Separate** — use only one presentation method at a time, e.g., demonstrate a movement *without* describing it at the same time.

● **Simplify** — break down the activity into a series of basic tasks that culminate in a successful movement experience.

● **Facilitate** — encourage students to think (rather than just to respond) by asking appropriate questions to stimulate their thinking.

These three components are expanded upon below.

Separate

There are three methods for presenting movement activities to a student: *demonstration, spoken directions,* or *hands-on guidance.*

When students work with a new movement or are introduced to a movement sequence, it is easier for them to respond to one method at a time. The teacher should use just a demonstration, just spoken directions, or just hands-on guidance. If we use two or more presentation methods simultaneously, our students have to integrate too much information. (Please note: We probably *would* use two or three of the methods in our presentations, but we would use only one of them at a time.) The next chapter, Presenting Movement Activities, includes a section on the key experience, Following Movement Directions, that expands on this concept.

Demonstration

Actively engage the students by asking them to watch for something specific, such as "Watch what my arms are going to do" (verbal start-up). Then continue by demonstrating the movement, but *do not talk* during your demonstration.

Spoken Directions

Say to your students, "Please listen and follow my directions." Then continue with a description of the task but *do not demonstrate* during the description. After you have given a series of directions, ask your students to tell you what they are going to do first, second, and so on, before they actually begin the activity.

Hands-on Guidance

Say to a student, "I'm going to straighten your arms and then bend them" (verbal start-up). Without speaking, proceed to straighten and bend the student's arms but *do not talk* during the hands-on guidance. Before using this method, describe it to your students and ask each of them if it is permissible to touch them in this way.

Simplify

To simplify, consider the task to be performed. If the task involves a sequence of two or more movements, you may be able to divide it into smaller, more manageable units. If you are going to ask your students to synchronize their movements, allow time for everyone to practice in their own tempo first — I call this "trying it on for size."

If the task involves an object, such as a ball, a musical instrument, or a pencil, try presenting it first without the object to establish the movement. If the task requires the correct use of right and left sides, let the students first try the task on either side and then try it on the opposite side, before having everyone use the correct side. If the task involves the use of a rhyme or song, have the students develop the sequence of movements first, before adding the words and melody.

The following guidelines will help you break down a movement sequence to its simplest tasks:

● A *static movement* (one that involves a stopped movement, such as placing both hands on the shoulders) is simpler than a *dynamic movement* (one that involves continuous movement, such as patting the shoulders).

● A movement in which the arms or hands touch the body is easier than one in which they do not, because the latter does not have a tactile endpoint.

● Movement of the upper body is usually simpler than movement of the lower body.

• Movement of the trunk is easier than movement of the limbs. Movement of the limbs is easier than movement of the fingers.

• Gross-motor movements are usually easier than fine-motor movements.

• Most nonlocomotor movement (no weight transfer) is easier than locomotor movement (weight transfer). Nonlocomotor or locomotor movement using *either* the arms *or* the legs is easier than integrated movement that involves using both the arms and legs at the same time.

• Movement without objects is easier than movement with objects.

• *Bilateral movements* (movement of paired body parts — two hands, two legs) are easier to do than moving one side of the body several times followed by moving the other side several times; but moving body parts on one side at a time is easier than alternating movements from side to side.

• *Symmetrical movements* (paired body parts moving in the same way) are easier than *asymmetrical movements* (paired body parts moving in different ways).

• Single movements are easier than sequenced movements (two or more movements in a row). Most sequenced movements are easier to do than continuously changing movements.

• When moving in groups, using *personal space* (the area around the body available as one engages in movement while remaining in one spot) is easier than using *general space* (the area available when one moves about the room).

• Movement without a partner or group beat is easier than movement timed with a partner or group beat.

• Movement alone without a specified beat is easier to do than movement alone to a specified beat.

• Nonlocomotor movement to a slower beat is easier than nonlocomotor movement to a faster beat.

• Locomotor movement to a beat that is close to the student's internal tempo is easier than locomotor movement to a beat that is either faster or

slower than the student's natural tempo.

Here are some specific examples of how tasks can be simplified:

• A two-movement task, such as PAT, CLAP or OUT, IN, can be introduced as two separate movements before the two movements are done in sequence. (Please note: The entire sequence may be tried first to see if the students can succeed without simplification.)

• A four-movement task, such as OUT, IN, UP, DOWN, can be introduced and rehearsed as two separate movement sequences: First practice the OUT, IN, then practice the UP, DOWN; then put the whole task together, remembering the "try-it-on-for-size" concept.

• An *integrated movement* (purposefully combining arms and legs with a combined movement) can also be introduced first as two separate movements. Introduce the locomotor leg movement first, because it is the most difficult, then add the nonlocomotor arm movement to it (if it is a logical extension of the locomotor movement). But if the tasks do not mesh easily, do the locomotor movement alone, then the nonlocomotor arm movement alone, and then show how they fit together.

• Movement with an object, such as a jump rope or a recorder, should be rehearsed first without the object. The timing of the movement should be well established before the object becomes part of the routine.

Facilitate

It is not enough that your students simply execute a movement task you have introduced to them; it is just as important that the students fully comprehend what they are being asked to do. To stimulate this level of student awareness, ask leading questions about the task and encourage your students to *think* about what they are doing. Ask them to talk about or to re-enact the task after you present it. Students who can accurately recall a movement in these ways fully understand it. In these situations, consider yourself to be a *facilita-*

tor — asking leading questions to increase the students' comprehension of what they are being asked to do. For young children, such questions may call for the identification of the body part that is being touched or moved, or an action that is under way. In questioning older children and adults, you can ask them several types of questions. For example, ask them to describe a movement as they perform it, or to describe a movement being demonstrated; ask them to plan what they are going to do, whether it is a movement based on your spoken instructions or a movement they have created; or ask them to recall a movement they have just performed. The next chapter, Presenting Movement Activities, includes a section on the key experience Describing Movement that expands on the information presented here.

The types of questions you can ask your students can be organized as follows, from least to most thought-provoking:

1. **Questions that have a yes/no or correct answer.** While this type of question is useful on occasion, it should not be used exclusively. Example: "Where did we put our hands [legs]? Did they get there at the same time?"

2. **Questions that are thought-provoking because students are making a choice between or among various movement concepts.** Example: "Did you move your arms quickly or slowly? Did you move in a straight, curved, or zigzag pathway?"

3. **Questions that have no correct answer or that require a choice between or among solutions given *(divergent questions)*.** Such queries require the child or adult to think through the process and to use language. Example: "How did you move your body? Tell me how you moved across the room."

Summary

When you use this Teaching Model, you will be able to help your students achieve higher levels of performance. They will understand movement tasks better as they think through each movement process and then describe the process in some way. In brief, the elements of the Teaching Model are (1) **separate** — use only one presentation method at a time (only demonstrate or only describe or only provide hands-on-guidance); (2) **simplify** — break the task down into its simplest components (subtasks) and give the students enough time to do each subtask; (3) **facilitate** — ask leading questions about the task that will enable students to fully understand what they are doing.

Presenting Movement and Dance Activities 2

Teachers should present movement and dance activities in ways that help the students perform them successfully and without fear of failure. In this chapter, I offer specific presentation strategies that are directly related to two of the movement key experiences presented in the Introduction: **Following Movement Directions** and **Describing Movement**. These key experiences will help your students (1) understand which movement you wish them to do and (2) understand what their bodies are doing, plan the movement they are going to do, recall the movement once it is completed, and link single actions to single words. The goals for the student are as follows: increased accuracy in visual and auditory discrimination, and attention to the "feel" of the movement, increased attention-span and concentration, increased kinesthetic (movement) awareness, increased ease in using language, and enhanced thinking skills. If you adopt the Separate, Simplify, and Facilitate methods that compose the Teaching Model presented in Chapter 1, you will be able to help students acquire these skills.

Over the years, I have informally collected data on these issues from several age groups. The data reveal two problems that confront teachers who present movement and dance activities. The data indicate that children and adults who cannot walk to an external beat are 85 times more likely to have visual and aural decoding problems. And since only about half of our population can walk to an external beat, as indicated from my testing and the data collected informally by my trainers, we need an effective teaching method that will help more students achieve success.

When we present movement and dance activities, we must choose a specific type of movement. Our choices fall into four major movement categories: (1) **nonlocomotor movement** (without weight transfers); (2) **locomotor movement** (with weight transfers); (3) **integrated movement** (combination of nonweight transfers with weight transfers that occur at the same time); and (4) **moving with objects**. *Round the Circle: Key Experiences in Movement for Children* contains chapters on three of these major movement categories that are geared to the younger child: nonlocomotor movement, locomotor movement, and moving with objects. Since integrated movement is most suitable for older students (second grade and above), it is presented in Chapter 3 with the three other movement categories in terms of the needs of older children and adults.

Once we select a movement focus and break the activity down or simplify it into subtasks, we need to decide how to present it. It is important that we introduce movement activities to our students with easy-to-follow directions presented visually, or verbally, or by using hands-on guidance. Then, to actively involve the students in the learning process, we must pose questions that make them think about and describe the movement they are performing. The various methods of presenting movement activities are explored next.

Key Experience: Following Movement Directions

Perhaps the most critical stage in presenting movement activities is the introduction. It is at this point that we either win students over or turn them off. That is why I focus first on the movement key experience Following Movement Directions. It is essential that those of us who teach movement and dance use only one presentation method at a time when introducing a movement activity. Of course, we will use all of the methods at various times, but using two simultaneously creates too much sensory input for our students. Remember, if you give verbal directions *without moving,* or demonstrate the movement *without talking,* or use hands-on guidance *without talking,* you will make it easier for your students to successfully execute a movement.

A description of the **Stages of Aural, Visual, and Tactile/Kinesthetic Decoding** is presented next. In progressing through these developmental stages, your students will learn how to follow your movement directions successfully. By the time children enter second grade, they should be able to progress easily through the first five stages but they should not attempt the final two stages until second grade. (These stages are also presented in *Round the Circle* where they are specifically designed for teachers working with young children.)

Many children in the upper elementary grades, as well as many adults, have not mastered these simple skills, because they have never been taught to process movement information accurately. Following a review of the Stages of Aural, Visual, and Tactile/Kinesthetic Decoding are some guidelines for introducing the stages as well as some recommended activities for the older child or adult. If some of the terms are not familiar, please refer to the Glossary.

Stages of Aural, Visual, and Tactile/Kinesthetic Decoding

The student moves one hand or both hands or one leg or both legs in a single or sequenced motion.

Stage 1: Single Bilateral Symmetrical Movements

At this, the easiest stage, the students move both hands or both legs in a single motion, after which the motion is identified.

Spoken direction method (aural decoding). Without demonstrating, say "Put your arms in front of you." Wait for the group to respond and then say "Move your feet apart."

Visual demonstration method (visual decoding). Without speaking, put both your arms overhead. After the group responds, turn the toes of both feet in. To continue this process, you could place both your hands on your waist.

Hands-on guidance method (tactile/kinesthetic decoding). Without talking, move the student's arms or legs to one location and stop. After the student identifies the placement, encourage him or her to repeat the movement alone. Note: Be certain to ask permission to touch the student.

Stage 2: Single Predictable Alternating Movements

The student moves one side of the body (i.e., one hand or one leg) and then the other side, doing the same thing.

Spoken direction method (aural decoding). Say "Put *one* arm out to the side." Pause and then say "Put the *other* arm out to the side." The students respond to each direction after it is given. Wait for the group's response before giving the next direction.

Visual demonstration method (visual decoding). Place one hand on your hip. After the group duplicates the movement *with either hand,* place your other hand on your other hip.

**Hands-on guidance (tactile/kinesthetic decod-

ing). Move one side of the student's body to one location and wait for the student to identify it. Then move the other side to the same location. Encourage the student to repeat the movement. You may wish to ask which side they want to move first.

Stage 3: Single Asymmetrical Movements

The student moves both sides of the body together or separately, but to different places or positions.

Spoken direction method (aural decoding, alternating movement). Say "Put *one* hand on your knee." After the group responds, say "Put the *other* hand on your shoulder." To continue, you could say "Put *one* hand on your chin. Put the *other* hand in the air." (Note the use of *one* and *other* rather than right and left, and the use of one direction at a time.)

Visual demonstration method (visual decoding, bilateral movement). *Simultaneously* place one hand in front of your body and the other hand out to the side. After the group copies this movement, *simultaneously* move both hands to two different locations. (Note that both hands arrive at the location at the same time.)

Hands-on guidance method (tactile/kinesthetic decoding, bilateral movement). Simultaneously or one at a time, place the student's hands on the chin and on the knee and encourage him or her to identify and repeat the movement. If using one at a time, you may wish to ask which side the student wants to move first.

Stage 4: Single Asymmetrical Tracking Movements

The student moves a body part, on one side of the body, from one location to another and then moves the same body part, on the other side of the body, from its location to a new location.

Spoken direction method (aural decoding). Say "Move the arm in front of you to your shoulder." After the group responds say "Move the hand at your waist to your knee." (Note that it does not matter which hand is in each location.)

Visual demonstration method (visual decoding). Place your hands in two different locations, such as one at the waist and one above the head. Then move your hand from above your head to a new location, such as your ear, and *wait for the group to copy*. Then move your other hand from your waist to out in front of your body and wait for the group to copy. The students respond to a specific tracking movement by choosing the "correct" body part (by its location, not by right and left) and moving it to a new location.

Hands-on guidance method (tactile/kinesthetic decoding). Move a body part on one side of the student's body from one location to another and ask him or her to identify which body part was moved and what the new location is. Then move the body part on the other side to a new location. You may wish to ask which side they want to move first.

Stage 5: Sequenced Bilateral Symmetrical Movements

The student moves paired body parts to one location and then moves them again to a new location (e.g., both hands are placed on the head and then the shoulders). Once the student is comfortable with short, easy sequences, add more movements to the sequence to make it more complex. You can also add alternating and asymmetrical sequences.

Spoken direction method (aural decoding). Say "Put your hands on your waist and then on your shoulders." Wait for the response before giving two more directions. The student waits for both directions to be given.

Visual demonstration method (visual decoding). Put both hands on one body part and then on another body part, such as the hands on the shoulders, then on the knees, *before* the group copies the sequence of two movements.

Hands-on guidance method (tactile/kinesthetic decoding). Place the student's hands in one place, then follow by placing them in another (such as both hands on the ears, then on the chest) before asking the student to identify and/or imitate the movement.

The students should become comfortable with the movement or movement sequence and should not be concerned with "doing it right." With a little practice, older children should move through the first five stages fairly easily. It is important to progress through the stages often and to encourage individual students to be the leader.

Stage 6: Mirroring (Visual) and Correct Right/Left (Verbal)

This stage is appropriate beginning in second grade, because it requires that the student integrate two concepts at the same time — the correct

movement and the correct side of the body. It often helps to begin with the type of movements found in Stage 2, but then to specify a correct side.

Spoken direction method (aural decoding). Say "Put your right hand at your waist." Wait for the group to respond and then say "Put your left hand in front of you."

Visual demonstration method (visual decoding). As you put your left arm to the side, the students will put their right arms to the side. Use static movements, those that stop, before dynamic movements, those that require the group to continually track.

Hands-on guidance method (tactile/kinesthetic decoding). Move the student's arm or leg and then ask him or her which side of the body was moved.

Stage 7: Correct Right and Left Reversal (Visual)

This stage is a visual method appropriate for students in third grade and above. The students face the teacher and respond with the same arm or leg that is used in the teacher's demonstration. They must reverse the visual image to produce the correct (right/left) side of the body.

Visual demonstration method (visual decoding). Face the group and raise your right arm over your head. The group should respond with the right arm.

Guidelines for Introducing the Various Decoding Stages

1. **Use only one presentation method at a time.** Either describe *or* demonstrate *or* guide, but do not do two simultaneously.

2. **Use static movements or slow tracking.** The first four stages as well as Stages 6 and 7 use static movement, movement that stops and that the group follows; Stage 5 requires the student to track a sequence of movements. Static movements are much easier to follow than dynamic movements, which require tracking. The demonstration should be slow and the spoken directions should be simple.

3. **Make the movement age-appropriate.** Many older children need to experience the more basic stages, but teachers should present them in an age-appropriate manner. Work more with the hands off the body to increase students' space awareness. To increase students' lower-body coordination, use the legs more often, especially in a seated position.

4. **Keep the movement simple.** Do not make the process more difficult just because the audience consists of older children and adults. Begin each sequence with several Stage 1 movements so the group experiences immediate success and then proceed to the more difficult stages. Remember, it is important to suggest age-appropriate movements while working on something that may be necessary developmentally but that is below the chronological age of the group.

5. **Move slowly.** The skill of the group will dictate how quickly you can move from one verbal, visual, or tactile direction to another. The tendency is to move too quickly, which diminishes

the usefulness of the activity for those who really need it.

6. **Ask questions (facilitate).** It is important for the students to think and to use language, which is part of the decoding process. All the students can answer at once or students can volunteer individually.

7. **Avoid giving right/left or mirroring directions while working on Stages 1 – 5.** The purpose of these early stages is to help students of all ages respond quickly and easily so that they become comfortable with movement. Integrating two concepts at once, movement and correct side, is much more difficult than responding with movement only. Mirroring and correct right and left sides should not be expected until second grade.

8. **Keep the time blocks short when working on the stages.** The simple, static and dynamic movements used in the stages help individuals respond more easily and naturally. If used as a drill, the group may become bored and inattentive.

9. **Have fun with the group.** Think of yourself as a participant with the group. Be a little silly occasionally and use funny movements or movements that require balance.

10. **Develop strategies that set the group up to succeed with the more difficult stages.** Before giving specific verbal directions for one side of the body, say "Now listen carefully to which side of the body you are to use for the movement." Precede the correct visual demonstration with a statement such as "Watch for which hand I am going to use."

11. **Add music often.** As music is added be certain the music is **instrumental**, because vocal music is distracting. Any of the instrumental music on the *Rhythmically Moving 1 – 9* or *Changing Directions 1 – 4* series of records/cassettes is appropriate for introducing these stages.

12. **Encourage the students to assume leadership.** Being the leader promotes the development of a sense of independence and initiative in students of all ages. Progressing through the decoding stages should not be perceived as a teacher-directed process; your students will enjoy

being leaders and will become very skilled in the process.

When to Use the Stages and for How Long

In special classes, such as art, music, or physical education, a good time to use the stages is at the beginning or end of the class, for one or two minutes. At the beginning, these activities focus the students' attention on the task, and at the end of the class, they exert a calming influence on the group. Leading visually can also be used to replace such familiar directives as, "May I have your attention?" "Shhh." "Listen now." Transition times in the classroom are good times to involve the students in a brief movement activity. I often use a short right/left reversal (Stage 7) warm-up in adult dance classes because the circle formation constantly requires students use this technique, if they are across from the teacher.

Additional Activities That Use Visual or Verbal Processing

The following activities may be used in addition to the follow-the-leader ideas described in Stages 1 – 7.

1. Statues

● **Make a statue that the others in the group copy.** Your first statue should not require specific mirroring or right/left directions. Ask the partici-pants to talk about the placement of each part of the body.

● **Have the group work in pairs.** One partner makes the statue while the other copies it from any angle (e.g., facing same way, from behind, and so on). Suggest that they copy the statue part by part and talk about the placement of each part as they copy.

● **Have the group work in pairs and build statues.** Give verbal directions for the placement of each part of the body in the statue.

● **Have the group work in pairs and mirror the statue the leader makes.** Also have them re-verse the statue using the same arm and leg as the statue maker while facing the statue.

● **Have the statue makers keep a beat in one part of the body.** Suggest to those copying that they add the beat as the last thing copied in their statue. Play instrumental music for keeping the beat.

● **Have the group work in pairs to a beat.** One person, keeping beat, makes the statue while the partner moves about the space, walking to the beat, until the music stops. The partner returns to copy the statue and to keep the beat. See if all your students can keep the beat even though the music is no longer playing.

2. Line Scores and Visual Shapes

● **Draw or hold up a card with a stick figure drawn on it. Have the students copy.** Instead of an identifiable shape the drawing can be a series of lines (straight, curved, and zigzag) that the stu-dents trace with different parts of the body, or have the students walk the pattern of the lines.

3. Verbal Directions

● **Give the students a series of movements to perform, such as "Walk 4 steps in a straight line, then jump 3 times in a zigzag pattern."** Following the directions say "What are you going to do first? Second?" Vary this activity by asking the students to decide on three different movements. After they have been given a minute to think, say "What are you going to do first? Second? Third?"

● **Tell a story and have the students act out the story.** You could vary this activity by performing a sequence of movements that can tell part of a story and asking the students to make up a story from the movements. Then you could complete the story.

Key Experience: Describing Movement

When any movement activity is presented, the group should be able to describe it by integrating the information and acting on it, in addition to simply following movement directions presented by the teacher using one of the methods described earlier. Since language is a natural bridge to movement, it can make the learning process an active learning experience for the participants. My observations indicate that individuals who do a movement demonstrated by someone else often *do not understand what they are doing;* they are only copying the leader's actions. Likewise, many students who are told what to do often do not pay close attention to the directions and therefore cannot act on the instructions. By using language as a bridge to movement, we can help students increase their understanding of movement concepts. (Later in this chapter you will learn about my SAY & DO method designed just for this purpose.)

Four types of active learning methods are useful in movement. The first and easiest method requires that students **talk about the movement while they perform it. (Please note: The recipient of the directions should not be confused with the presenter of the directions. The presenter *does not* describe and do.**) The second method requires the student to **precede the movement with thought**, that is, to *plan* the movement before doing it. The third requires the student to **think about the movement while doing it**, and then to *recall* it **and describe it afterward** *without* **repeating the movement**. The final method **links one word with each part of the movement, to SAY & DO**. When linked together, the thought directs the movement. Each of these methods is described below, with examples.

Talking About Movement While Doing It

Elementary-age children are exploring different ways to move in straight pathways. The teacher asks the children to describe the different ways they are moving by saying, "Each time you change the way you are moving talk out loud about it. Be sure you are using sentences. What type of pathway are we all going to use?" After a short time, the teacher says, "Who would like to share one of the special ways you moved in a straight pathway?" Eric volunteers and the teacher says, "While Eric is moving, who would like to describe what he is doing?"

Describing while doing takes on two characteristics as illustrated in the scenario above. Students describe while they are doing or describe while someone else is demonstrating. The latter is a little more abstract, since the students who are talking are not doing, but it is an important element in describing movement. This latter abstraction is appropriate for children in second grade and above. Younger children at first need to *do* what they are describing.

The teacher **separates** by giving only verbal directions. You act as the **facilitator** by asking the questions and remaining interested in the answers, even though all your students may be talking at once. In addition, you facilitate the beginning of the task by asking the children what type of pathway they are going to use rather than giving the verbal instruction again, or assuming that all the children were paying attention at the time the original instruction was given.

Talking while doing is the easiest method of describing movement because the task is so concrete. Students who are not asked to think may merely be functioning at a subconscious level. Giving students an opportunity to use language increases their language development. Asking for sentences, rather than single words, increases their language production. If students do not know what they are doing, there is little likelihood you can successfully extend the movement activities to more difficult sequences.

Suggested Activities:

1. The students are exploring ways they can

balance with a different number of body parts touching the floor. The teacher says, "Fred, what parts of your body are touching the floor?" The class is asked, "What parts of Fred's body are bent and what parts are straight?"

2. The music teacher prepares the students to play octaves with two mallets on xylophones or similar instruments. She has them use their legs or the floor outside their legs as their bars to prepare the movement. She says to the group, "As you play each octave please identify the letter name of the octave you are playing."

3. The physical education teacher has the students moving through an obstacle course. The instructor says to the students, "As you approach each task in our obstacle course say what you are doing as you do it." (The tasks consist of going over, going under, going around, going between, going outside of objects so the students are working with these concepts as well as performing the tasks.)

Planning the Movement Before Executing It

The teacher asks the children to plan a locomotor movement to demonstrate the solution to a math problem. The teacher says, "Without doing it, tell me what locomotor movement you are going to use and in what direction you will move. Is the movement going to be performed quickly or slowly?" The teacher then gives the problem, "Two times five minus six."

In the above scenario, the teacher uses verbal instructions to start the activity and provides the students with choices as to which movement they will select. He or she asks the children to verbalize their plan before they are given the problem, a step that is often omitted. If the students are given a choice, the teacher acts as facilitator by asking for their plan. As an alternative, the teacher could ask individual students to volunteer their plans.

It is more difficult to think through a movement without simultaneously acting it out, than to describe the movement while doing it. The thought

now must come first, and the student must organize the movement to be performed. At first students may find it easier to think of only one aspect of the movement and do just that part, than to think about the entire movement before executing it.

Suggested Activities:

1. Physical education students are asked to put together four locomotor movements in a sequence of four beats. They can use one of the movements two times. The teacher gives an example of the task: step, hop, jump, hop. The students are given time to try out several sequences. Then they are asked to plan the sequence they will be using before doing the movements. Students are asked to explain their sequences by using complete sentences to describe them. Then they do their sequences. This activity can also be done with SAY & DO, a method described later in this chapter.

2. In a music class students plan a rhythm pattern they will use on an unpitched percussion instrument of their choice. Several students are asked to share their plan and then to play their pattern for the class.

3. In the classroom, students spell words by using one movement over and over for each letter. The teacher asks the children to plan a nonlocomotor movement for the task. The children first describe their movements without doing the movement. The spelling word is given after the children describe the movements.

Recalling a Movement After Executing It

After the football team learns a specific play, the coach asks the quarterback to talk about what he is going to do when the ball is snapped and asks the ends to talk about where they are going to run after the snap of the ball.

In this scenario the coach facilitates the players' understanding of the play by having them talk about the sequence of movements they will perform, rather than telling the players or reminding the players of their roles. The players must dem-

onstrate complete understanding of the play since they cannot communicate with the coach once they are on the field.

Recalling a movement or sequence of movements is more difficult than planning before the movement is executed or describing the movement while doing it. Unless the students are aware of what they are performing, it will be almost impossible to recall the movement without re-executing it. For example, have you noticed persons who, in giving driving directions, have to use their arms and change their body positions, or persons who cannot even recall well enough to give understandable directions?

Recalling the performance often helps students correct faults in that performance. The student does the movement again, concentrating on the part of the performance that is faulty. The student who steps on the right foot while throwing with the right arm can be helped more efficiently if the teacher asks him or her to say which foot is stepping as the ball is thrown. The teacher makes the child aware of the performance before trying to change the performance: "Show me which arm you are using to throw the ball. Now show me which foot you are stepping forward on." If the student cannot remember, the teacher has the student perform the task again, concentrating on which foot is stepping forward. After the task is completed, the teacher says, "Did the step occur on the same or opposite foot from the throwing hand?" The student identifies the same. The teacher now says, "Try stepping on the opposite foot as you throw the ball." In this sequence, the student is corrected without being told that he or she did it "wrong." The student recalls the performance and in the process learns the correct movement.

Most faulty motor patterns can be corrected in this manner. If the student is not aware of the way he or she performed a fingering movement on the recorder, the teacher does not just say, "Next time keep both fingers down when you play the A," or in helping a student with a tennis serve, "Next time throw the ball higher." Instead, the teacher leads the student to conscious awareness of the faulty performance through careful questioning that helps the student fully understand the problem and make the change; otherwise, the movement becomes another trial-and-error experience.

Suggested Activities:

1. Students in an art class are asked to draw a circle, a square, and a triangle on a piece of paper and to be aware of the placement of the shapes and the places they intersect. The teacher now says to the class, "Close your eyes and recall the placement of the shape and the intersection of the shapes without drawing them again."

2. Children in a classroom work with partners to make letters with their bodies. The teacher tells the children to be aware of how they make the letters. After each letter is made, one child in each pair is asked to recall, for his or her partner, how they made their letter.

3. In a physical education class, the students are paired and all are on one side of the gym or the other. The teacher asks one of the partners to begin a movement across the gym and asks the other partner to follow and copy the movement. When they reach the other side, the partner who has copied recalls the movement by describing it to the partner who initiated the movement.

Linking a Single Movement to a Single Word (SAY & DO)

The students learn a dance that is a partner mixer. Before putting on the music the teacher says, "One person in each pair tell your partner what you do in the first part of the dance. Use the Language-to-Dance Vocabulary. Now let's all SAY & DO the complete dance one final time."

In the above scenario the students both recall the movement sequence for the dance they learned and also link the movements to the words, using the **Language-to-Dance Vocabulary**, which is described more fully in Chapter 5. Linking movements to words is a very effective method of sequencing nonlocomotor movements and locomotor movements that require precise timing.

This method uses labels that are spoken in the same timing in which the movement occurs. For example, the arm pattern to be executed consists

of (1) straightening the arms in front of the body, (2) bending the arms and bringing the hands near the shoulders, (3) straightening the arms overhead, and (4) bending the arms as in (2). After practicing the movements, the students label the actions by saying "OUT, IN, UP, DOWN" as they continue the movements. They are performing with a SAY & DO. In having the students recall the movements the teacher might say, "Chant just the words of the sequence [the SAY] and when you feel comfortable add the movements [the SAY & DO]." The students are following the first two steps in the **Four-Step Language Process**. This process is described more fully below.

The Four-Step Language Process

The language process is designed to connect language (conscious thought) and movement. The four steps in the language process are:

- STEP I   *SAY*
- STEP II   *SAY & DO*
- STEP III *WHISPER & DO*
- STEP IV   *DO (THINK & DO)*

The steps should be followed at all levels of movement activity — from the simplest to the most complex. Table 4 illustrates the relationship between language and movement for each step. When a *new* movement is presented have the students practice it and then link the movement with Step I, the SAY to create the SAY & DO. When all are practicing in their own tempos encourage the students to say the words softly, WHISPER & DO, as those around them may be doing the movement faster or slower. Once this occurs and when you want everyone to perform together, begin the group with the SAY. Either you or a student can perform the movement, to give a concrete model, while the group performs with just the SAY. Encourage the students to add the movement as soon as they feel ready to do so. They now are using the SAY & DO. Move on to the WHISPER & DO and the THINK & DO, particularly if music is to be added, as these are the only two steps in the process to be used with music.

In presenting rhythmic movement activities, I recommend that teachers use the Four-Step Language Process with any age group. It is an especially important and effective technique in teaching patterns of organized dance.

Step I: SAY

In this first step the teacher asks the group to use simple descriptive labels to identify body parts,

to indicate motions, or to label locomotor movements that will be matched with those movements in the second step (SAY & DO). For example the students chant "CHIN, CHIN, CHIN, CHIN" or "PAT, PAT, PAT, PAT" or "WALK, WALK, WALK, WALK." The external beat is created by the repeated chanting of one word. No music is used for this step.

This step works most effectively after students have tried out a particular movement to their own timing and are using the SAY to create a group

---

TABLE 4

**Relationship Between Language and Movement
in the Four-Step Language Process**

Language: Body-Part Identification

		Movement
SAY	HEAD, HEAD, HEAD, HEAD	No movement
SAY & DO	HEAD, HEAD, HEAD, HEAD	Tap top of head while SAYING "HEAD"
WHISPER & DO	Same as SAY & DO, except whispered.	Same as SAY & DO
THINK & DO	Language is repeated silently.	Same as SAY & DO

Language: Action Words

		Movement
SAY	PUSH, PUSH, PUSH, PUSH	No movement
SAY & DO	PUSH, PUSH, PUSH, PUSH	Push the arms in any direction while SAYING "PUSH"
WHISPER & DO	Same as SAY & DO, except whispered	Same as SAY & DO
THINK & DO	Language is repeated silently.	Same as SAY & DO

Language: Movement Identification

		Movement
SAY	WALK, WALK, WALK, WALK	No movement
SAY & DO	WALK, WALK, WALK, WALK	Walk while SAYING "WALK"
WHISPER & DO	Same as SAY & DO, except whispered.	Same as SAY & DO
THINK & DO	Language is repeated silently.	Same as SAY & DO

Language: Dance Step

		Movement
SAY	CROSS, SIDE, BACK, SIDE	No movement
SAY & DO	CROSS, SIDE, BACK, SIDE	Execute dance steps simultaneously with language.
WHISPER & DO	Same as SAY & DO, except whispered.	Same as SAY & DO
THINK & DO	Language is repeated silently.	Same as SAY & DO

beat. This step is particularly useful as movement sequences or dance steps are practiced for group performance. Occasionally the movement is very simple and the SAY can be omitted. Special-needs groups may have difficulty expressing the exact words, but they should be encouraged to say them as well as they can.

Step II: SAY & DO

The leader asks the students to match a repetitious chant with the corresponding movements. As in Step I, no music is added. The leader begins the chant to establish the beat and tempo and adds the movement so that both the chant and movement occur simultaneously. For example, the leader chants "HEAD, HEAD, KNEES, KNEES" and then accompanies the words by touching the head with both hands two times and then the knees two times. The strategy mentioned above works well when the leader performs just the movement and the students chant the words. The students add the movement as soon as they are ready. This strategy organizes the thought and creates the tempo, before the movement is added.

Step III: WHISPER & DO

The leader asks the group to repeat Step II, but to whisper the chant. This step is used when music is playing and is a bridge to the next step when the students just think the words. Be certain students continue to verbalize the words so the thought process is maintained. My experience has shown that those who stop using the language, or who never use it at all, have difficulty performing the task with the group. This step is also used when all students are practicing together, but each to his or her own tempo.

Step IV: DO (THINK & DO)

The leader now asks the students to "think" the words while continuing the movement without music. If the students are able to "hear" the words in their heads, they will be able to maintain a consistent tempo. Otherwise, they most likely will increase the tempo unconsciously. If students practice movements using their own steady beat

and tempo, they are more apt to maintain this consistency when music is added.

The four methods of describing movement presented above should be mastered by the time a child reaches first grade, but unfortunately, many older children and adults have never had these experiences. At first, older children and adults may be surprised that they are being asked to behave in such a manner. They will not be accustomed to having movement and dance presented so simply and directly. Reassure them that this type of learning experience is the quickest and best method of helping them perform rhythmic movement successfully.

Summary

As you present movement and dance activities to your students, keep the following **key experiences in movement** uppermost in your mind: (1) **Following Movement Directions** — the ability

to comprehend and act on directions that are presented verbally, the ability to perceive and act on directions presented visually, and the ability to feel and act on directions presented with hands-on guidance; and (2) **Describing Movement** — the ability to use language to talk about the movement one is executing, to plan the movement before and to recall the movement after executing it, and to link a movement with a word using the SAY & DO method.

To help students follow movement directions, you can simplify the process by using only one presentation method at a time. To help students describe movement and to help them fully comprehend the movement, you can ask leading questions that will stimulate their thinking.

WAYS TO MOVE — A Teaching Progression Leading to Comfort With Movement 3

To succeed in rhythmic movement it is essential that students achieve **comfort with movement**, that is, the ability to move in a relaxed, comfortable manner. To achieve this type of movement, students at first must *not* be concerned with moving to an external beat; instead, they must be free to move to their own beat and tempo. Developing comfort with movement requires that students experience a variety of movement activities and have the opportunity to practice without fear of failure. The activities and teaching strategies presented in this chapter are designed to provide such opportunities and are directly related to four key experiences in movement: **Moving the Body in Nonlocomotor Ways, Moving the Body in Locomotor Ways, Moving the Body in Integrated Ways**, and **Moving With Objects**.

Comfort with movement can develop very naturally during the preschool years if children have the opportunity to play in mixed-age situations and without adult intervention. Because these opportunities are becoming increasingly scarce and because of the increased time children are devoting to television viewing, today's children are entering school with significant motor skill deficiencies. Many of them will carry these deficiencies into adulthood. They are uncomfortable when participating in movement activities, have little or no awareness of space and time concepts, are ignorant about what their bodies can do, and are unable to use language accurately to describe movement.

Because of their prolonged self-consciousness and fear of failure, older children and adults probably will experience more difficulty than younger children in developing basic movement skills as well as in learning to move comfortably in space. In my experience, many teenagers and adults are threatened by movement activities and dance because of unsuccessful experiences they had in elementary school and because of the manner in which organized after-school classes and sports activities are often presented. For example, students are often told they are moving in the wrong way, and they feel increasingly awkward and ill at ease in attempting to improve their performance; many students often are selected last for a team game; and many students are forced to be "creative" or to "be" an inanimate object, such as a tree or flower — activities they think are "dumb." In dance activities many of them feel conspicuous and are "turned-off" by having to move with a partner. The 7-year-old son of one of my assistants typified this level of self-consciousness when he prayed one night that some little girl would not ask him to dance the next day when the second graders were going to square dance in their physical education class. He told his mother he did not want to hold hands with a girl and he did not want to "touch arms."

Clearly, negative or positive feelings about movement and dance and a corresponding negative or

positive self-image are developed or at least greatly influenced by activities occurring in the primary grades. Unfortunately, many children fail or are "turned-off" before they really give movement activities a chance. If these children are the class leaders, their attitudes quickly permeate the classroom, making it that much more difficult for a teacher to create opportunities for success. In this chapter, you will learn how to avoid the pitfalls just described and how to help your students achieve comfort with movement in enjoyable, nonthreatening learning experiences.

As noted earlier, the teaching progression presented in this chapter revolves around four key experiences in movement. Three of these key experiences — **Moving the Body in Nonlocomotor Ways, Moving the Body in Locomotor Ways,** and **Moving with Objects** — are also discussed in detail in *Round the Circle: Key Experiences in Movement for Children* in relation to appropriate movement activities for preschoolers and kindergartners. The key experience labeled **Moving the Body in Integrated Ways** has been added to the teaching progression described in this chapter and is suitable for older students (second grade and above).

Guidelines for Following the Comfort With Movement Teaching Progression

1. Do *not* **use an external beat with movement activities and initial movement sequences until the students have had the opportunity to "try it on for size."** Allow the students to move comfortably without having to match their movements to a common *external* beat. (Matching movement to an external beat is a more complex activity and is discussed in Chapter 4.)

2. **Devise ways for students to be as inconspicuous as possible.** For example, have older elementary students do some movement seated in chairs, or standing behind chairs scattered about the room, or in a loose circle.

3. **Introduce activities that do not require specific use of the right or left side of the body.** If the movement is executed on one side, have the students repeat it on the other side.

4. **Present activities that do not require the students to have partners or to move in specific formations, such as a circle.**

5. **Suggest activities that allow the students to be successful because there is no right or wrong way to do the movement or to solve the problem.**

6. **Introduce activities that make use of personal space** (the area around the body when one engages in movement while remaining in the same location) **before those that use general space** (the area available when one moves about the room).

7. **Use movement and imagery activities that are age-appropriate.** *Touching parts of the body,* such as touching the head or chin or ears, is appropriate for younger children but may be perceived as juvenile by older children. *Movement away from the center of the body* (for example, reaching in all directions with the arms and legs) is more appropriate for the older children.

8. **Do not introduce a creative activity without first doing some simple problem-solving or guided exploration tasks.** The student who has not engaged in a great deal of movement exploration may have difficulty plunging right into

creative movement activities. See Chapter 4 for more information about ways in which students can express creativity comfortably.

9. **Introduce singing games, action rhymes and songs, and similar activities, by teaching the sequence of movements before adding the rhyme or song.** When we separate the movements from the rhyme or song and teach them first, our students only have to do one thing at a time. Once students learn the movements, they will be able to perform them automatically and will thus be able to concentrate on the words and/or melody.

The Comfort With Movement Teaching Progression

Key Experience: Moving the Body in Nonlocomotor Ways

Nonlocomotor movement is movement *without weight transfers* while a person remains in place. For example, it can be movement of the trunk, the

arms, the fingers, the legs, or the toes when a person is lying down, kneeling, standing or seated. Nonlocomotor movement can be executed with large (gross-motor) and small (fine-motor) movements. Nonlocomotor arm patterns are used for bouncing, tossing, or throwing a ball; in swinging a bat, golf club or tennis racket. Nonlocomotor

leg patterns are used when kicking or trapping a ball or when playing the organ. Finger or arm patterns are employed when playing an instrument, when writing, when painting, or when using tools. Nonlocomotor movement may be performed with or without objects. (See the section on Moving With Objects in this chapter.)

Nonlocomotor movement is usually easier to do than locomotor movement — movement with weight transfers — because it requires less strength, balance, and coordination.

How can nonlocomotor movement be used? Here are some ideas:

1. To help children and adults learn to follow movement directions, as described in Chapter 2.

2. To encourage language development and thinking skills when students are asked to talk about the movement (see the section on describing movement in Chapter 2).

3. To help the student develop body awareness — what each part of the body can do, what body parts can do together, and what the whole body can do.

4. To help students develop creativity through problem-solving activities, guided exploration, and imagery. (See Chapter 4 for information on expressing creativity in movement.)

5. To strengthen students' space and time awareness.

6. To help students with the following key experiences: Expressing Creativity in Movement, Feeling and Expressing Beat, and Moving With Others to a Common Beat. These key experiences are discussed in greater detail in Chapter 4.

7. To accompany locomotor movement, thus creating **integrated movement**; this concept is explored later in this chapter.

8. To do while holding objects in the key experience Moving With Objects, which is discussed later in this chapter.

Developing Body Awareness and Language Awareness Through Nonlocomotor Movement

The third graders are in groups of three and have been asked to find all the ways they can swing dif-

ferent body parts and all the positions they can use for the task. They have paper and pencils to write down their discoveries. After a few minutes each group is given an opportunity to share one of its ideas.

In this scenario the children are using non-locomotor movements to solve a problem, to work with variations of a concept, to cooperate, and to express their thoughts in writing. To encourage the students to explore various movement positions, the teacher could also ask, "Can you find a position on your side with no hands or legs touching the floor? How can you move one leg in this position? If only one foot and one hand touch the floor, what positions can you get your body into? Who would like to describe the position they are in?" In addition to identifying the possible positions for nonlocomotor movement, the children also are practicing static balance, that is, balance without movement. Good balance is an important element in attaining comfort with movement.

By the second grade most children will know the names and locations of body parts. If a group has not yet acquired this information, developing such an awareness should become one of the group's goals. The Stages of Aural, Visual, and Tactile/Kinesthetic Decoding described in Chapter 2 can be used to encourage this type of awareness.

If your students have not explored how two body parts that are the same can move together in the same way or in opposition, you could ask, "Can you move both arms together in the same way, so they go to the same place at the same time? Can you move both arms at the same time but to different places? Can you move one arm and one leg at the same time? The opposite arm and leg?"

There are eight basic categories of nonlocomotor movement: *bending, straightening, twisting, turning, swinging, rocking, curling,* and *stretching.* These categories are often grouped in four pairs:

● **Bending and straightening movements** — ways one can move the knee and elbow joints, the wrist and ankle joints, the neck, the waist.

● **Twisting and turning movements** — ways one can rotate the entire arm at the shoulder or the entire leg at the hip, the head at the neck, the spine. "Turning" implies movement that goes all the way around, whereas "twisting" is a partial rotation.

● **Swinging and rocking movements** — ways one can perform back-and-forth movements with the arms and legs or with the trunk. Rocking, sometimes referred to as swaying, is a back-and-forth movement in which there is a *partial* shift of weight and balance.

● **Curling and stretching movements** — ways one can move the fingers, toes, or entire body. The shape of a curling and stretching movement is curved, then straight.

In addition to these basic nonlocomotor movements, many action words can be explored using movement. Consider the following action words as you plan nonlocomotor movement activities: *shake, thump, pound, flick, dab, float, touch, pat.*

Developing Space and Time Awareness Through Nonlocomotor Movement

The fourth graders are working in pairs. They have been given a list of the eight categories of nonlocomotor movement and have been asked to find as many variations as they can for each movement. After a period of time the teacher asks each pair to share and has the class discuss the movement and the variations that the pair has demonstrated.

Two specific areas are involved in developing an individual's space awareness using non-locomotor movement: **spatial relationships** and **variations in nonlocomotor movement**. Specifically, a number of spatial relationships give meaning to the four nonlocomotor movement pairs of bending/straightening, twisting/turning, swinging/rocking, and curling/stretching. These spatial relationships can be viewed as *contrasting elements in movement* and may include the following:

in(side)/out(side)	*large/small*
around/through	*same/different*
on/off	*up/down*
push/pull	*high/low*
rise/fall	*over/under*
in front of/in back of	*weak/strong*
near/far/alongside	

Also, by exploring a number of variations in nonlocomotor movement, individuals can enhance their level of **space awareness** as they come to a deeper understanding of how the body is moving. They could, for example, explore these variations:

● The **direction** of the movement — whether it goes up or down, away from or toward the body, around

● The **size** of the movement — whether it is large or small (big or little)

● The **level** of the movement — usually occurring in three body regions (high, middle, or low)

● The **intensity**, or force, of the movement — whether it is strong or weak

● The **pathway** of the movement — whether it is curved, straight, zigzag (angular)

● The **shape** of the movement — whether it is wide or narrow, straight or angular, curved or round, symmetrical or asymmetrical

● The **flow** of the movement — whether it is smooth or bumpy

Moreover, all movement also requires an awareness of **time**. To develop an appropriate level of **time awareness** individuals must explore *movement variations that center around tempo and duration*. Time in movement may be thought of as

- Start/stop

- Fast/slow

- Getting faster/getting slower — a gradual increase or decrease in the tempo

- Even/uneven — movements that take the same or different amounts of time

- Sudden/sustained — abrupt, quick movements or movements that last, such as movements involved in skating

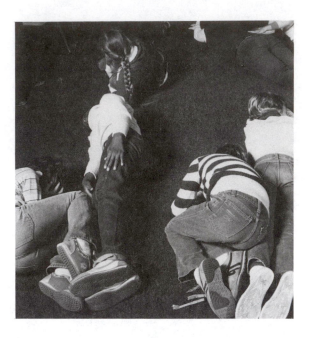

As your students explore these nonlocomotor movement variations, it is important that you make them feel secure in their attempts; *there should be no fear of failure*. To start off, either you or a student leader can perform nonlocomotor movements that the other students copy and describe. In addition, use the following questions to encourage nonlocomotor awareness activities. Remember, do *not* demonstrate as you pose the problems.

"How can we lift our arms slowly? How can we put them down quickly?"

"What shape can you draw in the air? What part of the body are you going to use? Where are you going to make this shape? Can you make the same shape with other parts of the body?"

"What type of large movement can you make? Can you make the same movement small? What pathway did the movement take?"

Excellent body awareness movement activities include making letters and shapes:

"Put your body in the shape of a T, now S, V, C."

"Draw a triangle with both hands held together."

"Draw a square with one leg, with the other leg."

Making letters and shapes can be done in pairs: One partner draws the letter or shape on the back of the other partner, who then identifies and replicates the letter or shape. You can suggest different ways of duplicating the letter or shape if your

group runs out of ideas. For example, suggest that they make a letter or shape with both hands held together; with a shoulder; by "drawing" it with a foot on the floor; by putting the whole body into the shape. For a more difficult variation, have one partner make the letter or shape in front of the body as the other partner is drawing it on the back. The partner doing the drawing must move slowly.

You could also hold up a shape on a card and ask your students to represent the shape with a nonlocomotor movement. Show a second shape card and have the students use a different nonlocomotor movement to represent it. At first, use just two shapes and have each student decide which movement will be performed when each is held up; then add a third and fourth shape to the sequence. The activity can also be performed with two or more sounds. The student represents each sound with a nonlocomotor movement. A variation would be to use the time relationships of musical notes; the students can represent the time values of the notes with their nonlocomotor movements.

You will find that the world of nonlocomotor movement is very broad. It offers numerous spontaneous exploratory activities for your students as well as activities that you suggest for exploration. If students are given opportunities to experience these types of movement without fear of failure, the results can be very rewarding.

Key Experience: Moving the Body in Locomotor Ways

In the previous section we learned about activities involving **nonlocomotor movement**; that is, the student moves the body without leaving the starting point or changing weight. In this section we examine **locomotor movement — movement that involves transfers of weight.** (Five basic weight transfers are described later in this chapter.) Basic locomotor movements include *walking, running, jumping,* and *hopping.* Extensions, combinations, and variations of weight transfer result in the movements of *leaping, galloping, sliding,* and *skipping.*

To succeed in either locomotor or nonlocomotor movement, your students must exhibit **strength, balance, coordination,** and **basic timing.**

In addition, they must pay attention, be willing to attempt the activity, and not be afraid of failure. As their teacher, you should keep in mind that having students move around the room will make many of them feel awkward, particularly if your group is composed of older children and adults. This awkwardness may manifest itself as silly or "acting-out" behavior. In locomotor movement activities, this type of behavior is difficult to direct into more appropriate behavior because the students are moving about, rather than remaining in one area. Therefore, it is very important that students being introduced to locomotor movement be relaxed and understand what they are doing *before* they attempt more difficult rhythmic movement activities.

To manage a class in which locomotor movement activities are being introduced, I follow a strategy I learned years ago in teaching folk dance to teens. Folk dance is not a popular choice of teens, and their discomfort often results in a great deal of anxiety, silliness, and "acting-out" behavior. Therefore, several years ago I decided to set some basic ground rules in dealing with teens *before* beginning the first movements. These "rules" have worked well for me over the years, which is why I am sharing them with you. I begin my teen classes by acknowledging that some of the students must be feeling uncomfortable and must be wishing they were elsewhere. *I acknowledge their discomfort; then I ask for their cooperation and set some limits.* I ask them not to run into or touch others; I tell them I will not embarrass them; and I assure them that they will be successful if they give me and the activity a chance. You will find that this type of introduction makes a tremendous difference and eliminates the need for constant discipline when working with older children. You are acknowledging the fact they may be uncomfortable; you are telling them you care and want to protect them; and you are setting limits and expectations.

Developing Body Awareness and Language Awareness Through Locomotor Movement

The fifth grade students are preparing to learn the triple jump, which consists of one hop from the take-off foot, followed by a step to the other foot, followed by a jump that lands on two feet. Before learning this jump, the physical education teacher asks the students to explore ways to combine stepping, hopping, and jumping. They work in groups to create foot patterns of locomotor movement. They use felt "feet" and a piece of flannel to work out their patterns. They say the words in their sequence as they perform their patterns (SAY & DO). They might say the following: "STEP, HOP, HOP, JUMP."

In the above scenario, the students explore the movements rather than receive instructions from the teacher. When students come up with their own ideas for locomotor movements, they are often more relaxed and their bodies are in better balance. The triple jump, which is the goal in the above scenario, becomes easier to master once students have experienced the weight transfers in their own patterns. After they have experimented with the various weight transfers, the triple jump then becomes just one more pattern to try.

Five basic weight transfers are executed with the feet in locomotor movement. Words like WALK, JUMP are the labels for these weight transfers. The weight transfers are listed in order of difficulty, with the easiest first:

Five Basic Weight Transfers	*Language Labels*
1. One foot to the other foot	WALK, RUN, JOG, MARCH, LEAP, GALLOP, SLIDE, STEP, and half of the SKIP
2. Two feet to two feet	JUMP
3. One foot to two feet	JUMP
4. Two feet to one foot	HOP, LEAP
5. One foot to the same foot	HOP, and the other half of the SKIP

Beyond the simplest one foot to the other foot, the next weight transfers involve the two-foot landing, which is in better balance than the one-foot landing. All the take-offs except the first require that an individual also go up and come down, a movement that demands a certain degree of strength and agility. Clearly, any combination of weight transfers requires coordination; the SKIP, for example, combines two weight transfers — one foot to the other foot and one foot to the same foot. Today, games like hopscotch are not played very often so children may not have developed the balance and coordination that would help them learn locomotor movement sequences.

In locomotor movement, **language awareness** means that the students understand and can use words that accurately describe the various movements they are doing. If you ask your students to GALLOP, for example, they need to know how to explain the word "gallop" in terms of the movements required. Always use the same label for a movement. Teachers frequently mix up labels, such as HOP and JUMP, when they give directions.

Teachers often mistakenly assume that locomotor movement activities performed in a class should be performed to an external beat — a drum beat, clapping, or music. They also often specify "right" and "left" foot or ask the participants to move in a circle with hands joined. These misconceptions set the stage for many beginners to fail in their first attempts. There are a number of reasons for these failures:

● First, an external beat may not match a student's natural beat and tempo; if it does not, the student must consciously deny a natural impulse in order to match the external beat.

● Second, the use of commands such as "right" or "left" creates a more complex activity because an additional thought is added. Now the student must integrate two things at once — the movement with the correct footwork. Also, those whose foot preference is on the opposite side from the one requested may find the adjustment difficult.

● Third, holding hands in a circle is another deterrent to immediate success. Students in a circle formation feel very visible and uncomfortable. In such cases, students become tense, because they feel the persons on either side will be aware of their failures. In addition, handholding itself is an intimate social interaction that many persons, particularly children, find distasteful.

The first rule for locomotor movement, then, is to allow students to move freely and successfully to their own beat and tempo. Try to design "failsafe" tasks. For example, the tasks of walking in a random fashion, walking quickly, walking more slowly *(without an external beat)* allow for immediate success. Another suggestion would be to have part of the group move about the space, while part of the group performs the same locomotor movement in place. Keep in mind that students who lack adequate balance and coordination, and who are not experienced in movements that require starting and stopping, may find it difficult to move about in a group situation.

Developing Space and Time Awareness Through Locomotor Movement

Elementary-age children are solving math problems by employing their space and time awareness skills. The teacher poses a problem such as $2 \times 3 - 2$. The students choose a locomotor movement, such as a JUMP, to express the answer. They JUMP four times. In the next problem they change the size of the JUMP as they move to answer the problem.

In the above scenario the students are thinking about the answers to the problems rather than how they look doing the locomotor movement. The movement called for in solving the first problem is just a simple locomotor movement without variations, whereas in solving the second problem, a variation is added to the movement (the size of the jump).

The variations found in locomotor movement are the same as those described earlier for

nonlocomotor movement. Several ideas for locomotor activities using *no* external beat or tempo follow:

1. **As a first step, have the students move from one designated spot to another, such as across the room.** You can structure the activity by suggesting, "Let's see you move across the room with three body parts touching the floor. Who has another idea of a way to move across the room with a different number of body parts touching the floor?" You might also use imagery, such as, "Let's pretend we are all walking with a cast on our legs the way Jamie has to walk with his cast. Let's move as if we are pushing a heavy object. Change your WALK in another way."

2. **As a second step, have the students move about freely in a designated space.** At first the group may need to start and stop frequently before new directions are given. Keep in mind that students who lack space and time awareness will have a difficult time moving easily in a crowded space. Do not specify a "correct" foot or direction.

3. **Vary the direction of the movement.** An activity that changes direction helps students become comfortable with movement. For example, have the students walk forward or backward. Then add special ways of walking forward or backward, such as skating forward or walking on tiptoes backward. Pose the following problem, "WALK sideward as if you were going through a narrow doorway. WALK as if you were on a tightrope." Suggest other weight-transfer movements such as the JUMP or HOP, to explore direction, and have the students suggest variations.

4. **Vary the level or position of the body.** A new set of concepts involves asking students to change the normal level or position of their bodies. For example, you could say "WALK with your body 'tall.' WALK with your body 'short.' WALK with your body as 'wide' as possible. Turn your toes in as you WALK. Turn them out." Once the class has explored the dimensions of direction and level, suggest movement tasks that combine them. For example, "WALK sideward with your body 'short'." Pose a problem, "Choose a direction and a level in which to WALK. Before you begin tell us how you are going to move."

5. **Vary the intensity.** "Show us how you would move with very forceful steps. How would you move if you were very weak?" Suggest a task that combines intensity with direction and/or level: "WALK as a person who is happy (sad) (angry) (tired)." "WALK noisily (softly)".

6. **Vary the size of the movements.** Have the class explore various sizes of steps. You might say "Can you WALK with four big steps and then HOP with four little hops?" Suggest an activity that combines size with the other variations above, and have the students suggest variations.

7. **Vary the pathway.** "From where you are standing, how many steps will it take you to WALK

to the wall in a straight pathway? Once you make a guess, see if you can reach the wall in exactly that number of steps." Have the students combine straight, curved, and zigzag pathways with direction, level, intensity, and size of steps, as well as with other locomotor movements.

8. **Vary the flow of the movement.** Have the students move forward in a very smooth way or a bumpy way. Combine flow with other variations.

9. **Vary the timing of the movement.** Have the students move quickly or slowly, evenly or unevenly and have them start and stop. Have them use imagery: "WALK as slowly as you would going up hill carrying a heavy object" or "WALK as quickly as a race walker." Try the GALLOP, SLIDE, and SKIP, all of which require uneven timing. Have them alter the duration of the movements: "Do three very slow movements and then one sudden quick movement."

10. **Vary combinations of locomotor movements.** Have the students practice combinations of WALKS and JUMPS or HOPS and JUMPS or GALLOPS and SLIDES. Give the students opportunities to decide on the combinations: "WALK eight steps in a straight pathway, then JUMP four times facing a different direction, then HOP six times with your hands on your hips."

An external beat, correct foot, and formations may be added to any of the above variations as soon as the students are comfortable with that movement. If you are posing a movement sequence to which an external beat is going to be

added, have the students try the movement sequence to their own natural beat and tempo first. If you are going to begin with a correct foot, have the students try the sequence starting with one foot, then repeat it starting with the other foot before specifying right or left.

Key Experience: Moving the Body in Integrated Ways

In the previous two sections of this chapter we examined *nonlocomotor movement,* movement during which one stays in place and does not use weight transfers, and *locomotor movement,* movement in which one transfers weight either in personal space or in general space. In this section we consider **integrated movement — the purposeful combination of** *nonlocomotor* **upper-body movement with** *locomotor* **lower-body movements.** Integrated movement activities, with

or without objects, include cross-country skiing, aerobic exercise and dance, marching band, and gymnastics routines. For persons to execute the activity successfully, their upper and lower body must function as a unit, even though the movements may be different. Consider the following scenario:

The students are practicing a sequence called the grapevine pattern that consists of stepping one foot sideward, crossing the second foot behind the first foot, stepping sideward again, and finally crossing the second foot in front of the first foot. They have already performed the sequence to their own timing and have used the language-to-dance vocabulary label, SAY & DO, "SIDE, BACK, SIDE, CROSS." The arm pattern consists of snapping the fingers two times and then clapping two times. The teacher asks the students to stand still and practice the snaps and claps a couple of times and then SAY the locomotor pattern (SIDE, BACK, SIDE, CROSS) while performing the snaps and claps, the nonlocomotor pattern. The teacher also asks the students to try to put the patterns together whenever they feel ready and to use a WHISPER & DO so they will not bother the persons near them. The class then performs the integrated sequence together beginning with the leg pattern and adding the snaps and claps.

Several things should be noted in the above scenario in relation to integrated movement. The students began with the locomotor movement pattern because it is easier to add the nonlocomotor movement than vice versa. Note that the nonlocomotor movement was practiced without the feet and without any words and then with the

SAY of the foot pattern. If a different SAY had been used for the nonlocomotor (snaps and claps) and the locomotor patterns, the movements would not have been integrated. Once each type of movement was established, the students put them together using their own beat and tempo.

This method of integrating movement works with any timed movement sequence. Children can learn to drop-kick a ball by first learning to STEP, KICK without the ball, then to pretend to drop the ball to the timing of STEP/DROP, KICK. In this example the nonlocomotor arm movement DROP was added because students were not moving their legs at that point. In the same way, it is very simple to add claps and snaps to dance sequences by just saying "clap with the word 'in' " or "snap with the word 'bend'."

An additional method for integrating movement, when the nonlocomotor and locomotor movements are fairly simple, is to "add on" arm movements to the established leg pattern. Example: The class begins a locomotor movement by stepping sideward and then bringing the second foot to meet the first. When this sequence is comfortable for all students, they add the arm movements — straightening their arms sideward on the side step and bending on the closing step.

All the variations described for nonlocomotor and locomotor movement can also be explored with integrated movement.

Key Experience: Moving With Objects

This key experience in movement is designed to enhance students' motor skill development. Activities that are part of this key experience require

the student to use objects in combination with nonlocomotor, locomotor, and integrated movement patterns.

To move with objects, students can **manipulate** the object; that is, they can use an object as part of a movement sequence. They also can use the object as a **prop**, which alleviates self-consciousness, especially for older children or adults.

Manipulating Objects

For most of us, "manipulating objects" means throwing, catching, kicking, or striking a ball. In addition to balls, however, students in physical education classes manipulate rackets, clubs, and jump ropes. Students in other classes manipulate musical instruments, brushes, crayons, sculpture materials, pens, pencils, and scissors. Regardless of age, students who use objects in movement activities have opportunities to use their motor coordination skills in new ways and to become comfortable and proficient in using the objects.

A wise approach to take when introducing an activity that involves moving with an object is to **first practice the motor pattern without the object.** The following scenario is an example of this process:

The students are practicing playing B, A, G on imaginary recorders. With their right arms held in front of their bodies, or paper towel tubes held in their right hands, the students practice manipulating the fingers. They get used to lifting the middle finger while the first finger stays in place and lifting the ring finger while the first and middle fingers stay in place. After some practice, the teacher says, "Play B, Play A, Play G," and so on, and the students respond. Then the teacher has the students pretend to play the song they are going to play when they use the real recorders.

Playing the recorder first requires that students practice moving the fingers, then moving the fingers and covering the recorder's holes, and then blowing while moving the fingers and covering the holes. In the example, the teacher *simplifies* the process by breaking it down to its basic components, thereby assuring that the students execute the motor task successfully before the object is added.

In physical education classes and sports activities, manipulative skills involve integrated movement, as upper-body and lower-body movement is coordinated. These skills also involve precise timing, if the student is to succeed. Consider, for example, the tennis serve. The student must throw the ball into the air with the non-preferred hand while moving the racket into position behind the back. The arm now is extended overhead so the head of the racket contacts the ball at precisely the right time. To all this is added a step on to the nonpreferred foot in the follow-through phase. If students do not possess basic timing ability — the ability to feel and express beat — then they begin with a handicap. If students cannot comfortably coordinate movement on both sides of their bodies, they have an additional handicap.

Moving with objects may be performed to one's own beat and tempo or can be performed with others to a common beat. The latter should not be introduced until persons are comfortable with their own timing. The Four-Step Language Process discussed in the previous chapter can be applied here. Example: A group working on bouncing a ball, catching it, tossing it into the air, and catching it has the goal of performing the activity to music. Thus, each student sets his or her own beat first with a WHISPER & DO, by saying "BOUNCE, CATCH, TOSS, CATCH." After a brief practice period, the group performs it together with the SAY & DO, and then with the music.

Using Objects as Props for Comfort

As noted earlier, individuals who have reached the age of eight or nine without having achieved basic comfort with movement are very likely to be threatened or "turned off" by rhythmic movement activities. Although they may have achieved general body awareness, they often lack the necessary balance and coordination to succeed in activities requiring rhythmic movement. They may understand space and time awareness concepts, but may be too tense to put them into practice comfortably. Also, they often lack basic timing ability and cannot perform movement *contralaterally,* that is, using the opposite arm and leg.

Props seem to be one of the best methods for helping individuals of any age feel more secure with movement. Older children and students who feel self-conscious because they believe "Everyone is watching me make a mistake" or "Everyone

is successful except me" feel less conspicuous when using props.

Chairs. Each student stands behind a chair. The chair allows the individual to "hide" and provides physical support when practicing movements while standing in one place. Students can begin learning a movement while seated. This allows them to use the lower body to practice the movement before they stand up. It is much more difficult to coordinate leg movements from a weight-bearing position. Lead movement sequences or exercise sequences with the students standing behind the chairs. Also use the chair for problem-solving movement or for the students to choreograph movement sequences.

Masks. Wearing a mask enables some people to be less inhibited, particularly in creative movement, because they can "hide" behind their masks.

Paper plates. Holding one paper plate in each hand makes people feel less visible because the plates become the focus of attention. The paper plates may be used for exploratory movement sequences, mirroring, and rhythmic sequences, too. Try the following movements with the plates:

● WALK while hitting the plates against the hips. Use the language "HIT, HIT."

● Have the student HIT the plates together on the first step of two walking steps or the first step of three or four walking steps. Also combine the patterns — first of two then first of three.

● Choreograph a sequence to music. HIT the

plates together, in front, overhead, and so on; use
them as cymbals; use them to hit the legs or other
body parts; RUB them together; use them as fans.

**Activity wands and cardboard paper towel
tubes, hoops, towels, balls, streamers.** These are
lightweight props that can be moved about easily.

Summary

This chapter introduced four major types of
movement: **nonlocomotor movement** without
weight transfers; **locomotor movement** with
weight transfers; **integrated movement**, the
combination of nonlocomotor and locomotor
movement; and **moving with objects**, using an
object with nonlocomotor movement, with locomotor movement, or with integrated movement.
Persons who cannot move their bodies in nonlocomotor and locomotor ways will find it
difficult to integrate movement or move with objects. Yet all these major motor patterns should be
established before a child is in second grade. Unfortunately, many of today's seven-year-olds seem
to be deficient in motor skill development. Our
task as educators is to provide opportunities for
children *and* adults to work on these deficiencies
in an age-appropriate manner. My experience
teaching folk dance to teens each summer leads
me to believe their motor skills are declining
because they do not have enough movement
experiences. I have worked with many 15-year-
olds who have the balance and coordination abil-

ity of a 6-year-old and who believe they will fail before they even try the activity.

In the previous chapter, Presenting Movement Activities, I discussed the importance of the key experiences **Following Movement Directions** and **Describing Movement** and offered suggestions for introducing activities in these key experience areas. In this chapter, you learned how to lead your students through various movement tasks and how to make them feel comfortable with the following movement key experiences: **Moving the Body in Nonlocomotor Ways, Moving the Body in Locomotor Ways, Moving the Body in Integrated Ways**, and **Moving with Objects**. Remember, you can come up with ideas for **ways to move** based on activities in your particular curriculum or program: physical education, music, art, or academic teaching. In any of these areas, active learning results when students are engaged in various forms of movement. In the next chapter, Extending Movement Activities, you will learn the importance of the key experiences **Expressing Creativity in Movement, Feeling and Expressing Beat**, and **Moving With Others to a Common Beat**.

Extending Movement Activities 4

We can extend movement activities to prepare students for organized dance, exercise routines, sports, and music participation by using the key experience in movement that builds **creativity** (**Expressing Creativity in Movement**) and the two key experiences that build **rhythmic competency** (**Feeling and Expressing Beat** and **Moving With Others to a Common Beat**). Combining the **comfort with movement** skill (discussed in the preceding chapter) with creativity and rhythmic competency gives us two broad movement categories: **creative movement** and **rhythmic movement**. For both categories of movement we can use the *presentation methods* that involve the key experiences **Following Movement Directions** and **Describing Movement** (see Chapter 2).

To engage in creative movement, students must understand how the body moves and how to vary movements, and they must have the confidence to try something new. To engage in rhythmic movement, students must be able to execute a movement pattern to an underlying beat; the beat can be either verbal or musical. Regardless of which movement form students engage in, they will use the four key experiences involving *ways to move*: **Moving the Body in Nonlocomotor Ways, Moving the Body in Locomotor Ways, Moving the Body in Integrated Ways,** and **Moving With Objects** (see Chapter 3).

In this chapter, we first examine the building blocks of creative movement: problem-solving activities, guided exploration, and imagery. These experiences give students body, language, space, and time awareness, which results in **comfort with movement,** a prerequisite for successful creative as well as rhythmic movement. Following this section, we explore the building blocks

of rhythmic movement: basic timing and beat coordination skill, which lead to **rhythmic competency,** the other prerequisite for successful rhythmic movement. Figure 5 illustrates these relationships. Due to its important role in the sequence leading to successful rhythmic movement, the **beat coordination teaching progression** is described in detail in this chapter.

Creative Movement

Key Experience: Expressing Creativity in Movement

The students are spread out about the activity space. The teacher says, "Find ways to move creatively in your own space. You may use nonlocomotor movement, locomotor movement, or integrated movement."

The activity described in this scenario may be very enjoyable for persons who have had lots of creative movement experience and may have ideas of their own about how to move, but it may be very threatening to persons who think they have to "invent" something new. Yet anyone who has had the opportunity to develop a movement vocabulary and to explore what the body can do in personal and general space can be successful with creative movement.

If your students participate in movement activities in which they can make choices, creative movement will not seem so new or threatening to them. But if you conduct movement activities in a highly structured environment in which *you*

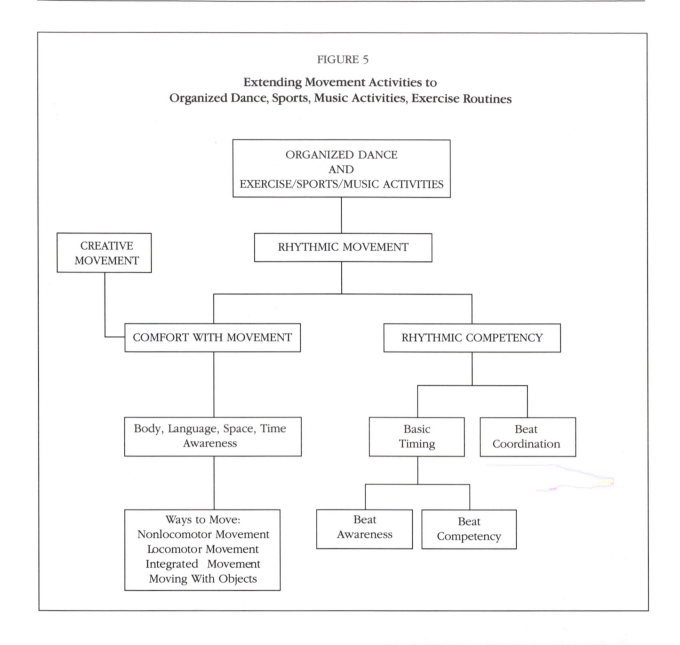

FIGURE 5

**Extending Movement Activities to
Organized Dance, Sports, Music Activities, Exercise Routines**

ORGANIZED DANCE
AND
EXERCISE/SPORTS/MUSIC ACTIVITIES

RHYTHMIC MOVEMENT

CREATIVE
MOVEMENT

COMFORT WITH MOVEMENT

RHYTHMIC COMPETENCY

Body, Language, Space, Time
Awareness

Basic
Timing

Beat
Coordination

Ways to Move:
Nonlocomotor Movement
Locomotor Movement
Integrated Movement
Moving With Objects

Beat
Awareness

Beat
Competency

make all the choices, your students will have difficulty putting their own ideas into practice. Students of all ages should be provided with opportunities for individual expression so that they will learn more about themselves and their environment and will develop increased self-confidence. In such situations, teachers guide and facilitate students' actions, rather than provide direct instruction. They ask such leading questions as these: "Can you find another part of the body that twists? Can you find another way to twist your arm?" It is important to note that teachers should use verbal instructions more than visual demon-

strations when introducing creative movement since a visual demonstration may inhibit students' creativity and individual expression.

Round the Circle: Key Experiences in Movement for Children contains a discussion about creative movement as it pertains to young children. The goal of that book is to assure that children are given opportunities to experience all kinds of movement, including creative movement, and that they feel successful and comfortable with movement activities before they enter first grade. The task here is to set the same goal for older children and adults. This section introduces three strategies that are helpful in building the ability to express movement creatively: **problem solving**, **guided exploration**, and **imagery**.

Problem Solving

The students are exploring swinging movements. After beginning the activity by having the students copy her swinging movements back and forth in front of the body, the teacher says, "Can you swing your arms in a different direction? Are you swinging them quickly or slowly? What is the size of your swinging movement?"

Problem solving is one of the easiest ways to help individuals develop their own creative movement ideas. In problem solving, the teacher does not continually provide specific instructions but gives an initial direction either by demonstrating as in the example, or by verbalizing. For example, a teacher could say "Swing your arms in front of you," and then encourage variations: "Now swing them somewhere else. Are you swinging them

quickly or slowly?" The students are being told to use a certain body part in a specified movement; they only have to decide how to vary the movement. The students are also being asked to talk about the various ways they solved the movement problem and to try out some of those solutions. In such a situation, if particular students are copying others, the teacher should make note of that fact but not call anyone's attention to it. The students may not have an immediate idea of their own, so rather than doing nothing, they are copying, or perhaps they were not paying attention when the direction was given and are trying to cover up the fact.

Guided Exploration

The students are exploring twisting movements. The teacher says, "Choose a body part that can be twisted and decide on the variation you wish to use in your twist."

Think of **guided exploration** as the beginning of some more advanced creativity in movement. In guided exploration, the movement is initiated by the student rather than the teacher, and few specifics are given. Example: "Can you find a new way to twist a part or parts of the body?" The student chooses the body part and the variation. It is important for teachers to vary the specificity of their directions.

In a different example, a teacher could say, "How can you move your arms? Your legs?" As with problem solving, it is important to support the efforts of the students, to make them feel that their ideas are valued, and to assure them that their ideas will not be compared to someone else's in a judgmental way.

Imagery

A group of middle-school students pretend they are driving a jeep on a very bumpy road. They get into the jeeps, fasten their seat belts, start the engines, put the jeeps into gear, drive down the bumpy road, turn sharp corners, stop at stop signs, and finally are pulled over by the police for driving too fast.

As this scenario illustrates, **imagery** can work very well with older children and adults, providing the imagery is age-appropriate. As teachers, we can ask numerous leading questions to help our students come to a more complete understanding of the movement through the imagery employed: "What foot did you use to step into the jeep? How did you fasten the seat belt? What did you have to do when you suddenly came to a stop sign?"

Please note that in this book the section on creative movement is short because "creativity" is inherent in *every* movement experience as students are encouraged to make their own choices. Students should be introduced to creative movement with **problem-solving situations** in which they have only one decision to make: The teacher chooses the body part and the movement, while the student decides how to do it. In other words, the body part, movement, and direction are given for the student, and the student decides on the "how" of the movement — the timing, the size, or the intensity. **Guided exploration** requires students to make more than one decision, such as which body part to use and/or where and how to use it. In **imagery**, students follow no specific directions. Instead, they interpret the imaginary situation in many ways. This prepares them for creative movement, in which there are few, if any, guidelines.

Rhythmic Movement

What exactly is meant by the term *rhythmic movement?* Used in a generic sense, rhythmic movement refers to *sequences or patterns of body movement that combine elements of time and space.* "Rhythmic" denotes a *time* relationship, ranging from the simple matching of an external steady beat to sequencing more complex movements. "Movement" denotes the use of the upper and/or lower body (motion in space). As noted earlier, in addition to achieving **comfort with movement**, there is another important component to successful rhythmic movement: **rhythmic competency**. Rhythmic competency results when students (1) can *feel and express beat,* thereby possessing **basic timing** and (2) can *move with others to a common beat,* thereby possessing the skill of **beat coordination**. Students cannot do rhythmic movement well unless they achieve rhythmic competency by mastering both skill areas.

Key Experience: Feeling and Expressing Beat — Basic Timing

The students choose a body position while listening to recorded instrumental music. They perform different nonlocomotor movements to the beat of the music. At the end of parts of the music, the teacher says, "Change the movement you are using" or "Change your position."

In this scenario, the teacher gives the students their choice of position and movement but neither demonstrates the movement nor demonstrates the beat for them to copy. Since the students are working independently, the teacher can assess their progress.

As the title of this section implies, the key experience Feeling and Expressing Beat can also be referred to as **basic timing**. To achieve basic timing, one must possess two related skills: **beat awareness**, the ability to feel and indicate the beat with a simple movement like a PAT, and **beat competency**, the ability to walk to the steady beat while engaging in a weight-bearing movement.

As noted earlier, the development of basic timing and beat coordination results in **rhythmic competency** and makes a significant difference in at least three skill areas related to rhythmic movement: (1) **motor skills**, from simple bending and straightening to dance or sports, involve timing; (2) **musical skills** require that students have a sense of basic timing and the beat coordination skill that enables them to perform with others; (3) **academic skills** such as those needed for reading and math appear to be stronger in students who possess basic timing and beat coordination skill. A Romulus, Michigan, pilot project, which I directed, showed this correlation. Individuals in my summer training program have found that children who possess rhythmic competency tend to score higher on standardized achievement tests than those who do not possess rhythmic competency.

Beat Awareness

Beat awareness is acquired through the process of *feeling* and *hearing.* An infant who is rocked, patted, jiggled, or stroked to a steady beat of a rhyme, song, or recorded music feels the beat that he or she hears. If this occurs often enough in the early years, a child will automatically be able to express beat as soon as he or she is old enough to move to the beat. Patting or bouncing the child to the *rhythmic pattern of speech* rather than to the steady beat, or having the preschool or school-age child pat or clap to the *syllables of names or word rhythms* makes them aware of *rhythm,* not *beat.*

To achieve a basic awareness of *beat,* children must experience it over and over again; feeling and expressing beat should become automatic *before* children learn to add movement to the rhythm of the words. Children are capable of patting the rhythm of the words by age three and often are encouraged to do so by teachers and caregivers. However, this encourages them to focus on the easier, more concrete word rhythm patterns and thus makes it difficult to establish or re-establish their feel of beat. For example, it is much easier to clap to all the letters in B-I-N/G-O than to clap four even beats with no clap on the letter G. It is much easier to move on all the syllables of "Hickory Dickory Dock" than to move once for each word and once at the end of each line when no word is spoken.

The **Four-Step Language Process** described in Chapter 2 is a good method for familiarizing the older child or adult with the feel of the beat of his or her own speech. With practice the students should develop beat awareness. If after repeated practice, some of your students are still having trouble with beat awareness activities, try the following sequence, which has been designed to help students gain skill in this area:

Step 1: To relax the student, have the student place his/her hands on top of your hands and keep them there as *you* move them in an up-and-down motion.

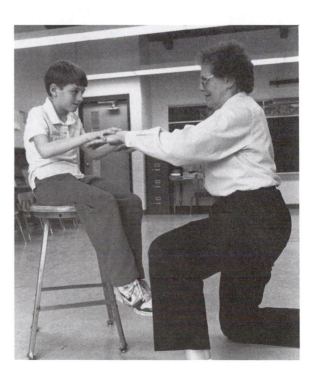

Step 2: Pat the student's legs — his/her hands on top of yours; then *you* SAY & DO.

Step 3: Keep patting the student's legs but have him/her say PAT every time your hands touch the legs.

Step 4: Slip your hands out and see if the student can do the SAY & DO alone.

Step 5: Now ask the student to choose another part of the body to use for SAY & DO.

When the students succeed with SAY & DO, have them practice simple movement sequences. Examples of sequences follow:

1. **Repeat one word four times.** While chanting the words, perform "KNEES, KNEES, KNEES, KNEES" or "SHOULDERS, SHOULDERS, SHOULDERS, SHOULDERS" with both hands at the same time, and later with alternating hands.

2. **Repeat two words two times.** While chanting the words, perform "SNAP, SNAP, PAT, PAT" or "WAIST, WAIST, CHIN, CHIN" with both hands at the same time and later with alternating hands.

3. **Repeat two words, each one time.** Perform "SNAP, PAT, SNAP, PAT" or "OUT, IN, OUT, IN" with both hands at the same time.

The last two examples also provide practice in beat coordination, a skill necessary to *move with others to a common beat.* Coordination will be discussed in greater detail in the following section.

Add a chant or song once a movement is learned. If at first the students have trouble doing both at the same time, try making them partners. Have one partner pat the other's shoulders, using both hands at the same time, while the other partner recites the rhyme.

Another activity that helps students feel the beat is four-beat voice echoes. You could ask your group to select a common beat, but have each individual choose how to perform it. Once the tempo is established, present four-beat, single syllable, verbal echoes; for example, "B, B, B/B, B" or "Ha, Ha/Ha, Ha/Ha, Ha." The group echoes while keeping the steady beat. **Note:** The leader should **not** demonstrate the beat in this activity because the students must learn to feel the beat, independent from a demonstration, for the skill to develop.

Other suggestions for learning to feel the beat include the following:

1. Pat the steady beat softly while singing or chanting rhymes. Start the group beat before adding the song or rhyme by chanting a single word, such as "PAT, PAT, PAT, PAT."

2. Pat the steady beat softly while chanting facts, such as times tables or counting by 5's or spelling words. Start the group beat first, as in 1.

3. Pat the steady beat softly while playing a category game in which each student suggests another item in the category (e.g., fruits, vegetables, states, state capitols, countries).

4. Pat the steady beat softly on a partner's shoulders while that partner is playing a rhythm pattern on a musical instrument.

5. Pat the steady beat softly on a partner's shoulders while that partner echoes the speech pattern given by the teacher or another student.

Please note, however, that you should always establish the patting movement with a single word chant before adding the rhyme or song, or before the partner begins the task.

Beat Competency

For students to have basic timing ability, it is necessary that they not only be able to feel and indicate the beat — beat awareness — but also be able to walk to a steady beat — beat competency. Beat competency is acquired through practice. Recently, I tested a group of teens and found that most could feel the beat when they pat-

ted the legs and most could walk their feet to the beat while they were seated, but half of the group could not stand up and walk to the beat. Many in the group were very tense when they stood up and became distracted when faced with the more difficult motor task. (See the Introduction for the specific results of this testing.) Since the teens could *feel* the beat, the key was making them more relaxed about applying a locomotor movement to that beat and raising their coordination level. Following are some suggestions that will help your students feel comfortable in practice situations:

1. Help them feel more comfortable with loco-motor movement; refer to the preceding chapter on the various ways to move.

2. Help them develop higher levels of beat coordination using nonlocomotor movement. See the following section, Moving With Others to a Common Beat.

3. Have parades in the classroom or do marching in the gym or cafeteria. Alternate between walking or marching in place and moving forward. If the group becomes distracted from the beat, return to the in-place movement.

4. Help them use the Four-Step Language Process with simple locomotor movement patterns in which they choose the starting foot. These patterns involve moving FORWARD, BACKWARD, IN, OUT. Once a simple pattern is established, put the sequence to music. Be certain to set the pattern in the tempo of the music before adding the music.

5. Perform side-to-side swaying on the slow beat while chanting or singing. Begin this with the group chanting "SIDE, SIDE, SIDE, SIDE" and then add the chant or song to the same beat.

6. Step the beat in place while chanting single words, such as "CHOCOLATE, CHOCOLATE" or "VACATION, VACATION." (In the second example, the step occurs with the second syllable.) Change the single repetitious word to two-word combinations, one step for each word: "CHOCOLATE PIE" or "SUMMER VACATION."

Students who cannot walk to the steady beat will have difficulty performing international folk dance, which is the focus of the second part of this book. They will also have difficulty with other forms of dance and other areas of rhythmic movement. It is clear to me that today's students lack **beat awareness** and **beat competency**. In other words, many of these students are "bonded" to rhythmic patterns of speech and to syllables of words and do not recognize the underlying beat. To reiterate, a great deal of practice *feeling and expressing beat* is required for the skill to become automatic, and we should provide students with many opportunities to practice moving to the steady beat. We also must remember to keep the motor task simple when helping students acquire the ability to express beat. See Levels I and II of the Levels of Beat Coordination in the next section for examples of these simple motor tasks. Remember, if the skill is not automatic, other rhythmic movement skills are not possible.

Key Experience: Moving With Others to a Common Beat — Beat Coordination

Groups of students have created 16-beat non-locomotor and locomotor movement sequences. They are using the SAY & DO method to organize the patterns into a common beat. Each group presents its 16-beat sequence to the entire class. After the groups perform, the teacher suggests a song and the groups sing and perform the movement.

In the preceding section, Feeling and Expressing Beat, we examined one of the two elements of **rhythmic competency — basic timing**. In this section we examine the other element — **beat coordination**.

In the above scenario, the students are using combinations of movement, all of which require beat coordination. The labels in the SAY & DO method are spoken to a steady beat and provide the organization for the movement sequences. The challenge at the end is putting the movement sequences to music. If students are not comfortable with the movement sequences, they will have difficulty when the song is added.

The capacity to move with others to a common beat requires a skill that I call **beat coordination**. The individual who possesses beat coordination is aware of beat and can move to the beat. Simple identification and matching of an external, steady

beat with movement is at one end of the rhythmic competency continuum; using beat coordination to do more complex movement sequences within groupings of beats is at the other end. Anyone who wants to successfully participate in organized dance or to perform other movement tasks that require accurate timing and coordinated movement must attain a level of beat coordination that results in rhythmic competency.

The Beat Coordination Teaching Progression

The **teaching progression** for beat coordination follows six activity levels of increasing complexity:

Activity Level	Movement	Beat
LEVEL I	Single Bilateral Symmetrical	1
LEVEL II	Single Predictable Alternating	2
LEVEL III	Sequenced Bilateral Symmetrical	2
LEVEL IV	Sequenced Bilateral Symmetrical Combined	4
LEVEL V	Sequenced Alternating	4
LEVEL VI	Sequenced Alternating Combined	8

The relationship between the activity levels and the **Four-Step Language Process** is illustrated in

Table 5. Children should have mastered the first four levels by the time they enter first grade. However, they will need additional practice at these levels throughout the first-grade year. In second grade, they should begin to progress through Levels V and VI. The major reason for having children wait until second grade to experience Levels V and VI is because they often lack "inhibiting" capability; in particular, boys often do not possess this capability until approximately the age of seven. Inhibiting capability is the ability to hold one side of the body *still* while moving the other side. Second grade is also an appropriate time to begin to add clapping to movement sequences, because second graders are able now to use one hand as the "target," the inhibited movement, while using the other hand as the "beater."

When dealing with older students and adults who are unable to perform the first four levels of beat coordination, it is important to start with the first two levels before performing the rest. Levels I and II will not need to be practiced as much once the students can perform with SAY & DO, that is, once they can link the movement to the words. However, it will be helpful for the students to return to these two levels periodically. These also are the levels to be used at first when chanting or singing, because the movement is easily made automatic. The more complex levels require much more practice time before students can succeed with chanting or singing when doing the movements.

To sequence movement, which begins with Level III, students will need frequent practice sessions. At the beginning of these sessions, students who are easily distracted from the task may perform the movement backward or say the words correctly but not perform the movement correctly. Interestingly, I have found a relationship between mastery of Level IV and beat competency skill. In 95% of all students informally tested, those who could not walk to the beat were unable to perform Level IV movements, and vice versa. Therefore, Levels III and IV seem to provide a bridge to beat coordination and basic timing.

The SAY in the Four-Step Language Process becomes more critical at Level III since it organizes the students' thought processes before the group moves together using the complete SAY & DO

TABLE 5

Combining the Four-Step Language Process With Movement to Achieve A Basic Level of Beat Coordination

Beat Coordination Activity Levels

Four-Step Language Process STEP	LEVEL I Single Bilateral Symmetrical Movement	LEVEL II Single Predictable Alternating Movement	LEVEL III Sequenced Bilateral Symmetrical Movements	LEVEL IV Sequenced Bilateral Symmetrical Movements Combined	LEVEL V Sequenced Alternating Movements	LEVEL VI Sequenced Alternating Movements Combined
I SAY	"KNEES, KNEES, KNEES, KNEES" or "BOUNCE, BOUNCE, BOUNCE, BOUNCE"	"KNEE, KNEE, KNEE, KNEE" or "WALK, WALK, WALK, WALK"	"HEAD, SHOULDERS, HEAD, SHOULDERS" or "WAIST, KNEES, WAIST, KNEES"	"HEAD, SHOULDERS, WAIST, KNEES"	"OUT, IN; OUT, IN" or "HEEL, STEP, HEEL, STEP"	"OUT, IN; UP, DOWN; OUT, IN; UP, DOWN" or "HEEL, TOUCH, KICK, STEP; HEEL, TOUCH, KICK, STEP"
II SAY & DO	Unite language and movement. Both hands *or* feet used simultaneously.	Unite language and movement. Alternate hands *or* feet.	Unite language and movement. Both hands *or* feet used simultaneously.	Unite language and two Level Three movements. Both hands *or* feet used simultaneously.	Unite language and movement using one side of the body for 2 beats and then the other side for 2 beats.	Unite language and movement using one side of the body for 4 beats and then the other side for 4 beats.
III WHISPER & DO	Continue STEP II using a whisper.	Continue STEP II using a whisper.	Continue STEP II using a whisper.	Continue STEP II using a whisper.	Continue STEP II using a whisper.	Continue STEP II using a whisper.
IV THINK & DO	Think the language and do the movements.	Think the language and do the movements.	Think the language and do the movements.	Think the language and do the movements.	Think the language and do the movements.	Think the language and do the movements.

NOTE: When music is added, begin with STEP III, WHISPER & DO, matching language and movement.
If difficulty is experienced, WHISPER the words to the music *before* adding movement.

procedure. One strategy for beginning the SAY is to have one student do just the movement sequence and have the other students add the SAY. This strategy gives the students a model for the words. Then have the students add the SAY & DO when they are ready, rather than requiring all to add the movement at precisely the same time. This strategy also works very well when groups are practicing dance patterns.

The Six Levels of Beat Coordination

Teaching techniques are provided for each of the six levels of beat coordination discussed in this section, and the section concludes with a summary of the general guidelines for presenting Levels I – VI.

Level I: Single Bilateral Symmetrical Movement

The students repeat the same movement for each steady beat, using both sides of the body. Example: Pat the chin and simultaneously chant "CHIN, CHIN, CHIN, CHIN" with each pat.

This coordination is the simplest because it involves only one repeated movement and because both sides of the body are doing the same thing at the same time. The older child and adult should be able to succeed at this level without much practice. As you work at this level with older children and adults, substitute *action words* such as PAT, TOUCH, TAP for *body part names*. Also have the students perform movements with the legs alone, such as bouncing heels or tapping toes, and movements that do not involve touching the body, such as PUSH and BOUNCE, as these will be more acceptable to the older student who still needs practice at this level.

Teaching Techniques for Level I: Single Bilateral Symmetrical Movement

1. **Use both hands, both shoulders, both thumbs, or both legs at the same time.** Begin seated and later, as students develop more self-confidence, do the movements standing. Keep the movements light and soft.

2. **Introduce each new movement without**

the SAY and then add the SAY to create the SAY & DO.

3. Repeat each SAY & DO a minimum of eight times. Then link several Level-I movements by doing each eight times, then four times.

4. Give students practice time without a common beat. Very often students are unsuccessful because we expect them to *move with others to a common beat* with no prior practice moving to their own beat.

5. Have the students pick their own Level-I movement and practice with a WHISPER & DO, using their own tempo. The WHISPER is used so each student can work to his or her own tempo. Follow this with a common group tempo with all using a SAY & DO. Try THINK & DO and challenge your students to stay together using their own movements. Have the students close their eyes during this activity — a useful strategy to help them function independently rather than copy other class members.

6. Add bilingual experiences, as appropriate.

7. Add chants, songs, or recorded *instrumental* music to familiar movements. Recorded music with words often distracts the students. The two series of records/cassettes, *Rhythmically Moving* and *Changing Directions,* contain instrumental music appropriate for this purpose.

8. When the group is sitting or standing make the movements aerobic. For example, push the arms down in front of the body or away from the chest, push the arms back, push them up or to the side, bounce the heels, or tap the toes on the floor.

9. Use hand movements to prepare students to play octaves on barred instruments.

10. Introduce echo movement in which the leader does a four-beat echo using Level-I movements and the students copy. Vary the echo by having the students echo with a different movement than the one presented.

Level II: Single Predictable Alternating Movements

The students perform a movement on one side of the body to the first beat, then repeat it on the other side of the body to the second beat. The beat coordination is continued by alternating the motion from one side to the other. Example: Students push one arm down in front of the body one time and then the other arm; the second movement occurs as the first movement ends with the arm returning to the starting position.

Level II is more difficult than Level I because the side of the body changes with every beat and because the nonpreferred side must work by itself. The visual confusion created as some students erroneously think they must figure out which side to use adds to the level of difficulty. Nevertheless, as with Level I, Level II will be mastered very quickly by older children and adults.

Teaching Techniques for Level II: Single Predictable Alternating Movement

1. Introduce the activity with the students seated; incorporate the standing position as they become more comfortable.

2. *Do not specify right or left* in the alternating patterns as this adds another dimension in the movement process.

3. WALK the legs from a seated position before trying the movement standing up. Say "WALK, WALK, WALK, WALK" with each step. Also alternate the heel bouncing as well as the toe tapping.

4. Repeat the alternating movement for a minimum of eight beats before changing the movement.

5. Introduce each new alternating movement without the SAY & DO. Add the label (the SAY) to the movement as soon as the students seem comfortable.

6. Let the students suggest new patterns and lead the activity. Also allow the students to move to a common beat with their own movements, so all are doing different things at the same time.

7. Add bilingual experiences, as appropriate.

8. Add chants, songs, and recorded instrumental music to the movements that have been practiced. (See the *Rythmically Moving* and *Changing Directions* series of records/cassettes.)

9. **Make the movements aerobic when seated or standing.** Alternate the aerobic-type movements suggested for Level I.

10. **Prepare students to use the alternating mallets on the barred instruments by practicing with the hands.**

11. **Use these alternating movements with echo movement.**

Level IIIA: Sequenced Bilateral Symmetrical Movements (Two Beats)

Using both sides of the body, students perform two movements. On the first beat they move both sides of the body to one location and, on the second beat, to another location. Example: Both arms reach out in front of the body on beat one and then both hands touch the shoulders on beat two. The chant is "OUT, IN, OUT, IN."

This is the easiest of the sequenced coordination movements because it is performed using both sides of the body at the same time and because it consists of only two movements. If you lead a group using this coordination, you might see several people who perform the correct movements but perform them in reverse. Their arms are OUT when yours are IN. One of the reasons for this is late processing — the leader goes on to the second movement before the follower begins the first. In such cases, doing the SAY first and then the SAY & DO is very useful to students of all ages.

Teaching Techniques for Level IIIA: Sequenced Bilateral Symmetrical Movement (Two Beats)

1. Use *both* hands or feet simultaneously (bilateral symmetrical movement).

2. Introduce the activity with the students seated; incorporate the standing position as they become more comfortable.

3. Make sure students use leg movements in a seated position at this level because this encourages the development of coordination before the weight is on the feet. Examples include legs APART then TOGETHER, both knees UP then DOWN, or both legs STRAIGHTEN then BEND.

4. One method for introducing a Level-III sequence is to stop after the first movement and have the students copy before doing the second movement; stop again before returning to the beginning movement. Repeat the two movements again slowly, add the labels, and begin the SAY & DO. This strategy gives the students who have difficulty a chance to fully understand and sequence the movements correctly.

5. If students have difficulty executing each part of the movement only once in the two beats, use two repeated movements for each half. Example: Do PAT, PAT, SNAP, SNAP before attempting PAT, SNAP, PAT, SNAP.

6. **Repeat each sequence a minimum of four times (eight beats).** Repeating a movement sequence eight times is often more helpful for less skilled groups.

7. **Ask different students to suggest new sequences and to be the leader.** Have the leader do the movement slowly while the group chants the SAY. Have them join the leader in the DO when they are ready.

8. **Give the students time to "try it on for size," using their own beat and tempo.**

9. **Have the group perform together in a common beat, with each of the students doing their own choice of sequence.** Suggest that they close their eyes as it will help them to concentrate and become less distracted.

10. **Try a variation on four-beat echo movement.** The leader uses just the movement and the students copy with SAY & DO. Example: Leader performs KNEES, SHOULDERS, KNEES, SHOULDERS and the students respond with the movement plus the words (SAY & DO).

11. **Avoid adding chants or songs until the movements can be performed automatically.** When using recorded instrumental music use only rehearsed sequences and have the students WHISPER & DO at first. Change the sequence at the end of the 16-beat parts.

12. **Link Levels I, II, and III and perform them aerobically to music.**

13. **Add bilingual experiences, as appropriate.**

14. **To evaluate the group, "pass" the four-beat movement sequence around the class.** You use a SAY & DO for "KNEES, EARS, KNEES, EARS," and each student in turn repeats your SAY & DO. Those who cannot SAY & DO the activity, or those who cannot sustain the beat and tempo passed around the group need more practice in feeling and expressing beat as well as in beat coordination tasks.

Level IIIB: Sequenced Bilateral Symmetrical Movements (Three Beats)

Students perform three movements on both sides of the body. On the first beat, they move both sides of the body to one location and on the second and third beats, to another location. Example: Using both hands, students pat their thighs on beat one and snap the fingers of both hands on beats two and three. The chant is "PAT, SNAP, SNAP; PAT, SNAP, SNAP."

This coordination sequence is a little more difficult than Level IIIA because of the groupings of three beats. Students who are distracted may do the first movement two times because it is a little easier to double up on the first of the movements. The reason for not teaching it this way is to preserve the integrity of the accent by doing that movement and then going on in the sequence. If students are not experienced in working with groups of three, SIMPLIFY the sequence by suggesting they pat one leg three times and then pat the other leg three times. This coordination is more like a Level-II movement, but the movement alternates after three movements.

Teaching Techniques for Level IIIB: Sequenced Bilateral Symmetrical Movement (Three Beats)

1. **Insert the third beat in the sequences used as two-beat examples.**

2. **The echo movement should be a six-beat sequence:** i.e., WAIST, SHOULDERS, SHOULDERS; WAIST, SHOULDERS, SHOULDERS.

3. **The evaluation should be a six-beat sequence.**

4. **Use music in 3/4 meter.** One good selection for this is "Southwind" on *Rhythmically Moving 1*.

Level IV: Sequenced Bilateral Symmetrical Combined (Four Beats)

Both sides of the body perform four movements — two sequences of two movements. For example, the first sequence could be OUT, IN and the second, PAT, SNAP. The chant thus becomes OUT, IN; PAT, SNAP.

This coordination is more difficult than the first three levels because it demands increased levels of concentration and because of the sequencing of four different motions and four different words. You could introduce the sequence as a Level-III sequence performed on the first two beats followed by another Level-III sequence performed on the second two beats. Learning the pattern as two known sequences linked together

is easier for students than learning four new movements.

Teaching Techniques for Level IV: Sequenced Bilateral Symmetrical Movements Combined

1. **Use both hands *or* feet simultaneously** (bilateral symmetrical).

2. **Introduce the sequence with the students seated. Incorporate the standing position as they become more comfortable.**

3. **Be certain to incorporate leg sequences.**

4. **Practice each half of the sequence before combining the movements into a four-beat pattern.** If students have difficulty combining the patterns, do the first three movements and stop, and then do the last two movements followed by the first movement and stop. Doing one movement beyond each two-beat movement provides a bridge that links the two sequences. Example: Using the pattern above, OUT, IN; PAT, SNAP, have the students do OUT, IN; PAT and stop. Then do PAT, SNAP; OUT and stop.

5. **Movements in one direction will be the easiest.** Example: HEAD, SHOULDERS; WAIST, KNEES is easier than KNEES, SHOULDERS; WAIST, HEAD.

6. **Sequences with a common movement will be easier than four different movements.** Example: HEAD, SHOULDERS; KNEES, SHOULDERS is easier than HEAD, SHOULDERS; EARS, CHIN.

7. **The four-beat echo movement is often more successful if done in two steps.** First have the group echo only the SAY and then echo with the SAY & DO. Usually if they cannot say it, they cannot do it.

8. **Remember, Level-IV sequences are very difficult to perform with chants and songs.** The movement must be automatic, on "muscle memory," before the chant or song is added.

9. **Add recorded instrumental music to the sequences that are established.** Have the students WHISPER & DO before they DO (THINK & DO).

Level V: Sequenced Alternating Movements (Four Beats)

Students perform a two-beat sequence on one

side of the body while holding the other side still; then they perform the same sequence on the other side while holding the first side still. Example: On the first side, students perform OUT, IN and then do OUT, IN on the other side.

This coordination requires that the student inhibit movement on one side while moving the other side. This level breaks Level III apart with one side performing the two-beat sequence before the other side. Students who have difficulty with this movement pattern usually end up doing a Level-II movement: When the first side is returning to the starting position the second side is beginning, thus establishing the single alternating pattern. Using the SAY & DO procedure is very helpful in these instances as a way of helping students organize the sequence of the movement properly.

Teaching Techniques for Level V: Sequenced Alternating Movements.

1. **The following steps assist the student in the development of Level-V movement sequences:**

Step 1: Have the students perform a Level-III movement, such as OUT, IN.

Step 2: Have the students repeat the same movement pattern with only one side of the body; then have them practice the pattern with the other side of the body. Repeat each sequence several times.

Step 3: Try alternating the sequence — the two-beat movement on one side followed by the other side. If any students have difficulty, stop on beat three — OUT, IN; OUT. Try it several times with one side starting and then with the other side starting. Now return to the alternating sequence. Stopping on beat three usually solves the problem.

2. **Let the students decide which side of the body to use first.** After they have practiced it both ways, specify a correct side to start with.

3. **Have the students practice the sequences with the upper body first.** Practice the lower-body sequences in a seated position, before attempting them in a standing position.

4. **Have the students suggest patterns and then** work with each of the students as they make their own selections.

5. **Allow some time for the students to "try it on for size,"** that is, let them practice at their own beat and tempo.

6. **Add chants, songs, and instrumental music** once the patterns are established.

7. **Incorporate the Level-V movements into** four-beat echo patterns.

8. **Add recorded instrumental music to the** sequences that are established.

Level VI: Sequenced Alternating Movements Combined (Eight Beats)

Students execute a four-beat movement sequence on one side of the body while holding the other side still; then they execute the same four-beat movement on the other side while holding the first side still. Example: On one side, students perform OUT, IN; PAT SNAP while holding the other side still; then they reverse the process — doing the same movement on the other side.

This level of coordination is more difficult than the previous one because students must hold one side of the body still longer while executing the sequence on the other side. This also means that students must use their nonpreferred side to execute a long pattern by itself. If students can perform Level IV and can sequence the alternating two-beat movements of Level V, they generally are successful with Level VI. We must be certain that our students understand the pattern of movement before they attempt to alternate it. The SAY organizes the pattern before the movement is added. The leg sequences will be more difficult because of the balance required to execute them successfully.

Teaching Techniques for Level VI: Sequenced Alternating Movements Combined

1. **Present the four movements in a bilaterally symmetrical way first (as in Level IV).** Then practice each side alone several times before attempting the alternating pattern.

2. **If students have difficulty, stop on the first**

beat of the opposite side. Example: OUT, IN, PAT, SNAP; OUT.

3. Allow the students to use the side they prefer first rather than specifying a particular side.

4. Practice Level-VI sequences with the upper body first. Then do lower-body sequences in a nonweight-bearing position, followed by a standing position.

5. Let the students practice using their own beat and tempo first.

6. Add chants, songs, and recorded instrumental music after the sequences are established.

7. Try eight-beat echos with Level-VI movements.

Summary of General Guidelines for Introducing Levels I to VI

1. **Have students sit in chairs to help them feel less conspicuous and to create a nonweight-bearing position that makes it easier for them to coordinate their leg movements.** In a standing position, students will be shifting weight, and weight-shifting positions are more difficult to coordinate than nonweight-bearing positions.

2. **Be certain students can SAY & DO at Level I before trying the more difficult levels.** If some of the students cannot SAY & DO, refer to the steps suggested in the earlier section on beat awareness activities.

3. **Note the use of bilateral symmetrical movements (both sides of the body doing the same thing) in Levels I, III and IV.** Remember, it is easier for students to do a movement on both sides simultaneously than for them to do a movement on one side at a time.

4. **Avoid movements that specify the use of the correct side of the body, as in right/left or mirroring.** Let the students choose the side of the body they wish to use first.

5. **Avoid adding claps and stamps in the first few levels because clapping and stamping are difficult for students to coordinate with movement.** Also, clapping and stamping are not bilateral movements.

6. **At first, avoid combinations of upper-body and lower-body movements in the same sequence,** e.g., OUT, IN (arms), APART, TOGETHER (legs).

7. **Allow the students to decide on the movement each will perform as you work on a specific level.** If you are working on Level III, for example, each student should decide how he or she is going to sequence the two movements.

8. **Remove yourself from the movement sequences in an inconspicuous manner.** If we are always there to provide students with a visual or auditory model, the students may not develop the independence of movement we are striving for.

9. **Give students opportunities to be the leader.** This creates changes in tempo and gives ownership of the process to the students.

10. **Work logically from level to level.** If students have been using both hands to pat their legs, suggest an alternating pat of the legs next, rather than changing location. Then use the leg pat as the first beat of the two-beat sequence in Level III.

11. **At first, present the Level-III sequence as two Level-I movements.** Present the Level-IV sequence as two Level-III sequences, Level V as Level III alternated from one side of the body to the other, or Level VI as Level IV alternated from one side of the body to the other.

12. **Add instrumental music, chants, or songs after the sequences have been practiced.**

Other Combinations

1. **Combine Level I with Level II.** Example: PAT the legs with both hands, then PAT one leg with the corresponding hand while the other hand rests. After practicing this several times, reverse the single hand PAT to the other hand, and then alternate the single hand. "PAT, ONE; PAT, OTHER." This corresponds to JUMP, HOP; JUMP, HOP in which the hopping foot alternates.

2. **Try Level-IV movements in which on the first two beats you use one part of the body, such as the arms, and on the second two beats you use the legs.** For a challenge, do beat one with the arms, beat two with the legs, beat three with the

arms, and beat four with the legs. Example: Arms go OUT, legs go APART; arms come IN, legs come TOGETHER.

3. **Combine arm and leg patterns while seated.** The arms and legs at first should do the same movement in a bilaterally symmetrical fashion, such as straightening and bending with a SAY of "OUT, IN" or "STRAIGHTEN, BEND." Then try the pattern with both arms and legs performing a sequenced alternating movement. Use the arm and leg on the same side first then on the other side.

4. **Combine arm and leg patterns while standing — integrated movement.** Try alternating weight-bearing movements from side to side. TOUCH the heel in front and STRAIGHTEN the arm on the same side of the body in front. STEP in place and BEND the arm. Repeat on the other side. Also, try it with the opposite arm and leg moving.

5. **Try a different pattern with the arms than with the legs — integrated movement.** Example: Use the SAY & DO with the leg pattern (APART, TOGETHER). Now rehearse the arm pattern, which consists of straightening and bending the arms in front of the body. Then apply the SAY of the leg pattern (i.e., arms are moved on the chant "APART, TOGETHER.") Finally, combine the arm pattern with the SAY & DO of the leg pattern.

As you begin to experiment with different patterns of movement, new ideas will come. You will find that your students also will come up with wonderful challenges, so use their ideas.

Summary

This chapter concentrates on two forms of movement, **creative movement** and **rhythmic movement**. The emphasis in this book is on **rhythmic movement** but both forms of movement are used to prepare students for organized dance, exercise routines, music activities, and sports. Three **key experiences in movement** are used to extend movement in these two areas: **Expressing Creativity in Movement, Feeling and Expressing Beat,** and **Moving With Others to a Common Beat.** In addition, **presentation methods** rely on two other key experiences, **Following Movement Directions** and **Describing Movement.** When engaging in either form of movement, students will rely on their **comfort with movement** skill resulting from all four key experiences in movement involving **ways to move: Moving the Body in Nonlocomotor Ways, Moving the Body in Locomotor Ways, Moving the Body in Integrated Ways,** and **Moving With Objects.**

The section on creative movement describes several methods for reducing the threatening nature of creative movement activities. The most important aspect of presenting creative movement activities is encouraging the active involvement of your students from the beginning — use them as leaders and adapt their ideas to the skill being practiced. This type of presentation will result in **comfort with movement** as students develop a sense of ownership of the movement process and related concepts.

For students to do **rhythmic movement** successfully, they must possess **rhythmic competency**: the ability to feel and express beat (**basic timing**) and the ability to move with others to a common beat (**beat coordination**). To develop these skill areas, students need practice in walking to the beat and in coordinating sequences of movement in relation to beat.

The following strategies are useful to remember when working on the development of rhythmic competency:

● Delay movement in rhythm until second grade — work instead on steady beat.

● Delay movement that requires "inhibiting"

until second grade — alternating movement sequences and clapping are examples of such movements.

• Learn the sequences in a seated position first and move to a weight-bearing position when students are comfortable with the coordination of the legs in the nonweight-bearing position sequences.

• Avoid specifying correct side to begin movement and do not ask for correct side until second grade. Practice the movement on both sides.

• Remove yourself from the activity as inconspicuously as possible. Frequently, we act as visual or auditory models for students, and as a result, students often do not develop the independence in movement we are striving to instill in them.

• When performing movement tasks to recorded music, be certain the music is **instrumental** rather than **vocal**.

Introducing Folk Dance to Beginners 5

Organized dance is defined as a **rhythmic movement sequence performed to music**. It should be a beautiful "marriage" between music and movement — the more unified, the more aesthetic the experience. The reason this book focuses on beginning international folk dance becomes clear when we compare the different types of organized dance.

Ballroom dance involves difficult rhythm patterns rather than a step or motion for each beat.

The dancer must begin with the correct foot and must have a partner. **Square dance** requires partners and entails an individual performing complex movement and directional patterns while keeping the beat. Current **dance fads** can involve a great deal of style and creativity; even if the footwork is simple, the impression created by the style can discourage a beginner. **Aerobic** and other **fitness-type dance** requires that the participants follow highly complex movements and

continuously changing movement sequences. Many aerobic dance routines require that individuals use both the arms and legs to perform either *integrated movements* (combining upper-body with lower-body movements) or *contralateral movements* (using the opposite arm and leg moving at the same time).

International folk dances, on the other hand, begin with simple movements that combine to become easy circle and line dances that do not require complex footwork, rhythms, or changes of direction.

This chapter offers a method for introducing folk dance to students from approximately age 7 to adulthood. By second grade, students should have been exposed to an introductory sequence of organized movements. If the students have not experienced the introductory sequences, the teacher should present them before attempting to introduce actual folk dances. Then the folk dances should be introduced by level of difficulty.

Chapter 6 contains the delivery system for teaching international folk dance to students *after* they have mastered the introductory sequence of activities presented here. You will find it helpful to read Chapter 6 along with this chapter to strengthen and deepen your knowledge base — providing a broader perspective on international folk dance.

Part Two of this book contains a variety of international folk dances that are suitable for beginners who have successfully completed these introductory steps. The dances in Part Two are organized by level of difficulty. (See Appendix C, List of Dances by Level of Difficulty.)

Remember, the dances described in this section and in Part Two are recommended for those students who have experienced many *ways to move,* for those students who possess *rhythmic competency* and for those students who possess the ability to SAY & DO. I have found that at least 50% of students of all ages do not possess the prerequisites to feel successful with folk dance. Teachers can provide these prerequisities by using the teaching model described in Chapter 1 and by applying the teaching progressions for the key experiences in movement described in Chapters 2, 3, and 4.

Students of any age can be successful. Therefore, assuming that our particular group of students is ready to be introduced to international folk dance, we are faced with three important questions: (1) What guidelines will we follow for selecting introductory organized movement and dance sequences and the corresponding music? (2) How will we plan and introduce the first experiences so that the participants (young or old) feel successful? (3) How will we introduce folk dance by level of difficulty?

Guidelines for Selecting Organized Movement and Dance Sequences and Music for Beginners

Music

1. The music should be instrumental.

2. The music should have a strong underlying beat.

3. The phrases of the music should be distinct and occur in groupings of 8 or 16 beats.

4. The music should be organized in either two or three parts that are predictable in their repetition.

5. The music should be organized in groupings of two beats rather than three beats and should have a metronome setting that is not too fast or too slow (120 – 132 usually works well).

6. Use music to which beginners can relate. Avoid music that uses unfamiliar instruments.

Please note that many of the musical selections recorded on the nine *Rhythmically Moving* albums and cassettes meet these criteria.

Movement and Dance Sequences

1. The sequences should follow the phrases of the music.

2. Each part of the sequence should be highly repetitive.

3. The sequences should not require organized formations, such as a closed circle; students should be able to move about the room freely.

4. The sequences should not require the specific use of the "right" or "left" foot.

5. The sequences should not require holding hands or taking partners.

6. The sequences should not require complicated directional changes. Turning 180° or performing movement to the side is difficult for beginners.

7. Begin with sequences that change feet on every beat, rather than combining nonweight-transfer movements with weight-transfer movements.

8. Avoid style movements or claps and snaps until the foot movements are organized.

9. Build a consistent Language-to-Dance Vocabulary for the sequences. See Table 6 for the commonly used word labels and the Glossary for the complete Language-to-Dance Vocabulary. The ability to SAY & DO is a great help to the beginner.

Building Success With the First Movement and Dance Sequences

There are not many simple folk dances in the literature that satisfy the guidelines mentioned above. The international folk dance material that is suitable for beginners (from second grade on) often requires understanding and abilities well beyond the level of rhythmic competency achieved by beginners, such as sideward patterns, alternating two-beat sequences (Level Five), recurring four-beat and alternating four-beat movement patterns, and the use of the divided beat. Thus, **before introducing organized folk dance, teachers must provide opportunities for** students to practice locomotor and nonlocomotor sequences in different combinations, in different directions, and to a variety of musical selections.

You may have to choreograph simple dance sequences based on the guidelines presented above to bridge the gap from the simple rhythmic movement activities presented in Chapter 4 to actual folk dances. Such introductory dances should employ the same Language-to-Dance (Movement) Vocabulary used in the preceding chapters. Students chant an action word, indicating the type of step or the direction, followed by a counting sequence. Use groupings of four beats. Some easy sequences that comply with these guidelines are provided below. They may be rehearsed in free formation, first with SAY & DO and then to music.

1. MARCH, 2, 3, 4; MARCH, 2, 3, 4; PAT, 2, 3, 4; PUSH, 2, 3, 4. (MARCH in place or in a specified direction, PAT the legs with both hands at the same time and then push the arms down in front of the body.) Note the use of groups of four, rather than counting to eight. This prepares the students for dance steps and sequences that use four beats.

2. WALK, 2, 3, 4; WALK, 2, 3, 4; DOWN, UP (4 times). (On the DOWN, UP bend and straighten the knees.)

3. MARCH, 2, 3, 4; PAT, 2, 3, 4; HOP, 2, 3, 4 (one foot); HOP, 2, 3, 4 (other foot). This is more difficult because the sequence changes after each four beats.

4. JUMP, 2, 3, 4 (in place); APART, TOGETHER, APART, TOGETHER (jump legs apart then together); KNEES, KNEES, SHOULDERS, SHOULDERS; KNEES, KNEES, SHOULDERS, SHOULDERS (pat knees two times and shoulders two times).

In addition, I recommend that you use two types of simple organized dances as your first dances: (1) **Two-Part, Three-Part**, and **Four-Part** dances that may be designed by you as well as by the students, and (2) **Big Circle** dances. These dances begin to incorporate more changes of direction and begin to involve the group in a common formation.

Two-Part Dances

Construct a dance from a musical selection that is grouped into two parts (such as "Blackberry

Quadrille," "Rakes of Mallow," and "Soldier's Joy," from *Rhythmically Moving 2* and "La Raspa," and "Irish Washerwoman" from *Rhythmically Moving 3*). The Two-Part Dance and the *Rhythmically Moving* recording on which it is found are described in Part Two of this book. Parts I and II (the A and B sections) should each have 16 or 32 beats, which allow for repeated movement, and each part should be easily distinguished. Use a locomotor pattern for Part I (the A section of the music). Walk one direction around the room for the first half of Part I and the other direction around the room for the second half of Part I. Use a nonlocomotor pattern for Part II (the B section of the music). Push the hands down in front of the body for the first half of Part II and push in a new direction for the second half of Part II. Have different students volunteer to be the leader for the nonlocomotor Part II. Encourage elementary-age students to decide which movements to use. Older students and adults prefer being directed at first. If the students can use space randomly, they feel less visible. Some groups, particularly older children, are unable to use space randomly. They get silly and use the occasion to crash into one another. In such a situation, it is better to have everyone go in the same direction.

A simple two-part dance developed for older children is the simplified version of "La Raspa." Part I (the A section) is nonlocomotor and Part II (the B section) is locomotor. Another simple dance is "Count 64." Part II (the B section) of the music uses a combination of nonlocomotor movements and locomotor movements.

Three-Part Dances

Music that is organized into three parts, such as "Zigeunerpolka" on *Rhythmically Moving 2*, "Sliding" on *Rhythmically Moving 1*, or "Little Shoemaker" on *Rhythmically Moving 3* provides a structure teachers and students alike can use to create a dance. Example: Part I (the A section), WALK one direction (or change direction in the middle of the Part); Part II (the B section), perform WAIST, WAIST, EARS, EARS (touching those parts of the body); and PART III (the C section), HOP on one foot for the first half and the other foot for the second half. Also see the choreo-

graphies for "Sliding" and "Zigeunerpolka" in Part II of this book.

Four-Part Dances

Use the same type of music described in Two-Part Dances in which the A and B sections of the music repeat. Part I (the A section) is played twice in a row as is Part II (the B section). You also may use music that has four 8-beat phrases, such as "Yankee Doodle" on *Rhythmically Moving 2*. The locomotor or nonlocomotor movement still changes with each part. What makes it four-part is the change of movement in the middle of each part. Example: Part I (first half of the A), walk with the body TALL or with the toes turned IN; (second half of the A, walk with the body SHORT or with the toes turned OUT; repeat Part I; Part II (first half of the B), perform OUT, IN movements of the arms; (second half of the B), perform UP, DOWN movements of the arms; repeat Part II. Be certain to link the parts together before performing the sequences to the music. Ask the students to recall the sequence: "What do we do first? Second? Third? Fourth?" Remember to involve the students.

It should be noted that these types of simple dances may be choreographed for limited space in which students convert locomotor patterns to in-place sequences — walking in place using any of the variations. The movement sequences also may be performed by persons sitting in chairs — chair dancing.

Big Circle Dances

Students now change from a more random pattern of movement to moving around the room in a more organized circle; either in a forward or backward direction, or toward or away from the center of the room. The goal is for the students to learn to change direction and not lose balance, while keeping the beat. When moving forward and backward around the room, it works best to change direction after 16 beats. Example: Walk FORWARD right 16 steps; walk BACKWARD left 16 steps. Movement toward and away from the center is most successful when 8 steps are used in each direction. There is not space enough for 16 steps,

and 4 steps create the change of direction too quickly.

As students gain more experience try calling out (cueing) the changes of directions right before the musical change. The students must listen and keep their good balance. With even more experience, try forming a single circle without joining hands, then try joining hands.

Big Circle Dances may be used as the first dance in a folk dance class for several class periods. I find that the students become oriented to walking to the beat and to directional changes. It serves as a warm-up for the class and ensures immediate success for all.

Introducing Folk Dances and Steps by Level of Difficulty

By this point students should be participating in simple dance sequences, should be comfortable changing direction, should have some body control and balance, and should be able to SAY & DO. They are now ready to begin learning the dances and steps that are classified as "beginning" folk

dance. It is advisable to introduce these steps and dances by level of difficulty, from the simplest to the more complex. Determining which dances to choose for your students depends on several factors:

● The chronological and developmental age of the participants

● Their familiarity with international music

● How comfortably the students move to the beat with changes of direction and movement patterns

● The amount of space available

I feel compelled to interject a note of caution at this point. After teachers become familiar with more complex organized dance material, they often tend to disregard the need to proceed by level of difficulty. An "apple-picking" analogy best explains this tendency; pickers reach to different limbs (some higher, some lower) in their search for the apples that are the biggest, reddest, and most free of imperfection. In like manner, dances often are chosen because (1) the teacher enjoys them, (2) they *appear* to the *experienced* teacher

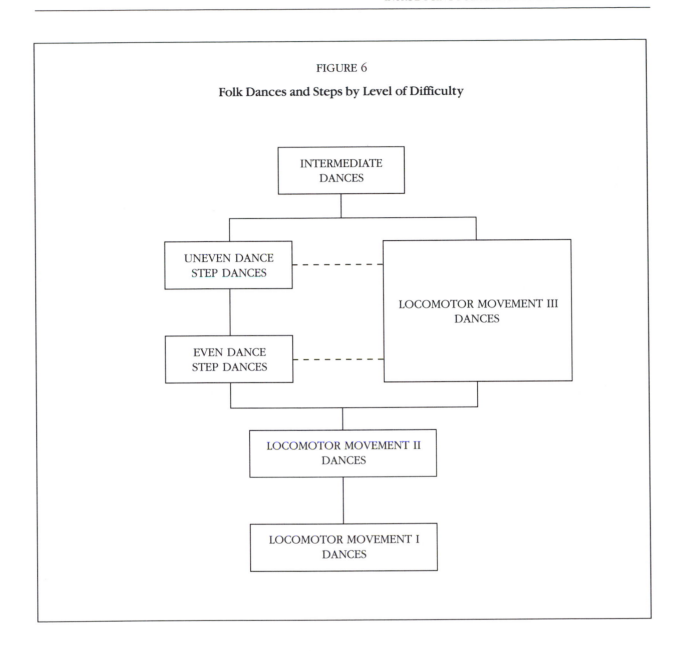

FIGURE 6

Folk Dances and Steps by Level of Difficulty

to be simple, (3) the teacher thinks the students will enjoy them, or (4) they serve to demonstrate the teacher's dance ability.

As illustrated in Figure 6, the first level of folk dance is called **Locomotor Movement I** because of the simplicity of the movements; this level is followed by **Locomotor Movement II** and **Locomotor Movement III**. The "locomotor movement" folk dances are so named because they *do not use any specific folk dance steps*. Dances using **Even Folk Dance Steps** are the easiest of the dances using specific dance steps and are similar in level of difficulty to the **Locomotor Movement III** dances. These steps are referred to as "even" be-

cause each movement in the step takes the same amount of time to execute. Dances using **Uneven Folk Dance Steps** are the most difficult beginning folk dances for students to master because of the required combinations of beat, divided beat, and resting beat. Fourth grade is usually an appropriate time to expect children to be successful with the **Uneven Folk Dance Steps** if they have had experience with the easier dances. *Motor experience, not age is the determining factor.*

Beginners should start with several **Locomotor Movement I** dances and, as they become ready, gradually move on to **Locomotor Movement II** dances. When the students have mastered the special characteristics found in **Locomotor Movement I** and **II** dances, they can either proceed to **Locomotor Movement III** dances or to **Even Folk Dance Steps.** In order of difficulty the **Even Folk Dance Steps** are the CHERKESSIYA; the GRAPEVINE, which is a moving Cherkessiya; the STEP HOP; and finally, the SCHOTTISCHE, which is the Step Hop preceded by two steps. **Locomotor Movement III** dances are similar in difficulty. The **Uneven Folk Dance Steps,** in order of difficulty, include the THREE; the TWO-STEP that puts a closing step into the Three; the YEMENITE, which is the same rhythmic structure as the Three and the Two-Step; and finally the POLKA, which is a Two-Step preceded by an up-beat.

Locomotor Movement Sequences by Level of Difficulty

Each of the Locomotor Movement Dance categories require development of certain skills in order to proceed to the next level of difficulty. These skills are described below. The dances in Part Two also are organized in this way. Introducing these skills requires the expanded use of the Four-Step Language Process as a bridge to movement (see Chapter 2). The beginner's Language-to-Movement Vocabulary expands to become a Language-to-Dance Vocabulary. The basic Language-to-Dance Vocabulary is listed in Table 6. The complete Language-to-Dance Vocabulary is included in the Glossary. Before the music is added use the SAY and the SAY & DO, then use WHISPER & DO and DO (THINK & DO) with the music. This progression of locomotor movement skills is intended as a guide to help the teacher select dances. See Appendix C for the dances listed by level of difficulty.

Locomotor Movement I

***Alternate the feet in movement sequences that employ* direction**

- FORWARD, 2, 3, 4; FORWARD, 2, 3, 4 (moving in the facing direction *around* the room); BACKWARD, 2, 3, 4; BACKWARD, 2, 3, 4 (moving away from the facing direction *around* the room). Note the use of groups of four rather than groups of

eight. This prepares dancers for more difficult sequences that generally use four-beat patterns.

- FORWARD, 2, 3, 4; BACKWARD, 2, 3, 4; IN, 2, 3, 4; OUT, 2, 3, 4 (in and out are toward and away from the center of the room)

- SCISSOR, 2, 3, 4 (alternate the kicking foot toward the center); IN, 2, 3, 4; SCISSOR, 2, 3, 4; OUT, 2, 3, 4.

Recurring two-beat movement sequences in one place with no weight transfers or "correct" sides

- HEEL, TOE, HEEL, TOE,

- UP, TOUCH, UP, TOUCH

Locomotor Movement II and III

Three recurring nonweight-transfer movements (e.g., TOUCH) plus a weight transfer (STEP) on the last beat of the four-beat sequence

- TOUCH, TOUCH, TOUCH, STEP

- UP, TOUCH, UP, STEP

Three alternating movements followed by a nonweight-transfer movement on the fourth beat of the four-beat sequence

- FORWARD, FORWARD, FORWARD, HEEL

- BACKWARD, BACKWARD, BACKWARD, TOE

- IN, IN, IN, KICK

- OUT, OUT, OUT, TOUCH

Recurring 2-beat movement sequences that move sideward, right or left, as the students face the center of the room (this is the first use of the "correct" foot)

- SIDE, CLOSE, SIDE, CLOSE

- SIDE, BACK, SIDE, BACK (crossing behind)

- SIDE, CROSS, SIDE, CROSS (crossing in front)

Two different two-beat sequences performed once

- SIDE, TOUCH; OUT, TOUCH

- SIDE, TOUCH; IN, HOOK

Alternating two-beat sequences (the second two beats begin on the opposite foot (Level V of the Levels of Beat Coordination)

TABLE 6

Introductory Language-to-Dance Vocabulary

*Words meaning **transfer of weight**, i.e., STEP/WALK*

STEP	A·step on the designated foot, in place.
FORWARD	A step on the designated foot moving in the facing direction (clockwise or counterclockwise) around a circle or one behind the other in a line
BACKWARD	A step on the designated foot moving away from the facing direction (clockwise or counterclockwise) around a circle or one behind the other in a line
IN	A step on the designated foot toward the center of a circle or in the facing direction when standing side by side in a line
OUT	A step on the designated foot away from the center of a circle or away from the facing direction when standing side by side in a line
SIDE	A step on the designated foot perpendicular to the facing direction when standing side by side
CLOSE	A step on the designated foot to bring it next to the other foot — in any direction
BACK	A step on the designated foot crossing in back of the other foot
CROSS	A step on the designated foot crossing in front of the other foot
TURN	A step on the designated foot that moves the body clockwise or counterclockwise 90° or 180° with a single weight transfer, or the step that begins a multistep rotation (90°, 180°, or 360°)
ACCENT	A forceful step on the designated foot

*Words meaning **no transfer of weight***

TOUCH	A motion of the designated foot against the floor
STAMP	A forceful motion of the designated foot against the floor
KICK	A motion of the designated leg in front, in back, or to the side of the body involving a straightening of the knee
LIFT	A motion of the designated leg in front of the body involving a bent knee. The lower leg is angled in front of the supporting leg
UP	A motion of the designated leg in front of the body begun by raising the knee
HEEL	A motion of the designated heel against the floor

*The complete Language-to-Dance Vocabulary appears in the Glossary.

- HEEL, STEP, HEEL, STEP

- KICK, STEP, KICK, STEP

- SIDE, TOUCH, SIDE, TOUCH

- SIDE, LIFT, SIDE, LIFT

Uneven timing

- TOUCH, TOUCH, STEP/STEP, STEP (one divided beat in four beats)

- FORWARD, FORWARD, FORWARD/FORWARD, FORWARD

- FORWARD, 2, 3, 4; FORWARD, REST, FORWARD, REST (use of rest in the second four beats)

Recurring four-beat movements (the second sequence of four beats begins on the same foot)

- STEP, KICK, STEP, TOUCH; STEP, KICK, STEP, TOUCH

- IN, CLAP, OUT, CLAP; IN, CLAP, OUT, CLAP

- SIDE, BACK, SIDE, CROSS; SIDE, BACK, SIDE, CROSS

Alternating four-beat movements (the second

sequence of four beats begins on the opposite foot (Level VI of the Levels of Beat Coordination)

- SIDE, BACK, SIDE, KICK; SIDE, BACK, SIDE, KICK

- SIDE, CLOSE, SIDE, TOUCH; SIDE, CLOSE, SIDE, TOUCH

- SIDE, CROSS, SIDE, LIFT; SIDE, CROSS, SIDE, LIFT

Complex use of space (the facing direction changes frequently)

- FORWARD, 2, 3, TURN; BACKWARD, 2, 3, 4

- Contra and square dances

Uncommon meter (dances executed in 3/4 or 5/4 meter are not as common or as easy for beginners as dance patterns organized in two and four beats)

- SIDE, BOUNCE, CROSS or SIDE, SIDE, CROSS

- FORWARD, 2, 3, HOP/STEP, STEP

To sum up, beginning international folk dance can be a most enjoyable educational experience for students from second grade to adulthood. The dances are arranged in a logical order from simple to more complex to permit students to experience success. This order takes into account balance, coordination, and stages of motor development.

As noted earlier, the beginning folk dance steps and sequences presented in this chapter and in Part Two of this book are grouped by categories: **Locomotor Movement I, Locomotor Movement II, Locomotor Movement III, Even Folk Dance Steps,** and **Uneven Folk Dance Steps.** Please note that the dances chosen for Part Two represent primarily circle and line dances or partner and mixer dances in which both persons do the same sequence. Students should be comfortable with dance and the group should be well balanced between male and female dancers, before couple dances are taught. Couple dances often involve different parts for the male and female dancer. Dances from many countries are not included in this book, since the dance heritage in those countries is represented by these types of couple dances.

Introducing Beginners to Locomotor Movement I Dances

The simplest of the folk dances include the previous movement experiences found in the Two-Part, Three-Part, Four-Part, and the Big Circle dances as well as the following characteristics:

1. **There is a step or motion for every beat.** No resting beats or divided beats are included.

2. **There is no reference to "right" or "left" foot.** All dances have a "correct" foot. The intent for the Locomotor Movement I dances is to permit the students to start on either foot in their beginning folk dance experience.

3. **There is no need for handholding.** Holding hands increases the level of difficulty and adds tension to the learning experience. Add handholds later.

4. **The formations can be modified easily for beginners.** This permits beginners to move around the room in an unstructured circle, and to avoid holding hands in partner dances.

5. **The music has a strong underlying beat.** Use instrumental music in which the beat is easily distinguished.

6. **There is repetition of sequences.** The sequences are short and uncomplicated. Each sequence is performed more than one time in a row, e.g., FORWARD, 2, 3, 4; FORWARD, 2, 3, 4.

7. **There are recurring 2-beat nonlocomotor movement sequences.** These nonlocomotor lower-body sequences do not require changing sides of the body before the eighth beat. An example is UP, TOUCH; UP, TOUCH; UP, TOUCH; UP, STEP.

Because it is difficult to find ethnic dances that satisfy the beginning criteria listed earlier, I have choreographed several dances and simplified some original folk dances for teachers to introduce to their beginning students. (These choreographed and simplified dances are described in Part Two of this book, and the music is found on the *Rhythmically Moving* albums.) The choreographed dances are *Count 64, Irish Stew, Sliding, Sneaky Snake, Yankee Doodle, Zigeuner-polka*. The simplified dances are *Bannielou Lambaol, Cherkessiya, Doudlebskà Polka, Fjäskern, Les Saluts, Plješkavac Kolo, Te Ve Orez*.

All the dances listed are appropriate for older children and adults. Refer to Appendix C, Dances by Level of Difficulty for additional suggestions for Locomotor Movement I dances.

Introducing Beginners to Locomotor Movement II Dances

Once students are comfortable with **Locomotor Movement I** dances they are ready to proceed to **Locomotor Movement II**. Second grade is an appropriate time to begin these dances if the students have the prerequisite abilities. The characteristics of **Locomotor Movement II** dances include the following:

1. **Use of nonweight-transfer movement (KICK or TOUCH) at the end of four or eight beats.** Example: FORWARD, FORWARD, FORWARD, KICK. Have the students choose the foot to begin with and have them step in place, stopping and balancing before the nonweight-transfer motion. Then have them start with the other foot. Now try it moving in a FORWARD direction. To link two 4-beat sequences together, try stopping on the first beat of the second four beats. (FORWARD, FORWARD, FORWARD, KICK; FORWARD) When students are comfortable doing this with both feet, specify a "correct" foot.

2. **Use of correct foot.** Work with alternating foot patterns and have the students try the preferred foot first and then try the other foot. Following this practice, try designating "right" or "left" side.

3. **Use of recurring two-beat sequences executed sideward.** Practice moving sideward using repetitious patterns of SIDE, CLOSE; SIDE, BACK;

or SIDE, CROSS. Students should practice to their own beat and tempo. If students have difficulty repeating the pattern, have them stop on the first movement of the next pattern (e.g., SIDE, BACK; SIDE).

4. **Use of alternating two-beat sequences.** Practice a sequence with the arms first (see Level V of the Levels of Beat Coordination in Chapter 4). Practice the following foot patterns from a seated position first if necessary and then from a weight-bearing position: HEEL, STEP; HEEL, STEP; or UP, STEP; UP, STEP. If students have difficulty, stop on the first beat of the next sequence (e.g., HEEL, STEP, HEEL). Be certain to try it with each foot as the starting foot.

5. **Holding a beat at the end of phrases.** Practice sequences of eight beats, substituting the word REST for the final beat. Example:
FORWARD, 2, 3, 4; FORWARD, 2, 3, REST;
BACKWARD, 2, 3, 4; BACKWARD 2, 3, REST
Be certain students know that the second sequence begins with the opposite foot.

6. **Use of single divided beat in four beats.** TOUCH, TOUCH, STEP/STEP, STEP. The third beat is divided. Have students stop at the end of each sequence, then link the first beat of the next sequence to the pattern (e.g., TOUCH, TOUCH, STEP/STEP, STEP; TOUCH).

7. **Use of four-beat recurring and alternating sequences.** These four-beat sequences combine two different two-beat sequences. Example: Recurring SIDE, LIFT, SIDE, STAMP (same foot begins each time and the two 2-beat sequences are SIDE, LIFT plus SIDE, STAMP). Alternating SIDE, CLOSE, SIDE, TOUCH (opposite foot begins each time and the two 2-beat sequences are SIDE, CLOSE plus SIDE, TOUCH). At first just do the four beats and stop. Then try it starting with the other foot and stop. Then link the first beat of the repeated sequence to the four beats (e.g., SIDE, LIFT, SIDE, STAMP; SIDE or SIDE, CLOSE, SIDE, TOUCH; SIDE).

A list of **Locomotor Movement II** dances can be found in Appendix C, Dances by Level of Difficulty. All are appropriate for second graders, *if* they possess the appropriate motor skills. Ask the students to choreograph sequences. Put several of the Language-to-Dance Vocabulary words on the chalkboard and ask them to make up dances using words. Add music to their choreographies. Examples using two-part music are as follows:

1. **Part I**: FORWARD, 2, 3, 4; BACKWARD, 2, 3, 4; FORWARD, KICK, FORWARD, KICK; BACKWARD, KICK, BACKWARD, KICK. Repeat if music repeats. **Part II**: IN, 2, 3, 4; SIDE, LIFT, SIDE, STAMP; OUT, 2, 3, 4; SIDE, LIFT, SIDE, STAMP. Repeat if music repeats.

2. **Part I**: SIDE, CLOSE, SIDE, TOUCH; SIDE, CLOSE, SIDE, TOUCH; IN, 2, 3, KICK; OUT, 2, 3, TOUCH. Repeat if music repeats. **Part II**: FORWARD, FORWARD, BACKWARD, BACKWARD; FORWARD, FORWARD, BACKWARD, BACKWARD; IN, TOUCH, OUT, TOUCH; IN, TOUCH, OUT, TOUCH. Repeat if music repeats.

You now can proceed to Locomotor Movement III dances or can introduce dances requiring Even Folk Dance Steps. I like to intersperse the Locomotor Movement III dances with dances using Even and Uneven Dance Steps to give variety. For the purpose of grouping similar experiences, however, the dances are presented separately in this book.

Introducing Beginners to Locomotor Movement III Dances

These dances are more difficult than the preceding dances for the following reasons:

1. **Quicker footwork may be demanded because the tempo is faster.** Have the students practice patterns of movement quickly to their own beat and tempo, e.g., SIDE, BACK or SIDE, CLOSE, SIDE, TOUCH.

2. **There may be several parts to the dance.** The dance may have four parts. Have the students SAY the parts in order to be certain they have memorized the correct sequence.

3. **The dances may require complex changes of direction.** Changes of direction require more

balance. Encourage the students to make up sequences that change direction quickly.

4. **There are groupings of beats other than in twos or fours. Movement sequences grouped in threes or fives are introduced.** Groupings of two or four beats are more common to our culture and are easier. Have the students practice moving to the combinations most often used in 3/4 meter. Have them walk on all three beats in each measure, to just the first beat of each measure, and to beats 1 and 3 of each measure. Have them do the same type of practice for the 5/4 meter.

5. **The music may have a more ethnic sound with a less easily defined beat.** Have the students listen to the music and discuss the instruments used.

Dances classified as **Locomotor Movement III** are found in Appendix C, Dances by Level of Difficulty.

Introducing Beginners to Even Folk Dance Steps

After students have mastered the combinations of steps and sideward patterns plus two- and four-beat sequences introduced in Locomotor Movement II, they are ready to proceed to **Even Folk Dance Steps**. The most basic of these steps are the CHERKESSIYA, the GRAPEVINE, the STEP HOP, and the SCHOTTISCHE. As noted earlier, these steps are referred to as "even" because each movement in the sequence takes the same amount of time to execute. Each of these steps is described below with suggestions for practicing and linking them into dances. The CHERKESSIYA step and the GRAPEVINE step should be mastered first because they are the easiest extensions of a basic walking pattern. The feet move in specified sequences. Rather than IN, 2, 3, 4, we have IN, STEP, OUT, STEP (CHERKESSIYA).

The CHERKESSIYA Step

The CHERKESSIYA (sometimes spelled TCHERKESSIYA) step is found most often in

Summary of Teaching Tips for Locomotor Movement I – III Sequences and Dance Steps

- Students should practice steps in place before traveling in the designated direction. Example: STEP, STEP, STEP, KICK *before* FORWARD, 2, 3, KICK.

- Students should practice steps beginning with one foot then beginning with the other foot *before* a correct foot is required.

- Students should practice steps in both directions before they step in a specific direction.

- Give students individual practice time to execute movement in their own tempo — the "try-it-on-for-size" strategy.

- When teaching the two-beat alternating sequence, have students stop one beat beyond the two-beat sequence and practice it starting with each foot. Example: HEEL, STEP; HEEL *before* HEEL, STEP; HEEL, STEP and SIDE, TOUCH; SIDE *before* SIDE, TOUCH; SIDE, TOUCH.

- When teaching the four-beat recurring sequence or dance steps, have students practice each two-beat sequence separately and then link the two 2-beat sequences together, applying the same teaching method as used in the two-beat alternating sequence, if

necessary. Example: IN, KICK plus OUT, TOUCH.

- When teaching the four-beat alternating sequence or dance steps, have students practice the two 2-beat sequences separately, link them together, and then stop one beat beyond the four-beat sequence. Example: SIDE, CLOSE, SIDE, TOUCH; SIDE.

- Have students do all the weight transfer movements first to establish footwork and balance and then add the nonweight-transfer movements. Example: FORWARD, FORWARD; SIDE (LIFT); SIDE (LIFT) — add the LIFT after practicing SIDE, REST; SIDE, REST.

- Students should leave out the HOP until they are comfortable with the remainder of the sequences involving the HOP. Example: IN, (HOP); OUT (HOP) — practice IN, REST; OUT, REST first.

- Have students practice the style of the dance after the footwork is secure. Continue to use the Language-to-Dance Vocabulary words, and SAY, when the upper-body movements are practiced, but stand still. Have students CLAP with the word OUT rather than say CLAP on beat one coming out.

Israeli dance. It originated with the Cherkassians, one of the current ethnic groups of Israel. These people emigrated from the Caucasus Mountains of the USSR when Israel gained her statehood.

Important Characteristics

1. The CHERKESSIYA step consists of a sequence of four movements executed in a FORWARD and BACKWARD or IN and OUT rocking motion.

2. This step is a combination of the two-beat sequences IN, OUT and OUT, IN or FORWARD, BACKWARD and BACKWARD, FORWARD.

3. The four movements alternate feet.

4. Each movement requires an equal amount of time.

5. The CHERKESSIYA step usually is executed in 4/4 or 2/4 meter:

CHERKESSIYA
4/4 METER

LR	L R	L R	R L	R L
START	IN (FORWARD)	OUT (BACKWARD)	OUT (BACKWARD)	IN (FORWARD)

4/4 Meter CHERKESSIYA R foot (facing center)

Beat 1	Step R foot in	"IN" ("IN")
2	Step L foot out (in place)	"OUT" ("STEP")
3	Step R foot out	"OUT" ("OUT")
4	Step L foot in (in place)	"IN" ("STEP")

2/4 Meter L foot CHERKESSIYA (facing around the circle)

Beat 1	Step L foot forward	"FORWARD"
&	Step R foot backward	"BACKWARD" ("STEP")
2	Step L foot backward	"BACKWARD"
&	Step R foot forward	"FORWARD" ("STEP")

6. Dancers face in any direction.

7. The CHERKESSIYA step is a recurring dance step, as opposed to an alternating dance step, because it repeats each time on the same foot.

8. Style may be added to fit the character of the dance, the music, or the wishes of the choreographer. For example, "leap forward on the first beat while raising the opposite leg behind with the knee bent" is a stylistic addition.

CHERKESSIYA Step Teaching Progression

1. Use the Four-Step-Language Process with the Language-to-Dance Vocabulary for the first half of the CHERKESSIYA ("IN, OUT" or "IN, STEP" or "FORWARD, BACKWARD").

2. Repeat step 1 with the second half of the CHERKESSIYA ("OUT, IN" or "OUT, STEP" or "BACKWARD, FORWARD").

3. Combine steps 1 and 2 to practice the full CHERKESSIYA.

4. Provide individual practice time, followed by practice to the group beat. Be certain that the students practice beginning with each foot.

5. Play a selection of music and have students identify the steady beat. Add the WHISPER & DO and DO (THINK & DO) steps to the music.

6. Combine the CHERKESSIYA with other locomotor patterns. For example:

- IN, 2, 3, 4; CHERKESSIYA; OUT, 2, 3, 4; CHERKESSIYA

  or

- CHERKESSIYA; CHERKESSIYA; SIDE, CLOSE, SIDE, TOUCH; SIDE, CLOSE, SIDE, TOUCH

7. Teach dances that use the CHERKESSIYA step, such as *Cherkessiya,* or *Mechol Hagat,* or *Ciocarlanul,* or choreograph your own sequences.

GRAPEVINE
2/4 METER

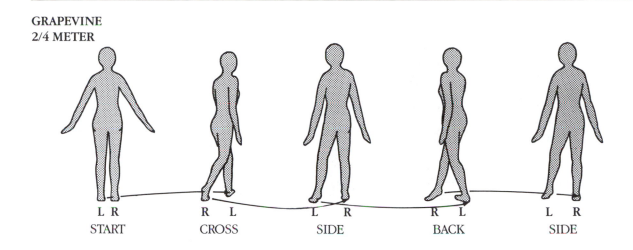

| L R | R L | L R | R L | L R |
| START | CROSS | SIDE | BACK | SIDE |

The GRAPEVINE Step

The GRAPEVINE step (referred to as a MAYIM step in Israeli dance) is common in dances from many countries. As a result, there are variations to the GRAPEVINE (which are still called GRAPEVINE) in many dance descriptions; this creates confusion for dancers and teachers. GRAPEVINE, as it is used in this book, always refers to the same sequencing of steps and the term "GRAPEVINE PATTERN" (described below) refers to a variation.

Important Characteristics

1. The GRAPEVINE step consists of a sequence of four movements executed in a sideward direction. It may be perceived as a CHERKESSIYA step moving sideward.

2. It is a combination of the two-beat sequences CROSS, SIDE and BACK, SIDE.

3. The four movements alternate feet.

4. Each movement takes the same amount of time to execute.

5. The GRAPEVINE step generally is executed in 4/4 or 2/4 meter:

4/4 Meter GRAPEVINE
(moving left)

Beat 1	Step R foot, crossing in front of L foot	"CROSS"
2	Step L foot sideward left	"SIDE"
3	Step R foot, crossing in back of L foot	"BACK"
4	Step L foot sideward left	"SIDE"

2/4 Meter GRAPEVINE
(moving right)

Beat 1	Step L foot, crossing in front of R foot	"CROSS"
&	Step R foot sideward right	"SIDE"
2	Step L foot, crossing in front of R foot	"BACK"
&	Step R foot sideward right	"SIDE"

6. Dancers may face any direction, although the GRAPEVINE step is usually performed facing center in order to travel sideward around the circle.

7. The GRAPEVINE step is a recurring step, as opposed to an alternating step, because it repeats each time on the same foot. Holding the fourth beat in sequence or hopping on the fourth beat are the most common alterations to allow the GRAPEVINE to travel in the opposite direction.

8. The GRAPEVINE step begins with the foot opposite from the traveling direction.

GRAPEVINE PATTERN

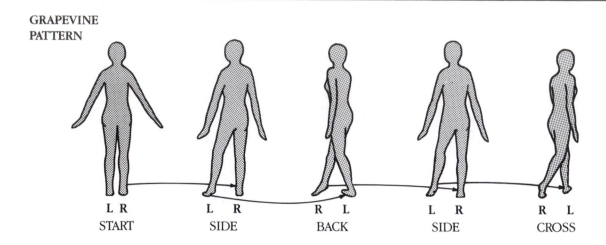

L R	L R	R L	L R	R L
START	SIDE	BACK	SIDE	CROSS

9. Style is added to fit the dance. In many Israeli dances, the first beat is accented and the fourth beat becomes a sideward leap. The dancer's hips generally rotate to make the front and back crossing steps easier to execute.

GRAPEVINE Step Teaching Progression

1. Use the Four-Step-Language Process with the Language-to-Dance Vocabulary for the first half of the GRAPEVINE ("CROSS, SIDE").

2. Repeat step 1 with the second half of the GRAPEVINE ("BACK, SIDE").

3. Combine steps 1 and 2 to practice the full GRAPEVINE ("CROSS, SIDE, BACK, SIDE"). Note: Be certain students face center as it is easy to turn the beginning of this step into a walking pattern, which makes the final two motions very difficult to execute.

4. Allow individuals time to practice using their own beat and tempo, followed by time to practice to the group beat. Practice both directions. It takes time to make the difficult crossing automatic on the first beat. Encourage students to begin with one CHERKESSIYA and to take small steps.

5. Play a musical selection and have students identify the steady beat. Add the WHISPER & DO followed by DO (THINK & DO) to the music.

6. Combine the GRAPEVINE step with other locomotor patterns and with the CHERKESSIYA:

● CHERKESSIYA; CHERKESSIYA; GRAPEVINE; GRAPEVINE

or

● IN, 2, 3, 4; OUT, 2, 3, 4; GRAPEVINE; GRAPEVINE

7. Teach dances that use the GRAPEVINE step, such as *Mayim, Hora Medura, Corrido, Romanian Hora,* or choreograph your own.

The GRAPEVINE PATTERN Step

The GRAPEVINE PATTERN step, sometimes referred to as the CARIOCA, is found in many dances. The sequence of steps is executed in one of two ways, either SIDE, CROSS, SIDE, BACK or SIDE, BACK, SIDE, CROSS. To avoid confusion, the GRAPEVINE PATTERN step should be taught separately from the GRAPEVINE step. Differences among GRAPEVINE and GRAPEVINE PATTERN:

1. The Language-to-Dance Vocabulary
   GRAPEVINE — "CROSS, SIDE, BACK, SIDE"
   GRAPEVINE PATTERN — "SIDE, CROSS, SIDE, BACK; SIDE, BACK, SIDE, CROSS"

STEP HOP
2/4 METER

R L   R L
STEP   HOP

2. GRAPEVINE uses a starting foot opposite to the traveling direction (R foot begins and the dance step travels left). GRAPEVINE PATTERN travels the same direction as the starting foot (R foot begins and dance step travels right).

The STEP HOP

The STEP HOP is found in dances from many countries around the world. It was often combined with the SCHOTTISCHE step in the ballrooms of western Europe and the United States toward the end of the nineteenth century.

Important Characteristics

1. The STEP HOP has two motions: a STEP in place or in a particular direction, followed by a HOP.

2. The STEP and the HOP use the same amount of time and the same foot. (The same two motions executed with unequal time duration become a SKIP.)

3. The STEP HOP generally is executed in 2/4 meter, but may occur in 4/4 meter as two STEP HOPS, or one STEP HOP executed very slowly:

2/4 Meter STEP HOP L foot

| Beat 1 | Step on the L foot | "STEP"** |
| 2 | Hop on the L foot | "HOP" |

4/4 Meter STEP HOP R foot

Beat 1	Step on the R foot	"STEP"**
2	Rest	"REST"
3	Hop on the R foot	"HOP"
4	Rest	"REST"

** FORWARD, BACKWARD, IN, OUT may be substituted.

4. The STEP HOP is an alternating dance step; if the first STEP HOP is executed on the R foot, the next one occurs on the L foot.

5. The STEP HOP as a dance step may be executed several times in sequence, in combination with other dance steps, as a transition from one direction to another, or as a transition in a recurring step (CHERKESSIYA or GRAPEVINE) to the opposite foot.

6. The STEP HOP is more difficult to learn than the CHERKESSIYA or the GRAPEVINE steps because two motions are executed on the same foot; the hop following the step demands timing and balance. The dancer's body actually leaves the floor before the beat in order to land on the beat. If the dancer's body is not in good alignment on the first step, the second step will occur too soon.

7. Style usually is added to include movements of the free leg during the step and hop. For example, dancers can lift their free leg backward while stepping, and swing it forward on the hopping

SCHOTTISCHE
4/4 METER

LR	R L	L R	R L	L R
START	WALK	WALK	STEP	HOP

motion. The hop is frequently used to change direction: 1/4 or 1/2 turns.

STEP HOP Teaching Progression

1. Practice hopping on one foot and then the other.

2. Use the Four-Step Language Process with the Language-to-Dance Vocabulary to practice the lead-up sequence of "STEP, HOP, HOP, HOP." Note: Be certain the hops and the step each take the same amount of time. The reason for the three hops is to prepare the body for the balance needed when only one hop is used.

3. Use the Four-Step-Language Process with the Language-to-Dance Vocabulary ("STEP, HOP") to practice the dance step.

4. Provide individual practice time with persons using their own tempo, followed by practice to the group beat. Ask your students to practice the STEP HOP more quickly (slowly). Ask students to try out different motions with the free leg.

5. Play a musical selection and identify the steady beat. Add the WHISPER & DO, followed by DO (THINK & DO) to the music.

6. Combine the STEP HOP with the GRAPE-VINE step, the CHERKESSIYA step, and other locomotor sequences. Give the students movement problems that they practice first to their own beat and tempo, such as "STEP HOP four times,

WALK eight steps, CHERKESSIYA two times."

7. Teach dances that use the STEP HOP, such as *Debka Kurdit, Hasapikos, Hora.*

The SCHOTTISCHE Step

The SCHOTTISCHE step originated with peasants in Germany. It was danced in ballrooms in Europe, the Scandinavian countries, and the British Isles during the nineteenth century. It also appeared in social dances in the United States, and in the twentieth century became a basic step of the *Jitterbug* and of the *Big Apple*.

Important Characteristics

1. The SCHOTTISCHE step pattern consists of a sequence of four motions: three steps followed by a hop.

2. It is a combination of two walking (running) steps plus a STEP HOP, and therefore should be learned after the STEP HOP.

3. Each motion takes the same amount of time to execute.

4. The SCHOTTISCHE step generally is executed in 4/4 or 2/4 meter:

4/4 Meter SCHOTTISCHE L foot

Beat 1	Step on the L foot	"WALK"**
2	Step on the R foot	"WALK"

| 3 | Step on the L foot | "STEP" |
| 4 | Hop on the L foot | "HOP" |

2/4 Meter SCHOTTISCHE R foot

Beat 1	Step on the R foot	"RUN"**
2	Step on the L foot	"RUN"
3	Step on the R foot	"STEP"
4	Hop on the R foot	"HOP"

** FORWARD, BACKWARD, IN, OUT may be substituted.

5. The SCHOTTISCHE step may be danced in place or in any direction.

6. It is an alternating dance step; beat one is executed with the opposite foot on each repetition.

7. The SCHOTTISCHE step can be used by itself in a dance or can be combined with other dance steps or locomotor patterns.

8. The greatest difficulty beginners encounter when learning this step seems to be with the HOP. Some students turn the HOP into a LEAP to the other foot. Because of this tendency, try presenting the STEP HOP first and use it in the SCHOTTISCHE step (i.e., explain to students that the SCHOTTISCHE step is a STEP HOP preceded by two walking steps — WALK, WALK, STEP, HOP).

9. Add style to fit the dance and music.

SCHOTTISCHE Step Teaching Progression

1. Use the Four-Step-Language Process with the Language-to-Dance Vocabulary ("WALK, WALK, STEP, HOP") to practice the SCHOTTISCHE. Note: The language may be converted to the usual "STEP, STEP, STEP, HOP" as soon as students are comfortable with the sequence.

2. Allow individual practice time during which beginners use their own beat and tempo, followed by practice to the group beat.

3. Play a musical selection and have students identify the underlying beat. Add the WHISPER & DO followed by the DO (THINK & DO) to the music.

4. Combine the SCHOTTISCHE step with the STEP HOP, GRAPEVINE, and CHERKESSIYA steps, and with locomotor sequences. Give the students movement problems: "SCHOTTISCHE IN; SCHOTTISCHE OUT; CHERKESSIYA two times."

5. Practice the SCHOTTISCHE step in different directions: forward, backward, sideward, turning. A sideward SCHOTTISCHE generally is executed as SIDE, BACK, SIDE, HOP.

6. Teach dances that use the SCHOTTISCHE, such as *Kuma Echa, Salty Dog Rag, Road to the Isles, Korobushka*.

Introducing Beginners to Uneven Folk Dance Steps

It is much more difficult for beginning students to organize sequences of movements that use resting beats or movements that combine divided beats with single beats. These types of dance patterns are referred to as **Uneven Folk Dance Steps** or "uneven rhythmic movement sequences." Elementary-age children should have reached the fourth grade before attempting uneven patterns and uneven movement sequences with the feet, if those patterns are longer than one measure. Although some third graders may be capable of executing these uneven patterns, it is best to wait until most of the class can be successful. Older children and adults who have not had appropriate dance experience will also need to master material that is "even" before they can be successful with "uneven" rhythmic movement. The lead-up activity for these steps use hand/arm patterns: PAT, PAT, PAT, REST, or three alternating PATS followed by a REST.

The four beginning folk dance steps using "uneven rhythmic movement" are the THREE, the TWO-STEP, the YEMENITE, and the POLKA. These steps, which prepare the students for intermediate folk dance are described below.

The THREE

The THREE ("BALKAN THREE") dance step originated in eastern Europe; the same sequence is also called "PAS DE BAS" and "BALANCE" in dances from other parts of the world.

THREE
4/4 METER

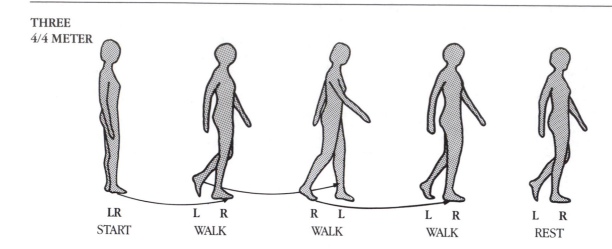

LR	L R	R L	L R	L R
START	WALK	WALK	WALK	REST

Important Characteristics

1. The THREE consists of three steps, executed either in place or while the dancer is moving. It is a SCHOTTISCHE step without a HOP.

2. The first two steps take equal amounts of time to execute, and the third step takes the same amount of time as the combination of the other two steps.

3. The THREE may be executed in 2/4 or 4/4 meter:

2/4 Meter THREE L foot

Beat 1	Run L foot	"LEAP"**
	(slight leap)	
&	Run R foot	"RUN"
2	run L foot	"RUN"

4/4 Meter THREE R foot

Beat 1	Step on R foot	"WALK"**
2	Step on L foot	"WALK"
3	Step on R foot	"WALK"
4	Rest	"REST"

** FORWARD, BACKWARD, IN, OUT may be substituted.

4. The THREE is an alternating dance step; beat one is executed with the opposite foot each time.

5. The greatest difficulty for beginners is in the step followed by the rest (the step of longest dura-

tion). No students should be expected to master this step until they have learned the steps described earlier. Many children below the fourth grade are not developmentally ready for these sequences.

6. Add style to fit the dance and music.

THREE Step Teaching Progression

1. Use the Four-Step Language Process with the Language-to-Dance Vocabulary "WALK, WALK, WALK, REST" to practice the THREE.

2. Practice the slower sequence before adding the faster one. Begin with the SCHOTTISCHE, eliminate the HOP, and replace it with a REST.

3. Allow individual practice time during which the students use their own beat and tempo, followed by practice to the group beat.

4. Play a musical selection and have the students identify the underlying beat. Add the WHISPER & DO followed by the DO (THINK & DO) to the music.

5. Practice the THREE in different directions and in place.

6. Combine the THREE with other dance steps and with locomotor sequences. Ask the students to execute "four THREES moving counterclockwise; one SCHOTTISCHE IN; one SCHOTTISCHE OUT."

**TWO-STEP
4/4 METER**

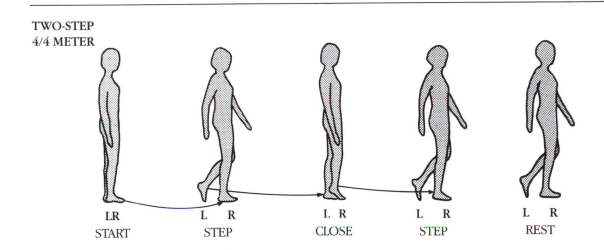

LR	L R	L R	L R	L R
START	STEP	CLOSE	STEP	REST

7. Teach dances that use the THREE such as *Hora Pe Gheaţa, Hora Bialik.*

The TWO-STEP

The TWO-STEP is believed to be of Hungarian origin; it was danced in ballrooms toward the end of the 1800s. The TWO-STEP is related to the FOX TROT and may be danced as a form of the FOX TROT. The movement sequence in 2/4 meter is identical to one form of the POLKA found in a number of countries (i.e., Mexico and Russia). The TWO-STEP is an important component of the POLKA step as often danced in the United States.

Important Characteristics

1. The TWO-STEP consists of three steps executed in any direction or in place. It is a THREE with a closing step as the second movement.

2. The first two steps take equal amounts of time to execute, and the third step takes the same amount of time as the first two steps combined.

3. The TWO-STEP may be executed in 2/4 or 4/4 meter:

2/4 Meter TWO-STEP L foot

Beat 1	Step on L foot	"STEP"**
&	Step R foot next to L foot	"CLOSE"
2	Step on L foot	"STEP"

4/4 Meter TWO-STEP R foot

Beat 1	Step on R foot	"STEP"**
2	Step L foot next to R foot	"CLOSE"
3	Step on R foot	"STEP"
4	Rest	"REST"

** FORWARD, BACKWARD, IN, OUT may be substituted.

4. The TWO-STEP is an alternating step; beat one of each repetition begins with the opposite foot.

5. The greatest problem beginners encounter in executing this step occurs with the CLOSE. A change in weight on that movement must occur; if the weight is shifted to both feet, one may not remember which foot to use next. As with the THREE, participants in the TWO-STEP should have prior dance experience, and children below the fourth grade should not be taught the step.

TWO-STEP Teaching Progression

1. Use the Four-Step Language Process with the Language-to-Dance Vocabulary ("STEP, CLOSE, STEP, REST") to practice the TWO-STEP.

2. Practice the slower sequence before adding the faster one. Begin with the THREE and add the CLOSE on the second step. Watch for uneven motions in the first two steps, particularly in

YEMENITE
4/4 METER

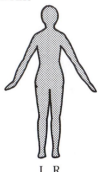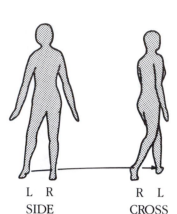

L R	L R	L R	R L	R L
START	SIDE	SIDE	CROSS	REST

the faster form; the students may revert to a GALLOP, which has unequal time in the first two movements.

3. Allow individual practice time during which the students use their own beat and tempo, followed by practice to the group beat.

4. Play a musical selection and add WHISPER & DO, followed by DO (THINK & DO).

5. Practice the TWO-STEP in different directions and in place.

6. Combine the TWO-STEP with other dance steps and locomotor sequences, for example: two TWO-STEPS IN; two TWO-STEPS OUT; SCHOTTISCHE SIDEWARD; SCHOTTISCHE SIDEWARD.

7. Teach dances that incorporate the TWO-STEP, such as *Misirlou* and *Nebesko Kolo*.

The YEMENITE Step

The YEMENITE is a dance step found in many Israeli dances. It is characteristic of the dances of the Yemenites who left Yemen to settle in Israel.

Important Characteristics

1. The YEMENITE step consists of three steps executed in a side-to-side pattern.

2. The first two steps take equal amounts of time to execute and the third step takes the same

amount of time as the first two combined.

3. The YEMENITE step may be executed in 4/4 or 2/4 meter, but is more frequently found in the slower form:

4/4 Meter YEMENITE L foot

Beat 1	Step L foot sideward left	"SIDE"
2	Step R foot sideward right	"SIDE"
3	Step L foot crossing in front of R foot	"CROSS"
4	Rest	"REST"

2/4 Meter YEMENITE R foot

Beat 1	Step R foot sideward right	"SIDE"
&	Step L foot sideward left	"SIDE"
2	Step R foot crossing in front of L foot	"CROSS"

4. The YEMENITE step is an alternating step; beat one of each repetition begins with the opposite foot.

5. The greatest difficulty for the dancer seems to be transferring weight on the crossing step. There is a tendency to TOUCH rather than CROSS with weight. The *uncross* to begin a second YEMENITE also poses a problem.

6. The YEMENITE step is very fluid; there is a great deal of bending and straightening of the knees. The step has a low-to-high-to-low movement pattern.

POLKA
2/4 METER

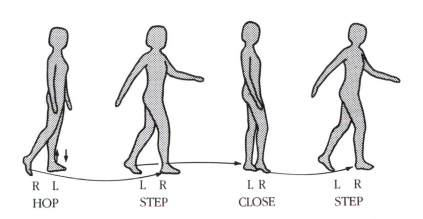

R L	R L	L R	L R	L R
START	HOP	STEP	CLOSE	STEP

YEMENITE Step Teaching Progression

1. Use the Four-Step Language Process with the Language-to-Dance Vocabulary ("SIDE, SIDE, CROSS, REST") to practice the YEMENITE.

2. Practice a series of front crossing steps with a resting beat after each step (CROSS, REST, CROSS, REST and so on). Do the first two steps in place followed by the CROSS (STEP, STEP, CROSS, REST); watch for students who TOUCH instead of CROSS.

3. Allow individual practice time during which students use their own beat and tempo, followed by practice to the group beat.

4. Play a musical selection and add WHISPER & DO, then DO (THINK & DO).

5. Practice the YEMENITE in combination with the TWO-STEP. Combine it with other dance steps and provide movement problems: two YEMEN-ITES beginning R foot; one SCHOTTISCHE IN; one SCHOTTISCHE OUT; two TWO-STEPS moving counterclockwise.

6. Teach dances using the YEMENITE, such as *Ma Na' Vu, Leor Chiyuchech, Hineh Ma Tov.*

The POLKA Step

The POLKA step originated in central Europe in the 1800s. It spread rapidly throughout the world both as a dance and as a step incorporated into other dances and retains its popularity today. The style of the POLKA step will vary from country to country, but its liveliness is a characteristic wherever it is danced.

Important Characteristics

1. The POLKA step, as it is most commonly danced in the United States, consists of four motions. It may be thought of as a TWO-STEP preceded by a HOP (or a "hiccup") into the TWO-STEP.

2. The HOP of the POLKA step is an upbeat into the TWO-STEP. The time that the HOP uses is borrowed from the step of longest duration in the TWO-STEP.

3. The POLKA step generally is executed in 2/4 meter:

2/4 Meter POLKA

Ah	Hop L foot	"HOP"
Beat 1	Step on R foot	"STEP"**
&	Step on L foot next to R foot	"CLOSE"
2	Step on R foot	"STEP"

** FORWARD, BACKWARD, IN, OUT may be substituted.

4. The POLKA is an alternating step; beat one of each repetition begins with the opposite foot.

5. Two problems exist for students learning the POLKA step. First, there is a tendency, as with the fast TWO-STEP, to execute the STEP, CLOSE portion of the step in an uneven fashion as a GALLOP. Second, students often turn the HOP into a LEAP (in error), or they leave out the HOP, turning the step into a TWO-STEP.

POLKA Step Teaching Progression

1. Use the Four-Step Language Process with the Language-to-Dance Vocabulary ("HOP, STEP, CLOSE, STEP") to practice the POLKA.

2. Allow students to practice their own beat and tempo, followed by practice to the group beat.

3. If students have difficulty, return to a GALLOP POLKA: GALLOP twice on one foot; GALLOP twice on the other foot. Then demonstrate the difference between the GALLOP POLKA and the POLKA step that follows a TWO-STEP rhythm.

4. Play a musical selection and add the WHISPER & DO followed by DO (THINK & DO).

5. Practice the POLKA step in combination with other dance steps in 2/4 meter and other locomotor movements.

6. Teach dances using the POLKA step, such as *Jessie Polka* and *Doudlebska Polka*.

Folk Dance — The Delivery System 6

When students have mastered the basic rhythmic movements described in Chapters 2 – 4, as well as the introductory steps and beginning dance sequences presented in Chapter 5, they are ready for full-fledged instruction in international folk dance. The teacher's guidance has been necessary throughout this process and is at the heart of a successful delivery system. While teachers may be very knowledgeable about folk dance and folk dance style, they must convert this knowledge into teaching methods that produce successful learning experiences, or the teaching/learning cycle will be incomplete and ineffective. Effective teachers provide their students with experiences that help them achieve an in-depth understanding of the material presented. One proof of effective teaching is found in the student's desire to pursue folk dance and other dance experiences when not in a teacher's presence. The delivery system outlined in this chapter is designed to help you achieve such success.

The delivery system described in this chapter is a culmination of the teaching progressions presented throughout Part One and provides you with additional guidelines and suggestions for introducing the international folk dances described in Part Two. Certain guidelines and techniques are emphasized because the teaching/learning cycle presented in this book consists of interlocking pieces. When these pieces fit together, the result is a solid foundation for successful rhythmic movement and beginning folk dance.

This chapter includes ideas for using space and equipment, it provides special recommendations for teaching the first few dances, and it suggests general teaching techniques that will lead to success for the student and feelings of accomplishment for you, the teacher. Also included are specific teaching techniques to apply when presenting a dance, and some ways to vary your teaching. Finally, this chapter includes more ideas for modifying selected dances for beginners (see Chapter 5), as well as a discussion of the uses of *chair dancing*.

This chapter is designed for the teacher who is teaching folk dance to children in the middle- and upper-elementary grades, to adolescents, and to adults (including special populations and senior citizens). The teaching suggestions included here also could be useful for teachers who are presenting other types of organized movement and dance activities.

Space and Equipment

You may not be able to choose the room you must work within or the equipment you must use; consequently, you may encounter space and equipment problems that create a less than adequate or desirable teaching environment. To counter such problems, most of the dances presented in this book may be modified for limited space by converting sequences that "travel" to steps in place. *Chair dancing* is useful in a confined space and is described in greater detail later in this chapter. The suggestions for chair dancing that are included with each dance in Part Two may also be converted to in-place, standing sequences. If you have poor equipment, discuss your needs with your administrators, helping them understand how important good sound reproduction is to the success of your classes. The following discussions of space and equipment provides suggestions that should help you make the best of whatever situation you are faced with.

Space

What type of room will you be using? A physical education teacher probably will have access to a gymnasium or activity room of adequate size in which all the students can move comfortably. Music and elementary classroom teachers may not have access to such a room and may have to use classroom space for the dance activities. If plans are made in advance, the physical education teacher will often work cooperatively with classroom and special teachers to permit use of the gymnasium or activity room. You should choose dances that are appropriate for the space you must use, or modify dances for limited space.

Since dance demands movement around a room, the floor surface is of special concern. A wood floor is ideal, particularly if it has been constructed with air space under it — the floating floor. Wooden floors can be very slippery, particularly if students move about in socks. Tile over concrete, a common surface, is very hard on the legs and back if the sequences include long periods of jumping and hopping. This type of surface may also be slippery. Carpeting, while providing some cushioning, makes it difficult for students to move about smoothly. Carpet also must be vacuumed frequently, as the dust raised from the carpeting may create problems for those students who have allergies.

The lighting, acoustics, and ventilation also are important considerations. You should consider all these factors if you have any input into choosing the room you will be using, as well as when you are planning the activities for the class.

Equipment

Can the record or tape be heard throughout the room without the volume being raised to levels of distortion? If using a record player, is the base of the turntable adequately sprung to prevent the needle from jumping as students move about? Is your equipment on a sturdy table to prevent unnecessary jarring and bouncing? Cassette tapes or reel-to-reel tapes are well suited for movement and dance activities and are more durable than records, but they require adequate playback equipment. A small portable tape recorder is not suitable for use in a classroom or activity room unless it can be "jacked" into a sound system or auxiliary speakers. If this modification can be made, cassette tapes (10 minutes in length) can be purchased in specialty shops and tapes can be made of appropriate musical selections from the records *you own,* thus preserving the records. One dance should be recorded on each side of a short tape. Try to avoid recording several dances on one side of a longer tape. Longer tapes are less convenient and require that you spend time locating the portion of the tape desired.

First Steps

Get to Know Your Group or Class

Before attempting to develop goals and objectives for a dance class, you should answer these preliminary questions about your students:

- What are their ages?
- How large is the class?
- What is the male/female breakdown of the class?
- What are the capabilities of the students? Has the group had any previous experience with dance or with other rhythmic movement activities?
- What is the probable receptivity of the group to dance?
- Will the participants be capable of vigorous activity, or is their level of fitness low?
- Are there special populations within the group, such as the physically or mentally handicapped?

● Are there students whose parents, grand-parents, or other relatives come from foreign countries?

● What activities precede and follow the dance class?

● Will the dance session be part of a music, physical education, or classroom experience, or will it be a separate class?

● How long will the session last?

By answering these questions first, you will be able to choose the most appropriate material and methods for teaching folk dance to your group. See Appendix D for a suggested folk dance unit.

Know Your Material

A dance has four important components — the music, the rhythmic sequence of movements, the combination of music and movement, and the style. Teachers must become thoroughly familiar with each of these components.

The music. Listen to the music several times to understand and be comfortable with it, and then answer the following questions:

● What is the dancer's beat? Is it slow? Is it fast? Is it easily perceived?

● What is the meter? Is the music organized in twos or threes?

● Is there an introduction? If so, when does the dance begin with respect to the introduction? If not, can the dance begin with the second part, omitting the first part the first time through the dance?

● What is the musical form — how is the music organized? Is it organized into two parts? Is it verse/chorus?

● How long are the phrases? How often do they repeat?

The rhythmic movement sequence. The teacher must clearly understand the steps and motions in a dance's rhythmic movement sequence. To achieve this understanding, you should

● Visualize the sequence from start to finish,

and dance it mentally. Use the identifying word (the Language-to-Dance Vocabulary term) for each step or motion.

● Know the directions the body faces throughout the dance. Is the "road map" for the dance clear?

● Recognize the transitions from one part of the dance to the next, and from the end of the dance back to the beginning.

Once the overall dance pattern is clear, you can concentrate on specific sections as needed. You may find it useful to write out a dance, using the Language-to-Dance Vocabulary to identify the dance sequence (refer to Glossary). To fully understand a dance and to know the language needed to teach it, a teacher must be able to describe a dance either mentally or in writing. For example, the simplified version of *Twelfth St. Rag* may be described as follows:

FORWARD, 2, 3, 4, TOUCH, TOUCH, STEP/STEP, STEP; Repeat; OUT, 2, 3, 4; IN, 2, 3, 4; IN, KICK, OUT, TOUCH; IN, KICK, OUT, TOUCH.

Thus, from the Language-to-Dance Vocabulary, the teacher knows that on the first 16 beats the dancers will travel around the circle, on the next 8 beats they will move away from the center of the circle and then toward the center, and on the final 8 beats they will face the center of the circle.

Combining music and movement. When combining music and movement, teachers should ask themselves:

● How do the movements fit the music? Do the different parts of the dance follow the musical phrases and the musical form?

● How does the rhythmic structure of the dance fit the steady beat of the music?

● How many repetitions of the dance will be executed to the music?

● Does the end of the dance coincide with the end of the recording?

Music and movement must converge. If we "feel" this unity, we will present dance to our students as a musical experience and not as a sequence of movements with music in the background.

The style. The handholds, the appropriate claps and snaps, and the use of the arms and body bring the special ethnic quality to the dance. It is important for teachers of folk dance to become as knowledgeable as possible about the style of the particular dance being taught. Talking with recreational folk dance teachers and leaders or attending folk dance sessions and workshops often will provide the teacher with this special information. If the style of the dance is not known, it is better to do the dance as presented, rather than creating your own way of performing the dance. In Part II of this book handholds and formations are given for each dance along with some special stylistic features.

"Warm Up" Your Class

At the beginning of a class, teachers need to "warm up" the group, dispelling any lethargy or fear that might be present in the students and providing for immediate success. You cannot expect most groups to be "ready" if you do not provide

warm-up activities. For example, you might involve everyone in simple movement from the "Levels of Beat Coordination" (Chapter 4). Or you might have music playing when the group arrives and immediately lead them around in a circle in a follow-the-leader experience. Or you might begin the session with a dance the group knows well and enjoys — a dance that does not need review.

Plan Each Class

When planning a dance class, teachers should ask themselves:

- What shall I do first?

- How shall I end the class?

- What new (and old) material shall I use?

- When in the lesson shall I present new material?

- How will the class be paced?

- Shall I honor requests to perform dances the class has learned before?

- Have I prepared enough material and a sufficient variety of material to respond to the needs of the group each day?

The major activities for a specific class should be planned carefully. Dances from the previous class should be reviewed during the body of the lesson. The material should be paced (i.e., alternate faster and slower sequences, vary familiar and unfamiliar music). Until students develop an accepting attitude about ethnic music and dance, teachers need to plan carefully the music and dances that precede and follow the ethnic sound, and to determine how to prepare the class for the unfamiliar sound. For example, if the Yugoslavian dance, *Djurdjevka Kolo,* is going to be taught, it might precede or follow *Alley Cat,* which uses the same "TOUCH, TOUCH, TOUCH, STEP" sequence. You might play a little of the ethnic music first and talk about the different sounds created by the combination of stringed instruments. Exhibiting a picture of one or more of the instruments or a map of the country of origin would help your students bridge the cultural gap. The next dance you present to the class should have more familiar sounding music, such as *Count 64.*

New movement patterns may be reinforced by planning a few dances in sequence that require the new pattern. For example, the beat structure "1, 2, 3 &, 4" can be reinforced through a review of *Limbo Rock, Plješkavac Kolo,* and *Dučec.* The alternating two-beat pattern of "STEP, LIFT" can be practiced in *Ugros, Hasapikos,* and *Dimna Juda.* The six-beat sequence found in dances from four countries can be compared and contrasted: *Hasapikos* (Greece), *Hora* (Israel), *Körtanc* (Hungary), and *Pravo Horo* (Bulgaria). (All of the dances mentioned in this chapter are described in Part Two.)

Do not forget to make a plan for the last few minutes of a class. A successful ending encourages a feeling of unity; the class closes on a high note with students looking forward to the next dance experience. Teachers can create good feelings by closing with a dance that students will enjoy immediately, or by repeating a favorite.

Plan a Series of Classes

The objectives for the entire course should be considered as teachers plan a series of classes. What aspects of the basic teaching progressions (Chapters 2 – 5) should be presented? What countries should be represented in dance? Are there people from the community who could bring costumes, art objects, or pictures to class to enrich the cultural experience for the students? How many classes will be offered? A sample lesson sequence for such a series is presented in Appendix D.

Special Recommendations for Teaching the First Few Folk Dances

Some of these recommendations have been mentioned in previous chapters. They are presented again to emphasize their importance in ensuring success at this level. These recommendations also form the basis for the next section in this chapter, which offers suggestions for modifying folk dances for special populations as well as for beginners. The composition of the class will dictate which of the techniques to use. These are "break-in tips" for middle- and upper-elementary students, adolescents, and adult beginners who are in classes in which it is not possible to spend sufficient time on the progressions outlined in Chapters 2 – 5. If your group experiences difficulty, however, you should refer to the sequencing of the beginning dance experiences presented in Chapter 5:

- Do not require holding hands.
- Make no reference to right or left foot.
- Do not require partners.

- Use dances composed of repetitions of short sequences.
- Make sure there is a step or motion for every beat.
- Choose music with a strong, underlying beat.
- Change movement sequences as the music changes.

Simplifying and Modifying Folk Dances

If certain elements of a folk dance are too difficult for beginners or for specific populations, such as older adults or the mentally and physically handicapped, a dance can be modified to suit that particular group. Simplifying or modifying dance steps provides more material for teachers and makes it possible to introduce many more ethnic dances to beginning students. Examine a more difficult dance to see what elements could be adapted: tempo, more difficult dance steps added to simple sequences, turns, right or left foot designations, the rhythmic structure, style, changes of sequence (parts), partners.

Simplifying a dance is not a license for us to be "creative" with another country's ethnic dance; American music should be used for creative endeavors. Simplifications or modifications of dances should closely follow the authentic dance movements, thus making it possible for students to perform the actual dance (when and if they are ready) without having to "unlearn" incorrect patterns. Be certain that the newly "simplified" dance is not just as difficult as the original.

During the process of adapting a dance for a particular group, we must be sure that we *are* modifying a dance to suit a group with certain needs and *are not* destroying or diluting cultural material. Retain the character and authenticity of the material and alter it just enough to create an appropriate movement sequence for a beginning class or special group. Replace the simplified dance with the authentic dance when the group is ready for the more difficult movements.

I have used the following dance modifications successfully with many special populations as well as with beginning folk dancers. (See "Introducing Beginners to Locomotor Movement I, II, and III Dances" for additional modifications.)

1. No right or left foot specified: *Alley Cat, Cherkessiya, Count 64, Djurdjevka Kolo, Haya Ze Basadeh*. Additional examples appear in Appendix C, Dances by Level of Difficulty and are marked with an asterisk.

2. Partner dances modified so the students learn only one part as a circle dance: *Doudlebska Polka* (the male part), *Haya Ze Basadeh* (the male part), *Good Old Days* (the male part), *Mexican Mixer* (the female part), and *Corrido* (the female part).

3. Sections of divided beats modified to WALKS or single motions, using the underlying beat: *Limbo Rock, Twelfth St. Rag,* and *Good Old Days.*

4. Four-part dances simplified to two-part dances, with each part repeated once if the musical form permits this alteration: *Popcorn, Alley Cat.*

5. BUZZ TURNS modified to TURNS using WALKS: *Ve David, Niguno Shel Yossi, Tant' Hessie.*

6. FULL TURN modified to STEPS IN PLACE: *Erev Shel Shoshanim, Bele Kawe, Pata Pata.*

7. A GRAPEVINE simplifed to WALKS in the specified direction: *Hora Medura, Mayim.*

8. A STEP HOP modified to a STEP REST, which leaves out the HOP: SIDE, STAMP modified to remove the STAMP and replace it with a REST.

9. Patterns that include resting beats modified to include STEPS on each beat: *Hora Pe Gheaţa, Hora Bialik.*

10. A SCHOTTISCHE modified to four WALKS; a POLKA modified to a GALLOP or GALLOP POLKA; a YEMENITE to three STEPS IN PLACE: see the dances that use these dance steps.

General Techniques for Teaching All Dances

Teachers should keep these general teaching techniques in mind for all their presentations.

Enthusiasm

Teachers who infect their beginning students with their enthusiasm and whose goal is to ensure immediate success for individual dancers will find students more willing to participate wholeheartedly and will find teaching much more rewarding. When students experience success, they tend to be more cooperative.

Sensitivity

A sensitive instructor who is responsive to the beginner's needs will be more likely to create a positive learning environment and thus a successful experience for the student. This means being aware not only of an individual's discomfort, but also of his or her progress. It also means being attuned to the chemistry of the group. Is there harmony or is there tension?

The Four-Step Language Process

Use the **Four-Step Language Process** (see Chapter 2) when teaching organized folk dance. SAY may be omitted if the sequence is short and easily understood by the students; use SAY & DO instead as the dance is presented. Follow up with WHISPER & DO and DO when the music is played. The single descriptive words used in the **Four-Step Language Process** are the organizing force behind understanding the rhythmic movement

sequences. The words must be simple, have meaning for the student, and be used consistently in all folk dances. As each word is introduced, make sure your beginning folk dancers understand completely the movement you are describing. This language-to-dance approach will help most students master a dance more rapidly because they will be actively involved in the learning process. There is no magic in watching a teacher's feet move unless the student can convert the visual image into successful action.

Note: When new sequences are introduced remember to separate your presentation using either visual or verbal techniques without SAY & DO. See "Separate" in the Teaching Model in Chapter 1. After the movement is understood, use the SAY & DO.

The Glossary contains the Language-to-Dance Vocabulary used to describe the dances found in this book.

Add a Visual Model

There will be times when you may want to demonstrate a movement sequence or use SAY & DO

to help your students master a movement. Two things should be kept in mind:

(1) **Avoid small, indistinguishable movements and steps**. Make each step or motion distinct, without distracting arm and body movements.

(2) **Change your location with respect to the formation the students are using**. For example, if you are demonstrating a dance while moving inside a circle formation, you should continually position yourself in front of different sections of the group, eventually covering the entire circle, because many of your students may experience mirroring and reversal problems. Remember, "Watch me and do as I do" is effective only for beginners who are rhythmically competent, and it should only be used with the Language-to-Dance Vocabulary and the Four-Step Language Process.

Teach From the Known to the Unknown

Dances are combinations of sequences that are learned over time. Very often you can use a dance step or movement sequence the group already has mastered and add new sequences. (See "Adding On" and "Combining Familiar Dance Steps into New Patterns and Dances" in the next section of this chapter.) It is easier to teach a new dance if the students realize that they already know parts of it.

Teach Quickly

It is important to teach dances quickly — no more than 5 minutes should be allotted for teaching a beginning folk dance. Almost all of the students in the class should be able to dance to the music with a minimum of errors within this time limit. If the teaching process takes longer than 5 minutes, the teacher should consider these questions:

● Is the dance too difficult for the students? Are they "ready" for it?

● Have I prepared the material carefully enough to permit a logical learning sequence? Am I organized?

● Have I tried to add style? The introductory session should include only the movement sequence.

When the whole dance is put together quickly it is easier to remember. A dance that is taught slowly, with each section practiced many times, does not provide the student with a sense of the whole. No matter what specific teaching technique is used to present the dance (see "Specific Techniques for Teaching Each Dance"), it is important to complete the practice within 5 minutes. Otherwise students lose track of what precedes and follows each part of the dance. *Once the sense of the whole is created, however, the parts can be practiced to perfection*. Remember, *teaching* and *learning* a dance are different from *perfecting* the dance steps. In this book, *teaching/learning* refers to the process of presenting the movement sequences of the dance, practicing them briefly, then dancing them to music. No special formations or handholds are added to the sequences. Do not ask your students to incorporate "style" until they feel comfortable with the movement sequence. A later section of this chapter, "Adding Style," provides further clarification of this point.

Teach Rhythmically

Time is an integral part of any movement sequence. **Rhythmic language** is an important bridge to **rhythmic movement**. Therefore, teachers should SAY the dance pattern rhythmically, then ask the students to SAY & DO the pattern rhythmically, thus creating the critical link between rhythm and movement. If the dance sequence is too difficult for your students at the tempo presented, practice the SAY & DO a little more slowly (see the following section), but be certain to retain the accuracy of rhythmic grouping. For example, the pattern of "TOUCH, TOUCH, STEP/STEP, STEP," which occurs in a beat structure of "1, 2, 3 & 4," should not be taught or executed as five beats then changed to the divided third beat. As your students practice sequences to their own beat and tempo, stress the need for them to retain rhythmic accuracy, regardless of the tempo they use.

Teach Close to Tempo

If the students are able to perform a sequence at the appropriate tempo, they should do so. It is much more difficult for students to learn a sequence well under tempo and then have to increase that tempo. If, however, the students are having problems with the tempo, reduce the tempo gradually — until you reach a point that permits student success. Sequences that are practiced too slowly become isolated pieces of single-beat movements rather than an integrated whole composed of longer sequences. An appropriate analogy may make this point clearer: reading slowly word by word does not often result in good comprehension. Therefore, when you work on a movement sequence at a slower tempo, the reduced tempo should be used only *after* the sequence has been presented to the students *at* tempo and *after* they have tried it. A slower tempo is useful for clarifying a complex sequence, for correcting a portion of the dance that has been perceived incorrectly, or for clarifying the style of a particular movement pattern.

Practice the Sequence at Tempo Before Adding Music

The movement sequence of the dance should be practiced at the actual tempo *before* adding the music. If you have been practicing at a slower tempo, use SAY & DO to bring the sequence up to tempo when your group is ready. Ask your students to SAY the sequence a little faster and they will naturally quicken their movements. This technique is preferable to asking students to "move more quickly." If a dance sequence is not up to tempo when the music is added, students may have difficulty making the transition from the practiced tempo to the musical tempo. Another useful technique to counter this problem is to play a little of the music for the students before teaching the dance, and then to ask them to identify the underlying beat. This should give the students a sense of the tempo and will help you recall the accurate tempo before beginning to teach or review the dance.

Specific Techniques for Teaching Each Dance

These techniques are designed to help teachers become familiar with a dance's unique combination of movement sequences. Chapter 5 includes additional techniques for use with two- and four-beat sequences. Some dances are constructed very logically from beginning to end and thus can be taught easily in sequential order. Other dances, however, are taught more successfully if the teacher begins with the most difficult movements, even if they occur at the middle or end of a dance. The following questions can guide you as you decide how to present a specific dance to your students. They are discussed in greater detail in the following sections.

- Is it logical to begin at the beginning and teach in sequence? Or are there more difficult sequences that should precede easier ones?

- Is it possible to begin with four beats and "add on" an additional two beats with each practiced repetition?

- Is it possible to teach new dances that include steps the students are already familiar with?

- How are the parts of the dance "glued" together, and how can I assure that the transition from the end of the dance to the beginning is executed smoothly?

- Are there sections of the dance that may be particularly troublesome?

- How will I ask the students to practice sections of the dance?

- When should I add style?

Presenting the Most Difficult Sequences First

Students usually master the difficult sections of a dance more quickly if they are presented first. Use the *Twelfth St. Rag* as an example. The teaching sequence should begin with the slightly more difficult movements of "TOUCH, TOUCH, STEP/ STEP, STEP" in a rhythm of "1, 2, 3 & 4." After the students have executed this sequence successfully, present the simpler sequence that immediately precedes it: "FORWARD, 2, 3, 4." Then combine the sequences "FORWARD, 2, 3, 4; TOUCH, TOUCH, STEP/STEP, STEP." Another good example is found in *Armenian Misirlou*. Teach the last four motions of "CROSS/SIDE, BACK/SIDE" first, then teach the sequence that immediately precedes it: "CROSS, CROSS." Finally, teach the first and easiest movement sequence: "TOUCH, TOUCH; TOUCH, TOUCH; CROSS, CROSS; CROSS/SIDE, BACK/SIDE." (Note the "/" between CROSS and SIDE denotes a divided beat. In this dance example, beats seven and eight are divided.)

Adding On

The dance, *Áis Giórgis,* provides an example of the "add-on" teaching technique, in which students do a short sequence and then learn the sequences that follow by "adding on" two more movements (two beats) at a time, linking these to the preceding sequences. For example, the first four beats of *Áis Giórgis* are "FORWARD, FORWARD, SIDE, TOUCH." Ask your students to execute these steps with the SAY & DO method. At the completion of these four beats, immediately ask the students to "add on" the next two-beat sequence, "SIDE, HEEL" then "SIDE, HEEL" again (another two-beat sequence). Finally, ask them to "add on" the last two-beat sequence of the dance, "SIDE, BRUSH." Another good dance for applying this technique is *Popcorn*: students first learn the alternating two-beat sequences of "HEEL, STEP, HEEL, STEP" then "KICK, STEP, KICK, STEP" then "SIDE, BOUNCE, SIDE, BOUNCE" followed by "RUN, 2, 3, 4."

Combining Familiar Dance Steps into New Patterns and Dances

Another way to introduce your students to a new dance is to find dances that incorporate steps or sequences they are already familiar with and have mastered. This process ensures that the students will fully integrate a particular step into their dance repertoire. Once a dance step is mastered, the students should know how that dance step

begins and ends, its directional movements, the steps needed to create a change of direction, and how to combine it with other familiar movement sequences. For example, students will know that the GRAPEVINE step begins with a CROSS and ends with a SIDE; the dancer moves sideward with four even steps and cannot move sideward in the opposite direction without altering one sequence. (See the sections of Chapter 6 on **even** and **uneven dance steps** for information on specific dance steps and on linking dance steps.)

By combining dance steps with other steps (SCHOTTISCHES and STEP HOPS or SCHOTTISCHES and GRAPEVINES), with two-beat sequences (SCHOTTISCHES and SIDE CLOSES), or with locomotor movements (HOPS and WALKS), students will learn to be flexible in their approach to dance. This technique enables students to practice the basic steps of international folk dance in a variety of contexts. By using this integrated approach, you show students that many new dances are really just different combinations of already familiar movements. A student's dance ability improves dramatically when this integrated problem-solving technique is used and students combine familiar sequences into new patterns. For example, they learn that the first half of the dance, *Kuma Echa,* is a combination of two SCHOTTISCHE steps and two GRAPEVINE steps, while *Salty Dog Rag* combines two SCHOTTISCHE steps and four STEP HOPS.

Transitions

It is often difficult for students to make the transition from one major part of a dance to the next and from the end back to the beginning; because frequently dances are presented by teaching one part at a time. Students practice each part over and over again, creating mental stopping points between parts. Dancers will have great difficulty with transitions unless the teacher consciously links the sequences together, thus preparing the student to go from one part to the next, or from the end to the beginning. Just as the sequences within a part are practiced, so should the transitions between parts be practiced. If a dance has only one part, ask the students to practice the sequence by starting and ending at different places.

If a dance has more than one part, ask the students to practice moving from the end of one part through the beginning of the next, as well as from the last several beats of the dance back to the beginning. The work with transitions should take place after a dance has been presented, while the students are practicing.

In addition, remember the technique to be used when the students are having difficulty moving from one two- or four-beat sequence to the next sequence; stop after one beat of the new sequence, e.g., HEEL, STEP; HEEL or SIDE, CLOSE, SIDE, TOUCH; SIDE.

Anticipating Trouble Spots

By analyzing dance material carefully, teachers generally can predict which sections of a dance may be troublesome for their group or for certain individuals. Beginning with more difficult sections and then presenting the easier material has already been recommended as one way to avoid trouble spots. Occasionally, trouble may occur when students misunderstand a particular language-to-dance term; in such cases, the teacher must clarify its meaning for the students. Rhythmic groupings are often difficult for students to understand and extra help should be provided. Transitions, as discussed previously, may prove troublesome and may require practice.

Group Drill Versus Individual Practice

The basic difficulty with group drill is that a movement sequence usually is practiced at a constant tempo and an individual's problems are often ignored. If some of your students are having trouble learning a dance or sections of a dance, group drill usually will be counterproductive. When all of the students understand the material and have mastered it, repetitions (group drill) can be used to increase their familiarity before the music is added. In such cases, individual practice time is not necessary. Individual practice time, however, is essential for students who do not understand the movement sequences. Remember, once your students can SAY the sequence, they can practice it to their own tempo. In such situa-

tions, you are then free to move about the group and provide assistance to those students who need help, without creating an embarrassing situation for them by putting them in the spotlight. Individual practice time can entail 1 to 2 minutes for persons to work alone, for small groups to practice with one student put in charge of each group, or for two or three students to work together informally.

Reviewing a Dance

Students should not be expected to master a dance in a single session. If you are teaching a large group of students, you may not notice everyone's errors the first time a dance is introduced; incorrect movements are very difficult to change once the student has integrated them into a routine. Since students often are not aware of their mistakes during the first teaching session, a review of the dance during the next class enables both the students and the teacher to catch and correct errors before the movement patterns need to be altered. Reviewing a beginning dance should take no more than 1 or 2 minutes.

Adding Style

Style, the movement of the arms and body, is a very visible part of a dance and it is important to students to do it right. Consequently, when style is presented too early students focus on the stylistic elements instead of the movement sequences. Teachers should wait to add style until footwork becomes "automatic" and students are able to combine the movement sequences with music. This prevents the students from becoming frustrated when a dance "falls apart" because they are concentrating on style and not on the movement sequences.

Certain elements of style may be incorporated almost immediately into some dances. In Israeli circle dances, for example, the arms are often *raised* and *lowered* as the dancer moves IN and OUT of the circle. These movements are a logical outgrowth of the sequence and should be easily incorporated by beginners. The kicking motion of "FORWARD, 2, 3, KICK," may also be added as the sequence is taught. The key question you must keep in mind is whether or not the style of a dance is a very natural part of the dance sequence. If you decide the style might be difficult for beginners, do not introduce it until the movement sequence has been established. In addition, handholds should be avoided until the students are comfortable with the dance.

Do not add extra language when students are practicing style. For example, in *Bannielou Lambaol,* students say "SIDE, CLOSE" as they execute the foot movements and, at the same time, move their arms in an *around* and *back* motion. To avoid confusion, first demonstrate the arm motions (without the foot patterns) with *no* language and ask the students to copy the motions. Then do the arm movements while *saying* the foot pattern, *without moving the feet* (say "SIDE, CLOSE" as the arms are moving). Finally, demonstrate the complete movement — the arm motions with the SAY & DO foot movements. Then have the students follow your lead. In the second part of *Bannielou Lambaol* follow the same procedure. First, practice the pushing and pulling of the arms *away from* and *toward* the body twice, followed by one *around* and *back* motion without language, then add the language of the foot pattern "TOUCH/ TOUCH, TOUCH/STEP; SIDE, TOUCH," and finally SAY & DO the entire sequence, including the arm movements. Adding the arm movements to the sequence of leg movements is much more successful than attempting both arm and leg movements at once.

One last point about style — most folk dance style is understated rather than overstated. If you are uncertain about the style of a particular dance, it is wise to use a regular handhold and omit any special stylistic features.

Strategies for Varying Your Presentations

Teachers can present dances in a variety of ways. By varying your presentations, you heighten the interest and curiosity of your students. Following

are ten different methods you can use, with appropriate dances as examples.

1. **Present the language-to-dance words (the SAY). Ask the students to move to the language without prior demonstration.** Ask the students to listen to the music and identify the underlying beat and the phrases. The students may translate the language into dance movement individually, in pairs, or in small groups. Then the music is played and the dance executed. The group then discusses any variations in interpretation. This method should be employed only with material that is completely clear. *Zemer Atik* or *Djurdjevka Kolo* are good dances for this method.

2. **Verbally describe a segment of a dance (SAY) to the students and ask them to respond with SAY in a "verbal echo."** Then demonstrate the dance segment with SAY & DO, asking the students to respond with a SAY & DO echo. This method and the one described above foster independence because the students must rely on their own thought processes to execute the movements. *Bele Kawe* or *Alunelul* could be taught this way.

3. **Present a dance through "echo moving"; you execute a movement sequence without using any language and your students copy your movements.** Then ask the students to add the appropriate language to the movement pattern. This is a good way to help students achieve a more complete understanding of a dance; and it enables you to test your students' comprehension of the language-to-dance patterns. *Bannielou Lambaol* or *Áis Giórgis* may be used for this method.

4. **As suggested earlier, present a sequence that incorporates familiar dance steps into a new dance.** For example, you could ask the class to face counterclockwise in a circle and do a "SCHOTTISCHE sideward right (OUT)," a "SCHOTTISCHE sideward left (IN)," and four "STEP HOPS FORWARD" around a circle. In this way you have presented the first part of *Salty Dog Rag* without mentioning to the class that they are actually learning a new dance. The working Language-to-Dance Vocabulary is used in a very

natural way. Relying on movements the students have already learned, you can then present another new dance, *Nebesko Kolo:* "four TWO-STEPS counterclockwise (beginning right foot), four TWO-STEPS clockwise, two CHERKESSIYA steps facing center, four THREES in place, and a STAMP with the right foot." Once they have mastered the basic dance steps, students will respond enthusiastically to this teaching method. The popularity of this method seems to be that each dance becomes a different sequence of "known" pieces.

5. **Demonstrate an entire dance with the music.** This teaching technique, if used carefully and with appropriate dances, is a great motivational tool. Following the demonstration, present the parts of the dance to the students in sequence from beginning to end using SAY & DO without music. Then lead students through the dance sequence with music. *Işte Hendek* or *Dučec* are appropriate dances for this method.

6. **Present several parts of a dance "one at a time."** You may wish to add the music after each segment is mastered or may not add music until after several parts have been mastered. A good dance for this technique is *Cumberland Square.* Your group could learn the first figure, or the first two figures, and then dance these two sequences to the music before they learn the rest. The same technique could be used with *Debka Kurdit;* students could dance the first three figures with the music before going on to the remainder of the dance. Remember to practice the transitions.

7. **If a dance is very short, or each section is repeated often, you might choose to put on the music and encourage students to join you as you dance.** *Hasapikos* is a short and easy dance with a six-beat sequence that could be taught in this way. *Ugros,* a multipart dance with frequent repetitions of each part, also could be taught in this way. Presenting a dance in this manner may be frustrating for those students who have trouble learning movement sequences by visual imitation. Therefore, it is important to cue your students just prior to a change in sequence and to retain a WHISPER & DO for the first few repetitions. Watch for signs of frustration and failure, and change the teaching

method if students are unable to follow your lead immediately.

8. **Teach a dance to several students outside of class and have them teach the dance to small groups of students during the next class period.** This technique gives those students who learn very quickly and proficiently an opportunity to extend their knowledge. These students also will realize that *dancing* a dance and *teaching* a dance require different competencies. This technique encourages students to develop new areas of expertise. *Close Encounters* or *Debka Daluna* are suggested for this method.

9. **Write the language-to-dance sequence on a chalkboard and have the students recite with SAY and then SAY & DO.** This strategy will help students who are very visually oriented. The student is able to *see* as well as *hear* the language-to-dance words. A variation of this strategy would be to give each student a written description of a dance. Ask the students to execute the dance from the description — working alone, in pairs, or in small groups. This is an excellent way for you to help students understand the Language-to-Dance Vocabulary more fully. *Alunelul* or *Twelfth St. Rag* may be used with this method.

10. **Teach students a dance while they are sitting in a chair (I call this *chair dancing*).** This technique is described in more detail next and is especially appropriate for senior citizens and special populations. *Dučec* and *Pata Pata* work well with this method.

Chair Dancing: A Mainstreaming and Modification Technique

Chair dancing gives many beginning dancers and special populations the opportunity to "dance" while sitting in a chair. Many folk dances need only slight alterations or modifications to become chair dances. Movement sequences to music can be modified for senior citizens who are sitting in

than in a standing position. Almost any dance can be chair danced and suggestions for this form of modification are provided with each dance presented in Part Two of this book. To make the sequence more interesting for the chair dancer, arm patterns occasionally replace foot patterns in part of a dance.

The general rules for chair dancing follow:

(1) WALKS and other locomotor patterns are modified to in-place STEP sequences.

(2) Sideward two-beat sequences such as SIDE, CLOSE or SIDE, BACK are modified to alternating two-beat sequences (SIDE, TOUCH, SIDE, TOUCH) or are executed as described with very small steps.

(3) IN and OUT foot patterns are executed by moving away from and toward the chair.

(4) Partner sequences are modified to use only one of the parts.

(5) All foot/leg patterns can be converted to hand/arm patterns.

(6) Many dances are converted to wheelchair

a chair, as well as for persons who can use their legs while seated, but who cannot function in a standing position with the rest of the group. Persons who do not have the use of their legs but have the use of both arms can simulate the leg movements with their arms and participate with the group in a seated position. Teachers will find that chair dances are useful for *all* beginning folk dancers; in this nonweight-bearing position, many students can learn footwork more comfortably

dances by using one push on the wheels for each two or four beats and by modifying a sequence such as a DO-SA-DO, to moving toward a partner (four beats) and back to place (four beats).

Where Do We Go From Here?

Once you have guided your students through the beginning folk dance experiences presented in this book and your students can comfortably integrate **even** and **uneven dance steps** in the beginning dances presented in Part Two, they are ready for **intermediate folk dance**. Intermediate folk dance involves longer sequences, integration of more complicated movement patterns, new dance steps, unusual meters (such as sevens and nines), and more creative choreography. I recommend that you move on to the intermediate level of folk dance as soon as *you* are ready, to gain a broader perspective. Then, when your beginning students are ready for intermediate folk dance (if you are working with children, they should be ready by grade five), you will be able to meet their needs.

You can enlarge your dance repertoire by attending some of the many folk dance workshops that are presented in this country.* If there is a recreational folk dance group in your area, they should be able to recommend special workshops that are being conducted nearby. Folk dance "camps" are often scheduled on weekends, during holidays, and during the summer for teachers' convenience. The folk dance magazine *Viltis* lists many of these workshops.

The next book in this series, *Teaching Movement & Dance: Intermediate Folk Dance* contains the same Language-to-Dance Vocabulary used here. A set of recordings titled *Changing Directions* contains music for many of the dances in the intermediate dance book. The *Rhythmically Moving* nine-record series contains the music for all the dances in this book. In addition, some of the dances described in Part Two are demonstrated in the *Folk Dances Illustrated* videotape series.

---

* The author conducts summer institutes in Michigan and rhythmic movement and folk dance workshops and conference sessions across the country during the school year. To contact her, write to the High/Scope Foundation, 600 North River Street, Ypsilanti, MI 48198, or call (313) 485-2000 to obtain more information on training sessions already scheduled or about scheduling a session.

Beginning Folk Dances

Every attempt has been made to represent each dance as accurately as possible. The descriptions are drawn from choreographers' guides and from workshops led by teachers who have researched their dances in the countries of origin. The dances are organized as follows: **Locomotor Movement I, Locomotor Movement II, Locomotor Movement III, Even Folk Dance Steps, Uneven Folk Dance Steps.**

How to Follow the Dance Descriptions in Part Two

Each dance description is organized into the following categories: Record, Introduction, Formation, Part (with the Language-to-Dance Vocabulary words in box rhythmic notation), description of the part by Beat, Lead-Up Activities, Teaching Suggestions, Chair Dancing. Explanations on how to use each of these categories are provided here. When necessary, the dance *Twelfth St. Rag* is used for illustration.

RECORD: Each dance description contains information on the record to use when teaching that particular dance. The music may be found on the *Rhythmically Moving* albums 1–9.

INTRODUCTION: This section tells you that you must adjust your beat and tempo to conform to a certain number of beats. Identify the steady beat of the music and match that beat with the number of beats listed in the Introduction. For example, *Twelfth St. Rag* has an 8-beat introduction. If you identify a slow or quick tempo beat, you will count either 4 beats or 16 beats for the introduction and will have to adjust your beat and tempo to 8 beats.

FORMATION: Check the formation for the dance. If you do not understand the terminology, refer to the Glossary in the back of the book. Remember, the exact formation is used *after* the dance is learned.

RHYTHMIC NOTATION BOXES: Match the rhythmic pattern shown in the rhythmic notation boxes to the steady beat. (The notation system is explained in greater detail in the next section.) Pat the hands on the thighs to identify the rhythmic sequence, first without music and then with music. At this stage, *do not* try to follow the correct foot designated under each box or SAY the language.

PART: After you are comfortable with the rhythmic sequence, SAY the Language-to-Dance Vocabulary words (those in capital letters directly opposite each PART) as you continue to pat the rhythmic pattern without music, then WHISPER the words to the music. (Note that in *Twelfth St. Rag* the divided beat in box 7 of PART I is represented with a divided box and two words "CROSS/OUT" or "STEP/STEP." For the next step, sit in a chair and SAY the capital-letter words while using the correct foot (shown under each box). If you are familiar with the Language-to-Dance Vocabulary, you might try to SAY & DO the dance at this point. If you do not understand the Language-to-Dance Vocabulary (capital-letter words), refer to the Glossary in the back of the book for definitions.

DESCRIPTION OF THE PART BY BEAT: Read the descriptions directly opposite the numbered beat(s). These descriptions clarify the capital letter words for each dance. All the words in the description are important: The *movement* is given (STEP, KICK, TOUCH), the *foot to be used* for that movement, and the *direction* of the movement (counterclockwise [CCW], IN, OUT, and so on). Check for NOTE or TO SIMPLIFY to see if there are any special directions. (I often present the simplified version of a dance first.) SAY & DO the dance and then add music.

LEAD-UP ACTIVITIES: These activities are presented to provide experiences that will make it easier for your students to learn the dance.

TEACHING SUGGESTIONS: A specific sequence for teaching the dance is offered in this section. These suggestions have been tried in classes with many age groups.

CHAIR DANCING: Chair dancing suggestions may be used to create a nonweight-bearing position for students who are practicing a dance or may be adapted for special populations of older adults and individuals who cannot perform the dance in a standing or moving position.

The Visual Representation of Beat (Rhythmic Notation)

In organized dance, the movement sequences are executed to a steady beat, creating a rhythmic structure for the dance. I have designed a system to visually represent the sequence of movements in folk dance. Many students do not understand the time relationships of beat and divided beat. They do not understand symbolic representations such as " | " and " ⊓ " or " ♩ " and " ♫ " and that " ⊓ " or " ♫ " is " | " or " ♩ " divided into two parts of equal duration. But when a "box" ☐ representing the beat is drawn around the abstract symbols the time relationships become clearer for students. Thus, students can respond to representations that show one or more divided beats in a 4-beat sequence, such as ☐ ☐ ☐ ☐ and ☐ ☐ ☐ ☐ .

The rhythmic structure of each of the dances is represented in a series of boxes. Each box is equivalent to one steady beat of music. For example, four beats of music: ☐☐☐☐

When a word is placed in the box, it indicates a step or motion (TOUCH, KICK, STAMP) for that beat. Four steps or motions to the underlying beat of music:

Two words in one box:

refer to two steps or motions of equal duration, ½ beat each, the total equalling the single beat.

Thus,

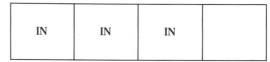

is translated to one step on beat 1, one step on beat 2, two equal steps that divide beat 3, and one step on beat 4.

A box with no word in it signals a "rest" (there is no movement for this beat):

IN	IN	IN	

means one step on beats 1, 2, 3 and no step (motion) on beat 4.

The following abbreviations are used for the footwork notations:

B   A weight transfer to both feet

(L)   Use of the left foot in a motion without weight transfer

L   Weight transfer to the left foot

(R)   Use of the right foot in a motion without weight transfer

R   Weight transfer to the right foot

Therefore, **R**, **(R)**, **L**, **(L)**, **B** under each box designate the "correct" foot to be used for that beat:

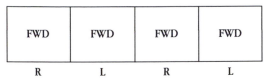

four weight transfers moving right, left, right, left foot;

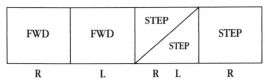

five weight transfers moving right foot, left foot on beats 1, 2; right/left foot on the divided beat 3; right foot on beat 4;

IN	KICK	OUT	TOUCH
R	(L)	L	(R)

one weight transfer to the right foot R on beat 1; one motion, KICK (no weight transfer) of the left foot (L) on beat 2; left foot weight transfer L on beat 3; one motion, TOUCH (no weight transfer) of the right foot (R) on beat 4.

Locomotor Movement I

Characteristics:

1. There is a step or motion for every beat.

2. There is no reference to "right" or "left" foot.

3. Handholds are not necessary.

4. The formations can be modified easily for beginners.

5. The music has a strong underlying beat.

6. Sequences are repeated.

> *Locomotor Movement I:*
> *The following dances alternate the feet in movement*
> *sequences that employ direction.*

Apat-Apat

Four by Four
Philippines

RECORD *Rhythmically Moving 4*

INTRODUCTION Pickup plus 8 beats

FORMATION Partners, double circle facing counterclockwise, inside hands joined

PART I

CCW   *CW*

FWD	FWD (2)	FWD (3)	TURN (1/2)	FWD	FWD (2)	FWD (3)	TURN (1/4)
R	L	R	L	R	L	R	L

AWAY	AWAY (2)	AWAY (3)	AWAY (4)	TOWARD	TOWARD (2)	TOWARD (3)	TOWARD (4)
R	L	R	L	R	L	R	L

FWD	FWD (2)	FWD (3)	FWD (4)	BWD	BWD (2)	BWD (3)	BWD (4)
R	L	R	L	R	L	R	L

CCW

TURN	TURN (2)	TURN (3)	TURN (4)	FWD (CHANGE)	FWD (2)	FWD (3)	FWD (4)
R	L	R	L	R	L	R	L

Beat 1-4	Step R, L, R, L foot forward counterclockwise (on beat 4 release hands and execute ½ turn right to face clockwise)
5-8	Step R, L, R, L foot forward clockwise, end facing partner
9-12	Back away from each other—R, L, R, L foot
13-16	Walk toward each other—R, L, R, L foot, end with ¼ turn right (men face clockwise, women counterclockwise)
17-20	Walk forward 4 steps (inside circle clockwise, outside counterclockwise)
21-24	Walk backward 4 steps to meet partner (turn to face partner)
25-28	Turn with partner 4 steps clockwise (R forearms together)
29-32	Outside person turn ½ turn in 4 steps while inside person walks R, L, R, L foot forward counterclockwise to new partner
NOTE	Keep steps small and the movements continuous. This should not be a march. No R foot or L foot is necessary.
LEAD-UP ACTIVITIES	Practice walking 4 steps, turning ¼, then moving in the new direction either FORWARD or BACKWARD until persons are comfortable with directional changes (individual tempo).
	Practice walking 4 steps, execute a ½ TURN on the 4th step; then WALK 4 steps in the other direction.
	Practice backing up 4 steps, followed by walking FORWARD 4 steps.
TEACHING SUGGESTIONS	Practice each combination of 8 beats with a partner (partner beat).
	Practice the transitions after each set of 8 beats.
	Practice the 4-step TURN with a partner (partner beat).
	Combine the parts of the dance (SAY & DO).
CHAIR DANCING	May be adapted for wheelchairs.

Fjäskern

Hurry Scurry
Sweden

RECORD	*Rhythmically Moving 2*
INTRODUCTION	8 beats
FORMATION	Partners in a single or double circle, facing counterclockwise
FORMATION (SIMPLIFIED)	Single circle, no partners

PART I

FWD	FWD (2)	FWD (3)	FWD (4)	FWD	FWD (2)	FWD (3)	FWD (4)
R	L	R	L	R	L	R	L

2X CCW   2XCW

Beat 1-16   Walk 16 steps forward counterclockwise turning on the final step to face clockwise

17-32   Walk 16 steps forward clockwise, partners turn to face each other on the final step

PART II

SCISSORS	SCISSORS (2)	SCISSORS (3)	SCISSORS (4)	TURN (CHANGE)	TURN (2)	TURN (3)	TURN (4)
R	L	R	L	R	L	R	L

4X

Beat 1-4   Leap 4 times alternating feet, extend the nonweight-bearing heel to the floor in front of the body

5-8   Step 4 times, changing places with partner. Clap with beat 1 and pass R shoulders

9-32   Repeat Part II, beats 1-8, three more times

PART II (SIMPLIFIED)

SCISSORS	SCISSORS (2)	SCISSORS (3)	SCISSORS (4)	IN (CLAP)	IN (2)	IN (3)	IN (4)
R	L	R	L	R	L	R	L

SCISSORS	SCISSORS (2)	SCISSORS (3)	SCISSORS (4)	OUT (CLAP)	OUT (2)	OUT (3)	OUT (4)
R	L	R	L	R	L	R	L

REPEAT PART II (SIMPLIFIED)

Beat 1-4	Repeat Part II, beats 1-4, in place facing center
5-8	Step 4 times moving to the center of the circle; clap with beat 1
9-16	Repeat beats 1-8 moving away from the center of the circle
17-32	Repeat Part II (Simplified), beats 1-16

| NOTE | No R or L foot is necessary. |

| LEAD-UP ACTIVITIES | WALK counterclockwise then clockwise in a continuous movement (individual tempo). SCISSOR 4 times then WALK forward 4 steps (individual tempo, then partner beat). |

| TEACHING SUGGESTIONS | Learn simplified version first. Change Part II to partner version. Practice using partner beat then group SAY & DO. Add music. |

| CHAIR DANCING | Use simplified version. Part I, WALK in place. Part II, WALK feet away from the chair then toward the chair. |

Haya Ze Basadeh

Once in the Field
Israel

RECORD	*Rhythmically Moving 2*
INTRODUCTION	8 beats
FORMATION	Double circle facing counterclockwise; directions given for left-hand person—man if co-ed group—person on right, opposite footwork
ALTERNATE FORMATION	Single circle

PART I *CCW*

FWD	FWD (2)	FWD (3)	FWD (4)	TURN	TURN (2)	TURN (3)	TURN (4)
L	R	L	R	L	R	L	R

CW

FWD	FWD (2)	FWD (3)	FWD (4)	IN	IN (2)	IN (3)	IN (4)
L	R	L	R	L	R	L	R

CCW

OUT	OUT (2)	OUT (3)	OUT (4)	FWD (CHANGE)	FWD (2)	FWD (3)	FWD (4)
L	R	L	R	L	R	L	R

Beat 1-4	Step R, L, R, L foot forward counterclockwise
5-8	Turn toward partner, R, L, R, L foot (end facing clockwise)
9-12	Step R, L, R, L foot forward clockwise (end facing partner with both arms joined in upper arm hold)
13-16	Step R, L, R, L foot toward center of circle (inside person backing up)
17-20	Step R, L, R, L foot away from center; clap on beat 20
21-24	Step R, L, R, L foot in place (outside person advances 4 steps counterclockwise to new partner)
NOTE	No R or L foot is necessary.
CIRCLE DANCE	Dance as outside person and substitute 4 accented steps in place for beats 21-24.

LEAD-UP ACTIVITIES Practice walking 4 steps in one direction, turning 180° in place using 4 steps, and then walking in the opposite direction with 4 steps (individual tempo).

Practice walking IN 4 steps, OUT 4 steps, adding a CLAP with the fourth step OUT.

TEACHING SUGGESTIONS Practice the first 12 beats (FORWARD, 2, 3, 4; TURN, 2, 3, 4; FORWARD, 2, 3, 4) with SAY & DO.

Add on IN, 2, 3, 4; OUT, 2, 3, 4.

Practice the final 4 beats with partners mixing or as a circle dance accenting 4 steps in place.

SAY & DO the dance and then add the music.

CHAIR DANCING

Beat 1-4   STEP in place

5-8   PAT thigh

9-12   STEP in place

13-20   WALK feet away from and toward the chair

21-24   ACCENT in place

Irish Stew*

Two-Part Dance
U.S.A.

RECORD	"Rakes of Mallow," *Rhythmically Moving 2*
INTRODUCTION	8 beats
FORMATION	Circle, no handholds

PART I

FWD	FWD (2)	FWD (3)	FWD (4)	FWD	FWD (2)	FWD (3)	FWD (4)
R	L	R	L	R	L	R	L

2X CCW   2X CW

Beat 1-16	Locomotor movement counterclockwise (walk or use variations)
17-32	Repeat locomotor movement clockwise

PART II

JUMP	JUMP	CLAP	CLAP	JUMP	JUMP	CLAP	CLAP
B	B			B	B		

IN	IN (2)	IN (3)	IN (4)	OUT	OUT (2)	OUT (3)	OUT (4)
R	L	R	L	R	L	R	L

REPEAT PART II

Beat 1-2	Jump 2 times (in place, apart-together, or scissors fashion)
3-4	Clap hands 2 times
5-8	Repeat beats 1-4
9-12	Step R, L, R, L foot toward the center
13-16	Step R, L, R, L foot away from the center
17-32	Repeat Part II, beats 1-16

NOTE	No R or L foot is necessary.
LEAD-UP ACTIVITIES	Practice different locomotor and nonlocomotor sequences.

TEACHING SUGGESTIONS   This type of two-part music gives students the opportunity to practice many sequences to music, alternating locomotor and nonlocomotor movements.

CHAIR DANCING   Do sequences in place.

Choreographed by Phyllis Weikart.

Les Saluts

French-Canadian

RECORD	*Rhythmically Moving 1*
INTRODUCTION	4 beats
FORMATION	Circle with or without hands joined

PART I

FWD	FWD (2)	FWD (3)	FWD (4)	FWD	FWD (2)	FWD (3)	FWD (4)
R	L	R	L	R	L	R	L
							2X CCW 2X CW

Beat 1-16 Walk 16 steps counterclockwise

17-32 Walk 16 steps clockwise

NOTE To give students additional experiences, vary the WALK or use other locomotor movements; no R foot or L foot specified.

PART II

IN	IN (2)	IN (3)	IN (4)	OUT	OUT (2)	OUT (3)	OUT (4)
R	L	R	L	R	L	R	L

IN	IN (2)	IN (3)	⌢ (BOW)	OUT	OUT (2)	OUT (3)	OUT (4)
R	L	R	L	R	L	R	L

Beat 1-4 Walk 4 steps in

5-8 Walk 4 steps out

9-12 Walk 3 steps in and bow; hold bow until music begins again

13-16 Walk 4 steps out

NOTE Fermata ⌢ : hold bow as long as music indicates.

LEAD-UP ACTIVITIES Experiment with locomotor movements.

Practice walking to the steady beat of music.

Practice walking IN 4 steps then OUT 4 steps.

TEACHING SUGGESTIONS   Practice Part II with SAY & DO, then add music. Practice Part I with the music.

CHAIR DANCING   Do sequences in place.

Little Shoemaker

Novelty Dance
U.S.A.

RECORD	*Rhythmically Moving 3*
INTRODUCTION	Pickup plus 8 beats
FORMATION	Double circle, partners facing each other
ALTERNATE FORMATION	Circle, no partners

PART I

FWD	FWD (2)	FWD (3)	FWD (4)	FWD	FWD (2)	FWD (3)	FWD (4)
R	L	R	L	R	L	R	L
						2X CW	2X CCW

Beat 1-16   Inside circle march clockwise (16 steps); outside circle march counterclockwise (16 steps)

17-32   Turn and march 16 steps opposite direction and turn to face partner

NOTE   Other locomotor steps may be substituted for the MARCH.

PART II

CLAP	HIT (R)	CLAP	HIT (L)	CLAP / CLAP	CLAP / CLAP	CLAP	

TURN (ELBOW)	2	3	4	5	6	7	8
R	L	R	L	R	L	R	L
					REPEAT PART II		OPP. ELBOW

Beat 1-2   Clap own hands, hit R hands together

3-4   Clap own hands, hit L hands together

5-8   Clap own hands 5 times (beats 5/&, 6/&, 7, rest 8)

9-16   Hook R elbows and turn 8 running steps

17-32   Repeat clapping sequence and hook L elbows

NOTE   This dance may be used as a mixer. At the end of Part I move ahead one person each time.

CIRCLE DANCE	Use Alternate Formation
PART I	MARCH
Beat 1-16	March 16 steps counterclockwise
17-32	March 16 steps clockwise
PART II	CLAP, PAT, CLAP, PAT; CLAP/CLAP, CLAP/CLAP, CLAP, REST; RUN
Beat 1-2	Clap own hands, pat thighs
3-4	Repeat beats 1-2
5-8	Clap own hands 5 times as above
9-16	Run in place with knees high or substitute scissors kicks, jumps or other in-place motions

LEAD-UP ACTIVITIES	Practice different locomotor movements to the music.
	Practice "hand-jive" with a partner.

TEACHING SUGGESTIONS	Teach the circle dance before the partner dance.
	Do Part I of the partner dance as described—practice with a new partner if the mixer is being used.
	Practice Part II with partner (use partner beat then SAY & DO).

CHAIR DANCING	CLAP, PAT thighs, CLAP, PAT thighs, CLAP 5 times as in the circle dance, then move feet APART, TOGETHER 4 times.
	The dance may be adapted for wheelchairs.

Sneaky Snake*

Novelty Dance
U.S.A.

RECORD	*Rhythmically Moving 4*
INTRODUCTION	8 beats
FORMATION	Individuals facing one direction

PART I

CLAP	CLAP	PAT	PAT	DOWN	UP	DOWN	UP

SCISSORS	SCISSORS (2)	SCISSORS (3)	SCISSORS (4)	TURN	TURN (2)	TURN (3)	TURN (4)

Beat 1-2	Clap hands 2 times
3-4	Pat thighs 2 times
5-6	Bend knees, straighten knees
7-8	Repeat beats 5-6
9-12	Scissor kick 4 times
13-16	Step in place 4 steps turning ¼ right; begin again facing new direction

NOTE	No right or left foot is specified.

LEAD-UP ACTIVITIES	Practice SCISSORS KICKS (individual tempo). Practice DOWN, UP, DOWN, UP.

TEACHING SUGGESTIONS	Practice each 4-beat sequence separately with SAY & DO and link together.

CHAIR DANCING	Beats 5-8—substitute raising and lowering both heels.
	Substitute steps in place for TURN.

Choreographed by Phyllis Weikart.

Te Ve Orez

Tea and Rice
Israel

RECORD	*Rhythmically Moving 1*
INTRODUCTION	8 beats
FORMATION	Three persons side by side facing counterclockwise
ALTERNATE FORMATION	Single circle

PART I   *CCW*

FWD	FWD (2)	FWD (3)	FWD (4)	FWD	FWD (2)	FWD (3)	TURN (4)
L	R	L	R	L	R	L	R

IN (SLIDE) / CLOSE	IN (2) / CLOSE	IN (3) / CLOSE	IN (4) / HOP	OUT (SLIDE) / CLOSE	OUT (2) / CLOSE	OUT (3) / CLOSE	OUT (4) / HOP
L R	L R	L R	L L	R L	R L	R L	R R

IN (CLAP)	IN (CLAP)	IN (CLAP)	IN (CLAP)	OUT (CLAP)	OUT (CLAP)	OUT (CLAP)	OUT (CLAP)
L	R	L	R	L	R	L	R

FWD	FWD (2)	FWD (3)	FWD (4)	FWD (CHANGE)	FWD (2)	FWD (3)	FWD (4)
L	R	L	R	L	R	L	R

Beat 1-8   Run 8 steps forward counterclockwise beginning L foot

9-12   Slide sideward left 4 times toward center of circle beginning L foot

13-16   Repeat beats 9-12 sideward right beginning R foot; turn to face center of circle (one behind the other)

17-20   Step L, R, L, R foot in (clap hands with steps)

21-24   Step L, R, L, R foot out (clap hands)

25-28   Run L, R, L, R foot forward counterclockwise

29-32   Middle person runs forward 4 steps to new group, outside persons run in place

CIRCLE DANCE SIMPLIFICATION This dance may be done in a single circle without handholds. Use a RUN on beats 1-8 and then JUMP on beats 25-32.

NOTE No R or L foot is necessary.

LEAD-UP ACTIVITIES Practice combinations of running and sliding (individual tempo).

Practice sliding IN and OUT, then walking IN and OUT (individual tempo).

TEACHING SUGGESTIONS Practice beats 1-16, the RUN followed by the SLIDE, with SAY & DO.

Add on the WALK IN and OUT and then the final 8 beats.

SAY & DO the entire dance and add the music.

CHAIR DANCING

Beat 1-8	RUN in place
9-16	SIDE, CLOSE, SIDE, TOUCH left and right
17-24	WALK feet away from the chair and toward the chair
25-32	KICK, STEP 4 times

Troika

Three
Russia

RECORD *Rhythmically Moving 2*

INTRODUCTION 8 beats

FORMATION Sets of 3 dancers side by side facing counterclockwise, inside hands held

PART I

FWD	FWD (2)	FWD (3)	FWD (4)	FWD	FWD (2)	FWD (3)	FWD (4)
R	L	R	L	R	L	R	L

REPEAT

Beat 1-16 Run 16 steps forward counterclockwise (light, long steps)

PART II

UNDER	2	3	4	5	6	7	8
R	L	R	L	R	L	R	L

REPEAT

Beat 1-8 Dancer on right runs 8 steps under arch formed by the other 2 dancers and returns to place; center dancer follows through the arch

9-16 Repeat with dancer on left going through the arch formed by the other 2 dancers; center dancer follows

PART III *CW*

TURN	TURN (2)	TURN (3)	TURN (4)	TURN	TURN (2)	TURN (3)	TURN (4)
R	L	R	L	R	L	R	L

CW

TURN	TURN (2)	TURN (3)	TURN (4)	STEP (ACCENT)	STEP (ACCENT)	TOG (ACCENT)	
R	L	R	L	R	L	R	

REPEAT   *OPP. DIR.*

Join hands in circle of 3 dancers

Beat 1-12   Run to left with 12 steps (3 Grapevine steps may be substituted for the runs)

13-16   Accent 3 steps and rest on beat 16

17-32   Repeat Part III, beats 1-16, running to the right; open out to original side-by-side formation on final 3 accents

LEAD-UP
ACTIVITIES

Practice running in groups of 3; synchronize the running steps.

Practice running clockwise and counterclockwise in a circle of 3 dancers; synchronize the running steps.

TEACHING
SUGGESTIONS

RUN 16 steps forward with SAY & DO.

Practice the arch sequence first with a beat common to the 3 dancers and then with a group SAY & DO.

Practice circling left 12 steps plus 3 accents then right 12 steps plus 3 accents (SAY & DO).

SAY & DO the entire dance and add the music.

CHAIR
DANCING

May be adapted for wheelchairs.

Yankee Doodle*

Novelty Dance
U.S.A.

RECORD   *Rhythmically Moving 2*

INTRODUCTION   8 beats

FORMATION   Free formation or open circle facing counterclockwise, no handholds

PART I   *CCW*

JUMP	JUMP (2)	JUMP (3)	JUMP (4)	JUMP	JUMP (2)	JUMP (3)	JUMP (4)
B	B	B	B	B	B	B	B

FWD	FWD (2)	FWD (3)	FWD (4)	FWD	FWD (2)	FWD (3)	FWD (4)
R	L	R	L	R	L	R	L

DOWN	UP	DOWN	UP	DOWN	UP	DOWN	UP
B	B	B	B	B	B	B	B

IN	IN (2)	IN (3)	IN (4)	OUT	OUT (2)	OUT (3)	OUT (4)
R	L	R	L	R	L	R	L

Beat 1-8   Jump 8 times

9-16   Walk 8 steps counterclockwise

17-24   Bend, straighten 4 times

25-28   Walk 4 steps in

29-32   Walk 4 steps out

VARIATION   Change locomotor movements to fit the age and interest of the group. Use only 2 different movement patterns (16 beats each). Have the group create the movement pattern.

LEAD-UP ACTIVITIES   Combine the locomotor and nonlocomotor movements to be used.

Have the students suggest sequences.

TEACHING SUGGESTIONS   Practice the sequence the correct number of times with SAY & DO.

CHAIR DANCING   Do any desired sequences while seated.

Choreographed by Phyllis Weikart.

Locomotor Movement I:
The following dances use recurring two-beat movement
sequences in one place with no weight transfers or "correct"
sides.

Big Circle Dance*
Movement Sequence
U.S.A.

RECORD "Cobbler's Reel/Gaspé Reel," *Rhythmically Moving 1* (other selections from *Rhythmically Moving 1-9* may be substituted)

INTRODUCTION 4 beats

FORMATION Circle, no handholds

SEQUENCE
1. FORWARD 16 steps right; BACKWARD 16 steps left
2. IN 8 steps, OUT 8 steps; repeat
3. FORWARD 16 steps left; BACKWARD 16 steps right
4. Repeat sequence 2
5. SIDE 16 steps right; SIDE 16 steps left
6. BEND and STRAIGHTEN (knees) 8 times (16 beats); HEEL, TOE, (3 times) HEEL, STEP; Repeat with other foot
7. IN 8 steps, OUT 8 steps; repeat
8. FORWARD 16 steps right; BACKWARD 16 steps right
9. Repeat sequence 7
10. FORWARD 16 steps left; BACKWARD 16 steps left
11. IN 4 steps, OUT 4 steps; repeat 2 more times IN 6 steps, STEP/STEP, STEP

NOTE This type of sequence is an excellent warm-up for any class and can be made more difficult by adding dance steps.

CHAIR DANCING Many follow-the-leader sequences may be executed while seated.

Choreographed by Phyllis Weikart.

Count 64*

Novelty Dance
U.S.A.

RECORD   "Peat Fire Flame," *Rhythmically Moving 2*

INTRODUCTION   8 beats

FORMATION   Circle, no handholds

PART I   *CCW*

FWD	FWD (2)	FWD (3)	FWD (4)	FWD	FWD (2)	FWD (3)	TURN
R	L	R	L	R	L	R	L

CCW

BWD	BWD (2)	BWD (3)	BWD (4)	BWD	BWD (2)	BWD (3)	BWD (4)
R	L	R	L	R	L	R	L

REPEAT PART I   OPP. DIR.

Beat 1-7   Step R, L, R, L, R, L, R foot forward counterclockwise around the circle

8   Step L foot turning halfway around to face clockwise

9-16   Step R, L, R, L, R, L, R, L foot backward continuing to move counterclockwise

17-32   Repeat beats 1-16 moving clockwise

PART II

UP (KNEE)	TOUCH	UP (KNEE)	TOUCH	UP (KNEE)	TOUCH	UP (KNEE)	STEP
(R)	(R)	(R)	(R)	(R)	(R)	(R)	R

IN	IN (2)	IN (3)	IN (4)	DOWN	UP	DOWN	UP
L	R	L	R	B	B	B	B

REPEAT PART II   OPP. FTWK (OUT)

Beat 1	Raise R knee up in front of the body
2	Touch R foot next to L foot
3-6	Repeat beats 1-2, two more times
7	Repeat beat 1
8	Step R foot next to L foot
9-12	Step L, R, L, R foot toward the center of the circle
13-16	Bend and straighten the knees slightly 2 times
17-32	Repeat beats 1-16 moving out of the circle on beats 25-28

NOTE No R or L foot is necessary.

LEAD-UP ACTIVITIES Practice walking with different variations (individual tempo); teacher calls out variations.

Practice walking forward and then turning and walking backward (individual tempo).

Practice bending and straightening one knee while balancing on the other leg. Repeat with the other side.

TEACHING SUGGESTIONS Have group WALK forward 8 steps counting the steps as they WALK (SAY & DO). Repeat and substitute the word TURN on the eighth beat and execute a 180° turn.

WALK backward 8 steps counting the steps (SAY & DO).

Sequence the forward and backward steps together.

Practice UP, TOUCH 3 times followed by UP, STEP (SAY & DO).

Add on IN, 2, 3, 4; DOWN, UP, DOWN, UP.

Practice the UP, TOUCH and UP, STEP sequence with the other foot and move OUT.

SAY & DO the dance and then add the music.

CHAIR DANCING Substitute steps in place.

Choreographed by Phyllis Weikart.

Sliding*

Novelty Dance
U.S.A.

RECORD	*Rhythmically Moving 1*
INTRODUCTION	8 beats
FORMATION	Open circle, no handholds

PART I   *CCW*

FWD	FWD (2)	FWD (3)	FWD (4)	FWD	FWD (2)	FWD (3)	FWD (4)

CW

BWD	BWD (2)	BWD (3)	BWD (4)	BWD	BWD (2)	BWD (3)	BWD (4)

Beat 1-8   Walk 8 steps forward moving counterclockwise

9-16   Walk 8 steps backward moving clockwise

PART II

IN	IN (2)	IN (3)	IN (4)	OUT	OUT (2)	OUT (3)	OUT (4)

REPEAT

Beat 1-4   Walk 4 steps in toward the center

5-8   Walk 4 steps out away from the center

9-16   Repeat Part II, beats 1-8

PART III

HEEL	TOE	HEEL	TOE	HEEL	TOE	HEEL	STEP

REPEAT   OPP. FTWK.

Beat 1   Extend one foot toward the center touching heel to the floor

2   Touch toe of the same foot next to the other foot

3-6   Repeat beats 1-2, two more times

7   Repeat beat 1

8   Transfer weight to the heel/toe foot

9-16   Repeat beats 1-8 using the other foot

NOTE   No R or L foot is necessary. Let the student choose the starting foot.

LEAD-UP ACTIVITIES   Practice walking FORWARD 8 steps and BACKWARD 8 steps (individual tempo).

Practice walking IN 4 steps and OUT 4 steps (individual tempo).

Practice HEEL, TOE with one foot and then with the other.

TEACHING SUGGESTIONS   SAY & DO Part I (group beat).

SAY & DO Part II and link to Part I.

Practice Part III with SAY & DO (group beat) and link with Parts I and II.

CHAIR DANCING   Substitute steps in place for FORWARD and BACKWARD.

Choreographed by Phyllis Weikart.

Two-Part Dance*

Novelty Dance
U.S.A.

RECORD	"Blackberry Quadrille," "Soldier's Joy," and "Rakes of Mallow," *Rhythmically Moving 2*; "Irish Washerwoman," "La Raspa," *Rhythmically Moving 3*, and others
INTRODUCTION	Depends on music chosen
FORMATION	Individual free formation

PART I

Beat 1-16	Walk 16 steps forward counterclockwise
17-32	Walk 16 steps forward clockwise

PART II

Beat 1-16	Pat thighs 16 times
17-32	Pat shoulders 16 times

NOTE	Part I consists of locomotor movement. Part II consists of nonlocomotor movement.

VARIATIONS PART I   WALK tall, WALK short, WALK wide, WALK pidgeon-toed, WALK with feet turned out, WALK on toes, WALK on heels, JUMP, or HOP.

VARIATIONS PART II   PAT legs, alternating hands; extend arms in front (OUT), bring arms back to shoulders (IN); extend arms overhead (UP), bring arms back to shoulders (DOWN); PAT, CLAP; SNAP, CLAP; BEND knees, STRAIGHTEN knees.

Repeat 15 more times.

LEAD-UP ACTIVITIES	Practice rhythmic coordination patterns. Practice walking to different pieces of music.
TEACHING SUGGESTIONS	Identify the walking beat and PAT the thighs, WALK to the music.
CHAIR DANCING	Do movements in place.

Choreographed by Phyllis Weikart.

Zigeunerpolka*

Novelty Dance
U.S.A. (German Music)

RECORD *Rhythmically Moving 2*

INTRODUCTION 8 beats

FORMATION Open circle, no handholds

PART I

FWD	FWD (2)	FWD (3)	FWD (4)	BWD	BWD (2)	BWD (3)	BWD (4)

IN	IN (2)	IN (3)	IN (4)	OUT	OUT (2)	OUT (3)	OUT (4)

Beat 1-4 Walk 4 steps moving forward counterclockwise

5-8 Walk 4 steps moving backward clockwise

9-12 Walk 4 steps moving toward the center

13-16 Walk 4 steps moving away from the center

PART II

REPEAT

Beat 1 Step one foot to the side (facing center)

2 Move the second foot next to the first (weight is on both feet)

3-4 Pat the hands on the legs 3 times (3&4)

5-16 Repeat beats 1-4, three more times

PART III

UP	TOUCH	UP	TOUCH	UP	TOUCH	UP	STEP

REPEAT   OPP. FTWK.

Beat 1	Raise one knee in front of body
2	Touch foot next to other foot
3-6	Repeat beats 1-2, two more times
7	Raise same knee up
8	Transfer weight to up, touch foot
9-16	Repeat Part III, beats 1-8 with opposite footwork

NOTE   No R or L foot is necessary.

LEAD-UP ACTIVITIES   Practice walking and changing directions every 4 steps (individual tempo).

Practice UP, TOUCH several times in a row for each leg (individual tempo).

Practice SIDE, TOGETHER, PAT/PAT, PAT (individual tempo).

TEACHING SUGGESTIONS   Practice Part I with SAY & DO (group beat).

Practice Part II with SAY & DO and link to Part I.

Practice Part III with SAY & DO and link to Part II; practice transition to Part I.

CHAIR DANCING   Substitute steps in place for FORWARD and BACKWARD steps.

Choreographed by Phyllis Weikart.

Locomotor Movement II

Characteristics:

1. There is reference to "right" and "left" foot.

2. There is a nonweight-transfer movement (KICK, TOUCH) at the end of 4 beats or 8 beats.

3. There are 2-beat sequences executed sideward.

4. There are alternating 2-beat sequences.

5. There is a resting beat at the end of an 8-beat or 16-beat phrase.

6. There is a single divided beat within 4 beats.

7. There are recurring and alternating 4-beat sequences.

> *Locomotor Movement II:*
> *The following dances use three recurring nonweight-transfer*
> *movements (e.g., TOUCH) plus a weight transfer (STEP) on the*
> *last beat of the 4-beat sequence.*

Alley Cat

Novelty Dance
U.S.A.

RECORD *Rhythmically Moving 3*

INTRODUCTION 8 beats

FORMATION Individual dance

PART I

TOUCH	TOUCH	TOUCH	STEP	TOUCH	TOUCH	TOUCH	STEP
(R)	(R)	(R)	R	(L)	(L)	(L)	L *REPEAT*

Beat 1 Touch R foot sideward right

2 Touch R foot next to L foot

3 Touch R foot sideward right

4 Step R foot next to L foot

5-8 Repeat beats 1-4 using L foot

9 Touch R foot backward

10 Touch R foot next to L foot

11 Touch R foot backward

12 Step R foot next to L foot

13-16 Repeat beats 9-12 using L foot

UP	TOUCH	UP	STEP	UP	TOUCH	UP	STEP
(R)	(R)	(R)	R	(L)	(L)	(L)	L

17   Raise R knee in front of body

18   Touch R foot next to L foot

19   Raise R knee in front of body

20   Step R foot next to L foot

21-24   Repeat beats 17-20 using L foot

UP	STEP	UP	STEP	JUMP (TURN ¼)		CLAP	
(R)	R	(L)	L	B			

25   Raise R knee in front of body

26   Step R foot next to L foot

27   Raise L knee in front of body

28   Step L foot next to R foot

29-30   Jump, turning ¼ right, or pat thighs without turn

31-32   Clap once and rest on beat 32

Repeat dance facing new direction (if turn has been executed)

NOTE   No R foot or L foot is necessary.

LEAD-UP   PAT the thighs and CLAP the hands to each 2 beats of music (PAT, CLAP).
ACTIVITIES
Balance on one leg for 3 beats and change feet on the fourth beat.

Practice touching the foot not bearing weight 3 times before changing feet. Encourage touching at different angles—sideward, forward, backward—individual tempo.

Practice raising and lowering each leg, touching the foot to the floor as the leg is lowered (individual tempo).

TEACHING SUGGESTIONS   Practice the TOUCH, TOUCH, TOUCH, STEP with each foot using the sideward touching patterns and then the backward touching patterns.

Practice 1 sideward pattern to each side followed by 1 backward pattern to each side. (Do not specify R foot or L foot.) SAY & DO.

Practice UP, TOUCH, UP, STEP with each foot.

Practice UP, STEP with each foot.

Combine 2 patterns of UP, TOUCH, UP, STEP (1 with each foot), with 2 patterns of UP, STEP (1 with each foot), SAY & DO.

Combine the sideward, backward, raising and lowering patterns and add the thigh PAT, CLAP or the JUMP, CLAP.

SAY & DO the entire dance and then add the music.

CHAIR DANCING

Beat 1-8	Do as in the dance
9-16	Extend touching foot diagonally backward
29-30	PAT the thigh

Djurdjevka Kolo

Yugoslavia (Serbia)

RECORD *Rhythmically Moving 2*

INTRODUCTION 8 beats

FORMATION Broken circle, hands joined in "V" position

PART I *CCW*

FWD	FWD (2)	FWD (3)	FWD (4)	FWD	FWD	STEP / STEP	STEP
R	L	R	L	R	L *REPEAT*	R L *OPP. DIR.*	R *OPP. FTWK.*

Beat 1-6 Walk 6 steps counterclockwise beginning R foot

7 & Step R foot, L foot in place

8 Step R foot and turn to face clockwise

9-16 Repeat beats 1-8 in opposite direction beginning L foot and turn to face center

PART I (SIMPLIFIED)

FWD	FWD (2)	FWD (3)	FWD (4)	FWD	FWD (2)	FWD (3)	FWD (4)
R	L	R	L	R	L	R *REPEAT*	L *OPP. DIR.*

Beat 1-16 WALK 8 steps counterclockwise and 8 steps clockwise with no R foot or L foot specified.

PART II

TOUCH	TOUCH	TOUCH	STEP	TOUCH	TOUCH	TOUCH	STEP
(R)	(R)	(R)	R	(L)	(L)	(L)	L *REPEAT*

Beat 1 Touch R foot in front of L foot

2 Touch R foot sideward right

3 Touch R foot in front of L foot

4 Step R foot in place

5-8 Repeat beats 1-4, beginning with L foot

9-16 Repeat Part II, beats 1-8

NOTE   No R foot or L foot is necessary.

LEAD-UP
ACTIVITIES

Practice standing on one foot for 3 beats and changing feet on the fourth beat (individual tempo).

Practice touching one foot for 3 beats and then stepping on the touching foot on the fourth beat. Alternate feet (individual tempo).

TEACHING
TECHNIQUES

Practice walking to the music (the walking beat is rather slow).

Practice TOUCH, TOUCH, TOUCH, STEP with SAY & DO.

SAY & DO the dance, and then add the music.

CHAIR
DANCING

Substitute steps in place for walking steps. Do Part II as described.

> *Locomotor Movement II:*
> *The following dances use three alternating weight transfer movements followed by a nonweight-transfer movement on the fourth beat of the 4-beat sequence.*

Close Encounters*

Novelty Dance
U.S.A.

RECORD "California Strut," *Rhythmically Moving 4*

INTRODUCTION 16 beats

FORMATION Partners side by side facing counterclockwise

PART I *CCW*

FWD	FWD (2)	FWD (3)	KICK	BWD	BWD (2)	BWD (3)	TOUCH
R	L	R	(L)	L	R	L	(R) *REPEAT*

Beat 1 Step R foot forward counterclockwise

2 Step L foot forward counterclockwise

3 Step R foot forward counterclockwise

4 Kick L foot forward counterclockwise

5-8 Repeat Part I, beats 1-4, moving backward beginning L foot (clockwise); beat 8, touch toe in back

9-16 Repeat Part I, beats 1-8, and turn to face partner (inside person has back to center of circle)

NOTE To increase complexity in Part I, move sideward right and left, beats 1-8.

PART II

AROUND (DO-SA-DO)	2	3	4	5	6	7	8
R	L	R	L	R	L	R	L

CCW

HIT	HIT	BUMP	BUMP	FWD (CHANGE)	FWD (2)	FWD (3)	FWD (4)
				R	L	R	L

Beat 1-8   Do-sa-do 8 steps (partners move forward, passing R shoulders; move back to back; then step backward to place, passing L shoulders)

9-10   Partners hit hands 2 times

11-12   Partners bump hips 2 times

13-16   Inside person: walk 4 steps forward counterclockwise to new partner; outside person: turn clockwise 4 steps or step in place 4 steps

NOTE   No R foot or L foot is necessary.

LEAD-UP ACTIVITIES   Step in place 3 steps and CLAP, then step in place adding KICK and TOUCH (individual tempo). Finally change to FORWARD, 2, 3, KICK and BACKWARD, 2, 3, TOUCH (individual tempo).

Review or learn a DO-SA-DO.

TEACHING SUGGESTIONS   Partners practice Part I with SAY & DO.

Partners practice transition from Part I to the DO-SA-DO.

Partners do the sequence HIT, HIT, BUMP, BUMP, then SAY & DO.

Partners SAY & DO Part II, adding the change of partners.

CHAIR DANCING   Move feet away from and toward the chair for the FORWARD and BACKWARD.

Step in place for the DO-SA-DO or away and toward the chair.

Substitute PAT, PAT, CLAP, CLAP for the HIT, HIT, BUMP, BUMP.

Choreographed by Phyllis Weikart.

The Hustle

Novelty Dance
U.S.A.

RECORD *Rhythmically Moving 9*

INTRODUCTION 8 beats

FORMATION Free formation

PART I

FWD	FWD (2)	FWD (3)	TOUCH	BWD	BWD (2)	BWD (3)	TOUCH
L	R	L	(R)	R	L	R	(L)

FWD	FWD (2)	FWD (3)	TOUCH	TOUCH	TOUCH	TOUCH	TOUCH
L	R	L	(R)	(R)	(R)	(R)	(R)

TOUCH	TOUCH	TOUCH	STEP	TOUCH	TOUCH	JUMP (¼ TURN)	HOP
(R)	(R)	(R)	R	(L)	(L)	B	R

Beat 1-3 Step L, R, L foot forward

4 Touch R foot forward

5-7 Step R, L, R foot backward

8 Touch L foot backward

9-12 Repeat beats 1-4

13-16 Touch R foot forward twice then backward twice

17-20 Touch R foot forward, backward, sideward, then step next to L foot

21-22 Touch L foot sideward, touch L foot next to R foot

23 Jump turning ¼ left

24 Hop R foot bringing L foot up in back

LEAD-UP ACTIVITIES   Practice balancing on one leg and touching the free foot in front, in back, to the side, etc. (individual tempo).

Practice FORWARD, 2, 3, TOUCH; BACKWARD, 2, 3, TOUCH (individual tempo).

Practice TOUCH 3 times followed by a STEP (individual tempo).

Practice JUMP, HOP executing a ¼ TURN (individual tempo).

TEACHING SUGGESTIONS   Begin with the first 12 beats and keep adding on the next section of 4 beats. Use individual tempo, then group SAY & DO.

Practice the transition from the end to the beginning.

SAY & DO the entire dance and then add the music.

CHAIR DANCING   Do the FORWARD and BACKWARD patterns with small steps away from and toward the chair and omit the TURN at the end.

Işte Hendek

Dig a Ditch
Turkey

RECORD	*Rhythmically Moving 6*
INTRODUCTION	8 beats
FORMATION	Short lines, shoulders touching, hands joined, arms straight

PART I *CCW*

FWD	FWD	IN	HOOK	OUT	TOG	DOWN / UP	BOUNCE / BOUNCE
R	L	R	(L)	L	B	B B	B B

Beat 1	Step R foot diagonally forward right
2	Step L foot diagonally forward right
3	Step R foot in toward center
4	Bend R knee bringing bent L leg behind R knee (lean body out)
5	Step L foot away from center
6	Step R foot next to L foot and transfer weight to both feet
7	Bend both knees then straighten knees
8 &	Bounce both heels 2 times
NOTE	Beats 7-8 may be simplified as a down, up.

PART I
VARIATION *CCW*

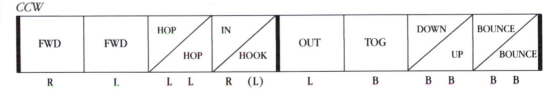

FWD	FWD	HOP / HOP	IN / HOOK	OUT	TOG	DOWN / UP	BOUNCE / BOUNCE
R	L	L L	R (L)	L	B	B B	B B

Beat 1-2	Repeat Part I, beats 1-2
3 &	Hop twice on L foot bringing straight R leg around to center
4 &	Repeat Part I, beats 3-4, as a divided beat
5-8	Repeat Part I, beats 5-8

PART II   *CCW*

FWD	FWD	IN	CHUG	OUT	TOG	DOWN / UP	BOUNCE / BOUNCE
R	L	R	(R)	L	B	B B	B B

Beat 1-3   Repeat Part I, beats 1-3

   4   Chug R foot out leaning body in, L leg as in Part I, beat 4

   5-8   Repeat Part I, beats 5-8

PART II
VARIATION   *CCW*

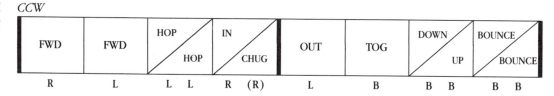

FWD	FWD	HOP / HOP	IN / CHUG	OUT	TOG	DOWN / UP	BOUNCE / BOUNCE
R	L	L L	R (R)	L	B	B B	B B

Beat 1-3   Repeat Variation to Part I, beats 1-3

   4 &   Repeat Part II, beats 3-4, as a divided beat

LEAD-UP
ACTIVITIES   Practice DOWN/UP, BOUNCE/BOUNCE in the rhythmic pattern of 1 &, 2 & (individual tempo).

Practice IN, HOOK (individual tempo).

Practice IN, CHUG (individual tempo).

TEACHING
SUGGESTIONS   Do IN, HOOK, OUT, TOGETHER beginning R foot (individual tempo), then group SAY & DO.

Precede the above with FORWARD, FORWARD, and add on DOWN/UP, BOUNCE/BOUNCE.

SAY & DO Part I.

Have students understand the change in beat 4 from HOOK to CHUG and point out that the rest of the sequence is the same.

Do the 2 parts with SAY & DO and then add the music.

Teach the variations whenever it seems desirable—at a session when the dance is reviewed, not during the initial teaching.

CHAIR
DANCING   Step in place and raise and lower the legs for beat 7.

Locomotor Movement II:
The following dances use recurring 2-beat sequences moving
sideward, right or left, as the students face the center of the
room.

Bannielou Lambaol

Banners of Lampul
France (Brittany)

RECORD	*Rhythmically Moving 8*
INTRODUCTION	8 beats plus 1 beat rest
FORMATION	Circle or broken circle facing center, little fingers joined

PART I *CW*

SIDE	CLOSE	SIDE	CLOSE	SIDE	CLOSE	SIDE	TOUCH
L	R	L	R	L	R	L	(R)

TOUCH / TOUCH	TOUCH / STEP	SIDE	TOUCH	TOUCH / TOUCH	TOUCH / STEP	SIDE	TOG
(R) (R)	(R) R	L	(R)	(R) (R)	(R) R	L	B

Beat 1	Step L foot sideward left on ball of foot
2	Step R foot next to L foot
3-6	Repeat beats 1-2, two more times
7	Step L foot sideward left
8	Touch R foot next to L foot
NOTE	During beats 1-8, arms make a forward circle with each 2 beats.
9	Touch R foot in, push arms in
&	Touch R foot next to L foot, pull arms out
10	Touch R foot in, push arms in
&	Step R foot next to L foot, pull arms out
11-12	Repeat beats 7-8, circling arms
13-14	Repeat beats 9-10
15	Repeat beat 1
16	Step R foot next to L foot, weight ending on both feet
NOTE	Music stops one beat so wait to begin dance.

LEAD-UP ACTIVITIES

Practice walking sideward in different ways, including the SIDE, CLOSE (individual tempo).

Practice the TOUCH, TOUCH, TOUCH, STEP sequence in different ways (individual tempo).

Practice SIDE, TOUCH, bringing the touching foot next to the stepping foot (individual tempo).

Practice moving both arms in a forward circle.

Practice pushing both arms forward and then pulling them in toward the body in 2-beat patterns.

TEACHING SUGGESTIONS

Practice moving sideward left with 3 SIDE, CLOSE steps followed by a SIDE, TOUCH (SAY & DO).

Practice TOUCH/TOUCH, TOUCH/STEP beginning R foot, first adding on SIDE, TOUCH (sideward left) and then adding on SIDE, CLOSE, SAY AND DO.

Learn the arm pattern after the foot pattern is established—use no language when moving the arms.

SAY the foot pattern while executing the arm pattern—do not move the feet at this stage.

Add the arm pattern to the foot pattern with SAY & DO and then with music.

CHAIR DANCING

Change sideward steps to steps in place, or do the arm movements alone.

Erev Shel Shoshanim*

A Night of Roses
Israel

RECORD	*Rhythmically Moving 3*
INTRODUCTION	8 beats
FORMATION	Circle facing center, hands joined in "V" position

PART I   *CCW*

FWD	FWD (2)	FWD (3)	FWD (4)	FWD	FWD	SIDE	TOUCH
R	L	R	L	R	L	R	(L)
					REPEAT	OPP. DIR.	OPP. FTWK.

CCW

SIDE	BACK	SIDE	BACK	SIDE	BACK	SIDE	TOUCH
R	L	R	L	R	L	R	(L)
					REPEAT	OPP. DIR.	OPP. FTWK.

Beat 1	Step R foot forward counterclockwise
2	Step L foot forward counterclockwise
3-6	Step R, L, R, L, forward counterclockwise and turn to face center
7	Step R foot sideward right
8	Touch L foot next to R foot
9-16	Repeat Part I, beats 1-8, forward clockwise beginning L foot

TO SIMPLIFY	WALK 8 steps counterclockwise, then 8 steps clockwise.
17	Step R foot sideward right
18	Step L foot crossing in back of R foot
19-22	Repeat beats 17-18 two more times
23	Step R foot sideward right
24	Touch L foot next to R foot
25-32	Repeat beats 17-24 sideward left beginning L foot

PART II

SIDE	SIDE	SIDE	SIDE	IN	IN	OUT	OUT
R	L	R	L	R	L	R	L

SIDE	SIDE	SIDE	SIDE	TURN	TURN (2)	TURN (3)	TURN (4)
R	L	R	L	R	L	R	L

REPEAT PART II

Beat 1   Sway right

2-4   Sway left, right, left

5-6   Step R foot, L foot toward center

7-8   Step R foot, L foot away from center

9-12   Repeat beats 1-4

13-16   Step R, L, R, L foot turning right (individual circle)

17-32   Repeat Part II, beats 1-16

BRIDGE

SIDE	TOUCH	SIDE	TOUCH
R	(L)	L	(R)

Beat 1   Step R foot sideward right

2   Touch L foot next to R foot

3-4   Repeat beats 1-2, sideward left beginning L foot

PARTS I & II

Beat 1-64   Repeat entire dance

ENDING   *CCW*   *CW*

SIDE	BACK	SIDE	TOUCH	SIDE	BACK	SIDE	TOUCH
R	L	R	(L)	L	R	L	(R)

Beat 1   Step R foot sideward right

2   Step L foot crossing in back of R foot

3   Step R foot sideward right

4   Touch L foot next to R foot

5-8   Repeat beats 1-4, sideward left beginning L foot

LEAD-UP ACTIVITIES   Practice walking in one direction and then the other, using SIDE, TOUCH as the transition (individual tempo).

Practice SIDE, BACK in each direction with SIDE, TOUCH as the transition (individual tempo).

Practice turning to the right in 4 steps without travelling sideward (individual tempo).

TEACHING SUGGESTIONS   SAY & DO Part I, beats 1-16; add Part I, beats 17-32 with SAY & DO.

SAY & DO Part II and add to the end of Part I. Practice the Bridge and the Ending.

Do the entire dance with the music.

CHAIR DANCING   Do walking steps in place. Substitute SIDE, CLOSE for SIDE, BACK. Substitute 4 steps in place for the TURN.

Choreographed by Phyllis Weikart.

Nigun*

Novelty Dance
U.S.A.

RECORD	*Rhythmically Moving 1*
INTRODUCTION	4 beats
FORMATION	Open circle, no hands joined, or closed circle, hands joined

PART I   *CCW*

SIDE	CLOSE	SIDE	CLOSE	SIDE	CLOSE	SIDE	TOUCH
R	L	R	L	R	L	R	(L)
					REPEAT	**OPP. DIR.**	**OPP. FTWK.**

Beat 1	Step R foot sideward right
2	Step L foot next to R foot
3-6	Repeat beats 1-2, two more times
7	Step R foot sideward right
8	Touch L foot next to R foot
9-16	Repeat Part I, beats 1-8 in the opposite direction, beginning L foot

PART II

IN	IN (2)	IN (3)	KICK	OUT	OUT (2)	OUT (3)	TOUCH
R	L	R	(L)	L	R	L	(R)
							REPEAT

Beat 1-3	Step R, L, R foot in toward the center
4	Kick L foot in
5-7	Step L, R, L foot away from the center
8	Touch R foot out
9-16	Repeat Part II, beats 1-8

PART III

SCISSORS	SCISSORS (2)	SCISSORS (3)	SCISSORS (4)	STEP (ACCENT)	STEP (2)	STEP (3)	STEP (4)
R	L	R	L	R	L	R	L

SCISSORS	SCISSORS (2)	SCISSORS (3)	SCISSORS (4)	TURN	TURN (2)	TURN (3)	TURN (4)
R	L	R	L	R	L	R	L

Beat 1   Leap on R foot in place while kicking L foot toward center

2   Leap on L foot in place while kicking R foot in

3-4   Repeat beats 1-2

5-8   Step R, L, R, L foot in place with accents

9-12   Repeat beats 1-4

13-16   Step R, L, R, L foot while turning a full turn right (body turns clockwise)

LEAD-UP ACTIVITIES   Practice moving sideward with SIDE, CLOSE (individual tempo).

Practice IN, 2, 3, KICK; OUT, 2, 3, TOUCH (individual tempo).

Practice SCISSORS KICKS (individual tempo).

TEACHING SUGGESTIONS   Practice SIDE, CLOSE 3 times and SIDE, TOUCH with SAY & DO (group beat).

Practice Part II with SAY & DO and then add to Part I.

Practice Part III with SAY & DO and then add to Part II.

Practice the final TURN, 2, 3, 4 and go back to Part I.

CHAIR DANCING

PART I   Do as described.

PART II   Move feet away from and toward the chair.

PART III   Substitute steps in place for the turn.

Choreographed by Phyllis Weikart

Oh How Lovely*

Novelty Dance
U.S.A.

RECORD *Rhythmically Moving 1*

INTRODUCTION 4 beats

FORMATION Circle or broken circle, escort hold (L hand on hip, R arm in crook of elbow of person in front)

PART I

FWD**	FWD (2)	FWD (3)	FWD (4)	FWD (5)	FWD (6)
R	L	R	L	R	L

SIDE	SIDE (2)	SIDE (3)	SIDE (4)	SIDE (5)	SIDE (6)
R	L	R	L	R	L

IN	OUT	IN	OUT	IN	OUT
R	L	R	L	R	L

Measure 1-6 Step R, L, R, L, R, L foot forward while moving counterclockwise and turn to face center

7-12 Step R, L, R, L, R, L foot side to side right and left

13 Step R foot toward the center

14 Step L foot away from the center

15-18 Repeat beats 13-14, two more times

LEAD-UP ACTIVITIES Walk to music in ¾ meter stepping only on beat 1.

Practice the sections of the dance (individual tempo).

TEACHING SUGGESTIONS Practice sections of the dance with SAY & DO (group beat), linking each section together.

CHAIR DANCING Use steps in place for 6 FORWARD steps. Do the rest of the dance as described.

Choreographed by Phyllis Weikart.
**Each box represents one ¾ measure of music.*

Locomotor Movement II:
The following dances use two different 2-beat sequences performed once.

Ajde Noga Za Nogama

Let's Go Foot Behind Feet
Yugoslavia (Croatia)

RECORD	*Rhythmically Moving 5*
INTRODUCTION	4 beats
FORMATION	Broken circle, escort hold (R hand on hip, L hand holding elbow of person to left)

PART I *CW*

FWD	FWD (2)	FWD (3)	FWD (4)	SIDE	TOUCH	OUT	TOUCH
L	R	L	R	L	(R)	R	(L)

Beat 1	Step L foot forward clockwise
2	Step R foot forward clockwise
3	Step L foot forward clockwise
4	Step R foot forward clockwise and turn to face center
5	Step L foot sideward left
6	Touch R foot next to L foot
7	Step R foot out (facing center)
8	Touch L foot next to R foot

LEAD-UP ACTIVITIES	WALK to the music.
	Do SIDE, TOUCH, SIDE, TOUCH without the music (individual tempo).
	Do OUT, TOUCH, IN, TOUCH without the music—begin R foot OUT (individual tempo).

TEACHING SUGGESTIONS

Practice SIDE, TOUCH, OUT, TOUCH beginning with L foot (SAY & DO).

Practice 4 slow walking steps to the left beginning with L foot and add the SIDE, TOUCH.

Practice the whole sequence, adding on the OUT, TOUCH.

SAY & DO the dance and then add the music.

CHAIR DANCING

Beat 1-4	STEP L, R, L, R foot in place
5	STEP L foot sideward left
6	TOUCH R foot next to L foot
7	STEP diagonally backward right
8	TOUCH L foot next to R foot

Gaelic Waltz*

Novelty Dance
U.S.A.

RECORD	*Rhythmically Moving 1*
INTRODUCTION	4 measures of ¾
FORMATION	Closed circle, L hand on the hip, R hand to neighbor's L elbow

PART I *CCW*

FWD	FWD (2)	FWD (3)	FWD (4)	SIDE	SIDE	IN	OUT
R	L	R	L	R	L	R	L

Measure 1-4	Step R, L, R, L foot forward, moving counterclockwise
5	Step R foot sideward right (facing center)
6	Step L foot sideward left
7	Step R foot toward the center
8	Step L foot away from the center

LEAD-UP ACTIVITIES	Practice walking to the music. Step on beat 1 of each measure.
	Practice SIDE, SIDE, IN, OUT (individual tempo).
TEACHING SUGGESTIONS	Do FORWARD, 2, 3, 4 with SAY & DO. Add on SIDE, SIDE, then add on IN, OUT.
CHAIR DANCING	Do FORWARD steps in place.
	Do IN, OUT toward and away from the chair.

*Choreographed by Phyllis Weikart.

Kendimé

To Myself
Turkey

RECORD *Rhythmically Moving 5*

INTRODUCTION 8 beats

FORMATION Broken circle, led from right; little fingers held, arms describe small circles forward in time to music

PART I *CCW*

FWD	FWD (2)	FWD (3)	FWD (4)	SIDE	TOUCH	IN	HOOK
R	L	R	L	R	(L)	L	(R)

Beat 1 Step R foot forward counterclockwise

2 Step L foot forward

3 Step R foot forward

4 Step L foot forward and turn to face center

5 Step R foot sideward right

6 Touch L foot next to R foot

7 Step L foot toward center

8 Hook R leg behind L knee (bend L knee)

LEAD-UP ACTIVITIES Practice stepping and bending the supporting knee while hooking the other leg behind the bent knee (individual tempo).

Practice walking 4 steps and then taking a step sideward to face center (begin with the R foot).

TEACHING SUGGESTIONS Practice SIDE, TOUCH, IN, HOOK (individual tempo), then SAY & DO.

Precede the practiced pattern with 4 walking steps, beginning R foot (individual tempo), then SAY & DO.

Practice the transition from the end to the beginning.

CHAIR DANCING STEP in place.

Locomotor Movement II:
The following dances use alternating 2-beat sequences.

Áis Giórgis

St. George
Greece

RECORD   *Rhythmically Moving 7*

INTRODUCTION   8 beats

FORMATION   Front basket (broken circle in "W" position may be substituted)

PART I   *CCW*

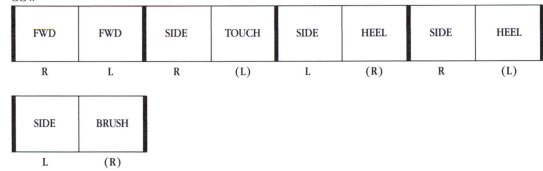

FWD	FWD	SIDE	TOUCH	SIDE	HEEL	SIDE	HEEL
R	L	R	(L)	L	(R)	R	(L)

SIDE	BRUSH
L	(R)

Beat 1-2   Step R foot, L foot forward counterclockwise and turn to face center

3   Step R foot sideward right

4   Touch L foot behind R foot

5   Step L foot sideward left

6   Extend R heel diagonally right

7   Step R foot sideward right

8   Extend L heel diagonally left

9   Step L foot sideward left

10   Brush R foot in and toward the right

LEAD-UP ACTIVITIES

WALK to the music.

Practice the 2-beat sequences as alternating foot patterns using individual tempo:
SIDE, HEEL, SIDE, HEEL
SIDE, TOUCH, SIDE, TOUCH
SIDE, BRUSH, SIDE, BRUSH.

TEACHING SUGGESTIONS

Practice SIDE, HEEL, SIDE, HEEL beginning L foot (SAY & DO).

Practice SIDE, TOUCH, SIDE, HEEL beginning R foot (SAY & DO).

Practice SIDE, HEEL, SIDE, BRUSH beginning R foot (SAY & DO).

Practice SIDE, TOUCH, SIDE, HEEL; SIDE, HEEL, SIDE, BRUSH beginning R foot (SAY & DO).

Practice FORWARD, FORWARD, SIDE, TOUCH beginning R foot.

SAY & DO the entire sequence, and then add the music.

CHAIR DANCING

FORWARD, FORWARD—step R foot, L foot in place

SIDE, TOUCH—step R foot, touch L foot behind R foot

SIDE, HEEL—step L foot, extend R heel; step R foot, extend L heel

SIDE, BRUSH—step L foot, brush R foot

Amos Moses

Novelty Dance
U.S.A.

RECORD	*Rhythmically Moving 8*
INTRODUCTION	8 beats
FORMATION	Individual free formation

PART I

HEEL	STEP	HEEL	STEP / PIVOT	SIDE	BACK	STEP / PIVOT	CLOSE
(R)	R	(L)	L (L)	R	L	R (R)	L

Beat 1	Extend R heel in
2	Step R foot next to L foot
3	Extend L heel in
4	Step L foot next to R foot and pivot ¼ left
5	Step R foot sideward right
6	Step L foot crossing in back of R foot
7	Step R foot sideward and pivot ½ clockwise
8	Step L foot next to R foot

TO SIMPLIFY Do not indicate a specific foot for HEEL, STEP. Do 4 steps forward in the facing direction and turn ¼ right.

LEAD-UP ACTIVITIES Practice OUT, IN with one arm and then the other, extending the arm forward from the shoulder (the arm not used should remain still with the hand touching the shoulder).

Practice HEEL, STEP with each foot (individual tempo).

Practice executing ¼ TURNS on the fourth step in place.

Practice ½ TURNS on 1 foot followed by a CLOSE to the other foot.

TEACHING SUGGESTIONS Practice simplified dance without reference to R or L foot.

Practice simplified dance beginning R foot (SAY & DO).

Practice beats 5-8 to incorporate the appropriate TURNS of the body. Tell the group which way they face for beats 5-6 and beats 7-8.

Practice the transition from ½ TURN, CLOSE to HEEL, STEP.

SAY & DO the dance and then add the music.

CHAIR
DANCING

Beat 1-4   Do as described

Beat 5-8   STEP in place

Bele Kawe

Creole-African (Caribbean Island of Carriacou)

RECORD	*Rhythmically Moving 3*
INTRODUCTION	8 beats
FORMATION	Free formation or circle, no handholds

PART I

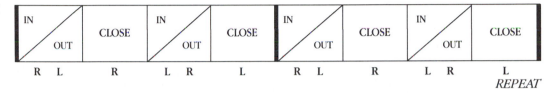

IN / OUT	CLOSE	IN / OUT	CLOSE	IN / OUT	CLOSE	IN / OUT	CLOSE
R L	R	L R	L	R L	R	L R	L *REPEAT*

Beat 1   Step R foot in with bent knees (men with backs of hands on hip pockets, women hold long skirts)

&   Step L foot out

2   Step R foot next to L foot

3-4   Repeat beats 1-2 with opposite footwork

5-16   Repeat Part I, beats 1-4, three more times

PART I (SIMPLIFIED)

IN	TOUCH	OUT	TOUCH	IN	TOUCH	OUT	TOUCH
R	(L)	L	(R)	R	(L)	L	(R) *REPEAT*

PART II

HEEL	OUT	HEEL	OUT	HEEL	OUT	HEEL	OUT
(R)	R	(L)	L	(R)	R	(L)	L

HEEL	IN	HEEL	IN	HEEL	IN	HEEL	IN
(R)	R	(L)	L	(R)	R	(L)	L

Beat 1   Touch R heel diagonally sideward right (arms extended sideward, elbows slightly bent)

2   Step R foot slightly out

3   Touch L heel diagonally sideward left

4   Step L foot slightly out

5-8   Repeat beats 1-4

9-16   Repeat Part II, beats 1-8, moving in

TO SIMPLIFY   8 steps OUT, 8 steps IN.

PART III

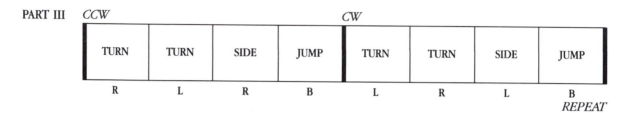

CCW   CW

TURN	TURN	SIDE	JUMP	TURN	TURN	SIDE	JUMP
R	L	R	B	L	R	L	B

REPEAT

Beat 1-3   Step R, L, R foot turning right a full wide turn (elbows sideward, hands behind back, body bent slightly forward)

4   Jump with feet apart (the jump is the men's part; women rest on beat 4 and may shake their shoulders)

5-8   Repeat beats 1-4, turning left and beginning L foot

9-16   Repeat Part III, beats 1-8

TO SIMPLIFY   Step in place without the TURN.

NOTE   No R foot or L foot is necessary if dance is simplified.

LEAD-UP ACTIVITIES   Practice a rocking motion of IN, REST, OUT, REST then IN, TOUCH, OUT, TOUCH (individual tempo).

Practice walking OUT and IN in a 2-beat sequence using a TOUCH before the STEP. TOUCH on beat 1 and STEP on beat 2 (individual tempo).

Practice turning right and left in 3 steps with a JUMP on the fourth beat (individual tempo).

TEACHING SUGGESTIONS

Part I—Use the simplification IN, TOUCH, OUT, TOUCH until dancers are able to do the IN/OUT, CLOSE successfully.

Practice 4 HEEL, OUT steps followed by 4 HEEL, IN steps. HEEL, OUT is much more difficult because the foot is moved farther following the TOUCH of the heel (SAY & DO).

Practice the transition of the IN, TOUCH, OUT, TOUCH to the HEEL, OUT (the TOUCH to the HEEL is difficult).

Combine Parts I and II, SAY & DO.

Practice the 3-step TURN followed by the JUMP moving right then left (SAY & DO). Practice the transition from the final HEEL, IN to the TURN right.

SAY & DO Parts II and III.

Practice the transition from the final JUMP to IN, TOUCH at the beginning.

SAY & DO the entire dance and then add the music.

CHAIR DANCING

PART I Do as described.

PART II Do the HEEL, OUT and HEEL, IN in place or begin with the feet away from the chair in order to move them toward and away from the chair.

PART III Do 3 steps in place and add a JUMP motion of both feet.

Debka Daluna

Israel (Arab)

RECORD	*Rhythmically Moving 9*
INTRODUCTION	8 beats
FORMATION	Short lines in the shoulder hold, "T" position

PART I   *CCW*

SIDE	BACK	SIDE	STAMP	SIDE	STAMP
R	L	R	(L)	L	(R)

4X

Beat 1	Step R foot sideward right
2	Step L foot crossing in back of R foot
3	Step R foot sideward right
4	Stamp L foot sideward left
5	Step L foot sideward left
6	Stamp R foot sideward right
7-24	Repeat Part I, beats 1-6, three more times
NOTE	Part I is done with knees slightly bent, backs straight.

PART II

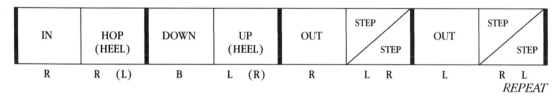

IN	HOP (HEEL)	DOWN	UP (HEEL)	OUT	STEP / STEP	OUT	STEP / STEP
R	R (L)	B	L (R)	R	L R	L	R L

REPEAT

Beat 1	Step R foot in
2	Hop R foot and extend L heel in
3	Jump into squat position with R foot slightly ahead of L foot
4	Rise up, extending R heel
5	Step R foot out
6 &	Step L foot, R foot
7	Step L foot out
8 &	Step R foot, L foot
9-16	Repeat Part II, beats 1-8

PART II (SIMPLIFIED)

JUMP	JUMP	DOWN	UP	OUT	OUT (2)	OUT (3)	OUT (4)
B	B	B	B	R	L	R	L *REPEAT*

LEAD-UP ACTIVITIES

Practice SIDE, BACK (individual tempo). Practice SIDE, STAMP (individual tempo).

Practice 4 JUMPS in sequence, squatting on the third JUMP (individual tempo).

Practice 4 JUMPS followed by 4 steps OUT (individual tempo).

TEACHING SUGGESTIONS

Practice SIDE, STAMP; SIDE, STAMP beginning R foot (SAY & DO).

Have students precede SIDE, STAMP; SIDE, STAMP with SIDE, BACK, beginning R foot. SAY & DO Part I several times.

Do JUMP, JUMP; JUMP, JUMP; OUT, 2; 3, 4 then substitute JUMP, JUMP; SQUAT, STRAIGHTEN; OUT, 2; 3, 4. SAY & DO Part II several times.

Practice the transition from the end to the beginning.

Practice the dance with SAY & DO and then add the music.

CHAIR DANCING

PART I Substitute SIDE, CLOSE for SIDE, BACK.

PART II JUMPS—bounce both feet to the floor 4 times. OUT, 2; 3, 4—step in place.

Dimna Juda

Yugoslavia (Macedonia)

RECORD   *Rhythmically Moving 6*

INTRODUCTION   8 beats

FORMATION   Broken circle, leader at right; hands joined in "W" position

PART I   *CCW*

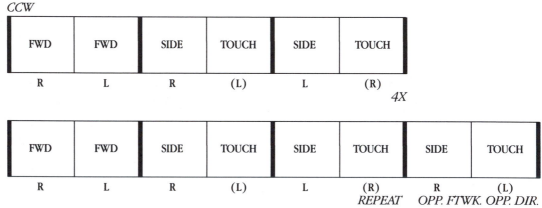

Beat 1	Step R foot forward counterclockwise
2	Step L foot forward counterclockwise
3	Step R foot sideward right
4	Touch L foot diagonally left
5	Step L foot sideward left
6	Touch R foot diagonally right
7-24	Repeat beats 1-6, three more times
25-30	Repeat beats 1-6
31-32	Step R foot sideward, touch L foot
33-38	Repeat beats 1-6 forward clockwise, beginning L foot
39-40	Step L foot sideward left, touch R foot

LEAD-UP ACTIVITIES   Practice SIDE, TOUCH; SIDE, TOUCH (individual tempo).

Practice walking in one direction followed by 3 SIDE, TOUCH patterns, then walking in the other direction beginning with the opposite foot (individual tempo).

TEACHING SUGGESTIONS   SAY & DO SIDE, TOUCH; SIDE, TOUCH beginning R foot.

Precede the SIDE, TOUCH; SIDE, TOUCH with FORWARD, FORWARD beginning R foot (SAY & DO).

Practice 3 SIDE, TOUCH patterns beginning R foot then reverse the FORWARD, FORWARD and do 3 SIDE, TOUCH patterns beginning L foot.

SAY & DO the entire sequence and then add the music.

CHAIR DANCING   Substitute steps in place for FORWARD.

Hasapikos

Butcher's Dance
Greece

RECORD	*Rhythmically Moving 4*
INTRODUCTION	8 beats
FORMATION	Broken circle in "T" position ("W" position may be substituted)

PART I *CCW*

FWD	FWD	SIDE	LIFT	SIDE	LIFT
R	L	R	(L)	L	(R)

Beat 1	Step R foot forward counterclockwise
2	Step L foot forward counterclockwise and turn to face center
3	Step R foot sideward right
4	Lift L foot in front of R leg
5	Step L foot sideward left
6	Lift R foot in front of L leg

VARIATION I *CCW*

FWD	FWD	SIDE	HOP	SIDE	HOP
R	L	R	R	L	L

VARIATION II *CCW*

FWD	FWD	SIDE	STAMP	SIDE	STAMP
R	L	R	(L)	L	(R)

VARIATION III *CCW*

FWD	FWD	SIDE	LIFT	SIDE	STAMP
R	L	R	(L)	L	(R)

VARIATION IV   *CCW*

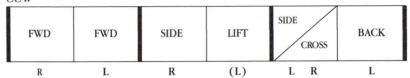

FWD	FWD	SIDE	LIFT	SIDE / CROSS	BACK
R	L	R	(L)	L R	L

Beat 1-4   Repeat Part I, beats 1-4

5   Step L foot sideward left

&   Step R foot crossing in front of L foot

6   Step L foot crossing in back of R foot

VARIATION V   *CCW*

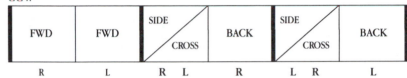

FWD	FWD	SIDE / CROSS	BACK	SIDE / CROSS	BACK
R	L	R L	R	L R	L

VARIATION VI   *CCW*

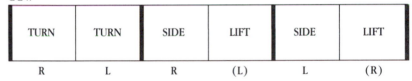

TURN	TURN	SIDE	LIFT	SIDE	LIFT
R	L	R	(L)	L	(R)

Beat 1-2   Step R, L foot while turning full turn right

LEAD-UP
ACTIVITIES   Practice SIDE, LIFT, SIDE, LIFT (individual tempo).

Practice FORWARD, FORWARD; SIDE, LIFT; SIDE LIFT (individual tempo).

Practice SIDE/CROSS, BACK in place (individual tempo).

TEACHING
SUGGESTIONS   Practice FORWARD, FORWARD; SIDE, LIFT; SIDE, LIFT with SAY & DO and add music.

SAY & DO the variation of SIDE/CROSS, BACK.

SAY & DO variations before adding them to the music.

CHAIR
DANCING   Do as described, substituting steps in place as necessary.

Pravo Horo

Straight Circle Dance
Bulgaria

RECORD *Rhythmically Moving 8*

INTRODUCTION 14 beats

FORMATION Broken circle, hands held in "V" position

PART I *CCW*

FWD	FWD	SIDE	LIFT	OUT	LIFT
R	L	R	(L)	L	(R)

Beat 1 Step R foot forward counterclockwise

2 Step L foot forward counterclockwise

3 Step R foot sideward right

4 Lift L foot in front of R leg

5 Step L foot out

6 Lift R foot in front of L leg

VARIATION *CCW*

FWD	FWD	SIDE		IN	
R	L	R		L	

OUT	OUT (2)	OUT (3)	LIFT	OUT	LIFT
R	L	R	(L)	L	(R)

Beat 1	Step R foot forward counterclockwise
2	Step L foot forward counterclockwise
3-4	Step R foot sideward right
5-6	Step L foot in
7-8	Step R foot, L foot out
9-10	Step R foot out and lift L leg
11-12	Step L foot out and lift R leg

LEAD-UP ACTIVITIES

Practice SIDE, LIFT, SIDE, LIFT (individual tempo), then change to SIDE, LIFT, OUT, LIFT (individual tempo).

Practice FORWARD, FORWARD, SIDE, LIFT (individual tempo).

TEACHING SUGGESTIONS

Practice Part I first with individual tempo and then with SAY & DO.

Add the music.

Practice the variation (individual tempo); SAY & DO after Part I is secure.

CHAIR DANCING

STEP in place.

Tipsy*

Novelty Dance
U.S.A.

RECORD	*Rhythmically Moving 6*
INTRODUCTION	4 beats
FORMATION	Individuals in free formation (may be done facing a partner)

PART I

TOUCH (CLAP)		STEP (PAT)		TOUCH (CLAP)		STEP (PAT)	
(R)		R		(L)		L	

2X

HEEL (SNAP)		STEP (PAT)		HEEL (SNAP)		STEP (PAT)	
(R)		R		(L)		L	

2X
REPEAT PART I

Beat 1-2	Extend R foot out, clap hands beat 1
3-4	Step R foot next to L foot, pat thighs, beat 3
5-8	Repeat beats 1-4 beginning L foot
9-16	Repeat beats 1-8
17-18	Extend R heel in, twisting torso right, snap fingers on beat 17 with arms up
19-20	Step R foot next to L foot, pat thighs on beat 19
21-24	Repeat beats 17-20 beginning L foot
25-32	Repeat beats 17-24
33-64	Repeat Part I, beats 1-32
NOTE	CLAP and PAT may be omitted; designating R foot, L foot is not necessary.

PART II

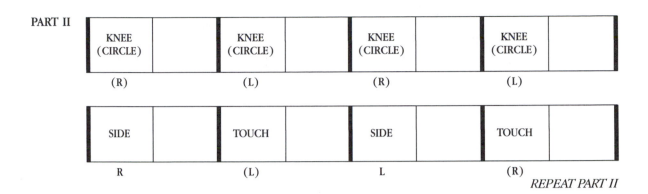

KNEE (CIRCLE)		KNEE (CIRCLE)		KNEE (CIRCLE)		KNEE (CIRCLE)	
(R)		(L)		(R)		(L)	

SIDE		TOUCH		SIDE		TOUCH	
R		(L)		L		(R)	

REPEAT PART II

Beat 1-2	Circle R knee right
3-4	Circle L knee left
5-8	Repeat beats 1-4
9-10	Step R foot sideward right
11-12	Touch L foot next to R foot
13-16	Repeat beats 9-12 with opposite footwork
17-32	Repeat beats 1-16

BRIDGE

DOWN	UP	DOWN	UP

Beat 1-2	Bend and straighten knees diagonally right
3-4	Bend and straighten knees diagonally left

LEAD-UP ACTIVITIES

Practice TOUCH, STEP, TOUCH, STEP (individual tempo).

Practice HEEL, STEP, HEEL, STEP (individual tempo).

Practice SIDE, TOUCH, SIDE, TOUCH (individual tempo).

Practice circling knees.

TEACHING SUGGESTIONS

Practice Part I with SAY & DO—omit hand movements until foot movements are secure.

Practice Part II with SAY & DO.

SAY & DO the entire dance and then add the music.

CHAIR DANCING

PART I   Reach foot diagonally backward alongside the chair.

BRIDGE

Beat 1-4   Raise and lower heels.

Choreographed by Phyllis Weikart.

> *Locomotor Movement II:*
> *The following dances use uneven timing (divided beat and rest).*

Chiotikos

Syrto from Chios
Greece

RECORD	*Rhythmically Moving 9*
INTRODUCTION	6 beats
FORMATION	Broken circle, hands joined in "W" position

PART I   *CCW*

FWD	FWD	SIDE	LIFT	SIDE	LIFT
R	L	R	(L)	L	(R)

4X

Beat 1	Step R foot forward counterclockwise
2	Step L foot forward counterclockwise and turn to face center
3	Step R foot sideward right
4	Lift L foot in front of R leg
5	Step L foot sideward left
6	Lift R foot in front of L leg
7-24	Repeat Part I, beats 1-6, three more times

PART II   *CCW*

TURN	TURN	SIDE	LIFT	SIDE	LIFT
R	L	R	(L)	L	(R)

4X

Beat 1-2   Step R foot, L foot turning full turn counterclockwise, clap on beat 1

    3-6   Repeat Part I, beats 3-6

   7-24   Repeat Part II, beats 1-6, three more times

PART III *CCW*

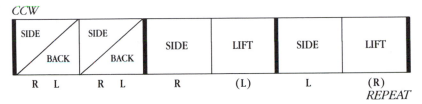

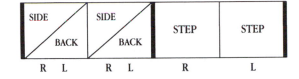

Beat 1   Step R foot sideward right

    &   Step L foot crossing in back of R foot

   2 &   Repeat beat 1 &

   3-6   Repeat Part I, beats 3-6

   7-12   Repeat Part III, beats 1-6

  13-14   Repeat Part III, beats 1-2

  15-16   Step R foot, L foot in place

LEAD-UP ACTIVITIES   Review the basic step of the *Hasapikos* (individual tempo).

Practice a 3-step TURN followed by a LIFT on the fourth beat (individual tempo).

Practice SIDE/BACK in a divided beat rhythm (individual tempo).

TEACHING SUGGESTIONS   SAY & DO Part I and then add the music. Help the students understand the change of the first 2 FORWARD steps in Part I, to the full TURN in Part II, to 2 SIDE/BACK steps in Part III.

Do the sequence of Part III that ends with 2 steps in place and practice the transition to Part I; SAY & DO.

SAY & DO the dance and then add the music.

CHAIR DANCING   Change the FORWARD and TURN to steps in place and the SIDE/BACK to SIDE/CLOSE.

Cumberland Square

England

RECORD	*Rhythmically Moving 3*
INTRODUCTION	4 beats
FORMATION	Square sets

PART I
SLIDE

ACROSS

SIDE	CLOSE	SIDE (2)	CLOSE	SIDE (3)	CLOSE	SIDE (4)	CLOSE	SIDE (5)	CLOSE	SIDE (6)	CLOSE	SIDE (7)	CLOSE	SIDE (8)	HOP
*R	L	R	L	R	L	R	L	R	L	R	L	R	L	R	R

REPEAT   OPP. DIR. OPP. FTWK.

Beat 1-8   Head couples do 8 slides across the set, men passing back to back

9-16   Head couples do 8 slides back again, women passing back to back

17-32   Repeat beats 1-16 (side couples)

PART II
STAR

CW

TURN	TURN (2)	TURN (3)	TURN (4)	TURN	TURN (2)	TURN (3)	TURN (4)
R	L	R	L	R	L	R	L

REPEAT   OPP. DIR.

Beat 1-8   Head couples walk 8 steps clockwise with R hands joined in the star formation (skipping steps may be substituted)

9-16   Head couples walk 8 steps counterclockwise with L hands joined in star formation

17-32   Repeat beats 1-16 (side couples)

PART III
BASKET

CW

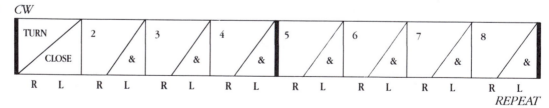

TURN	CLOSE	2	&	3	&	4	&	5	&	6	&	7	&	8	&
R	L	R	L	R	L	R	L	R	L	R	L	R	L	R	L

REPEAT

Beat 1-16   Head couples form a back basket and buzz turn clockwise

17-32   Repeat beats 1-16 (side couples)

PART IV
SKIP

CW

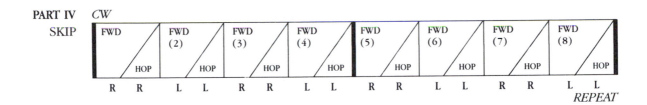

FWD		FWD (2)		FWD (3)		FWD (4)		FWD (5)		FWD (6)		FWD (7)		FWD (8)	
	HOP		HOP		HOP		HOP		HOP		HOP		HOP		HOP
R	R	L	L	R	R	L	L	R	R	L	L	R	R	L	L

REPEAT

Beat 1-16   All join hands and walk (or skip) 16 steps clockwise

PROMENADE   *CCW*

FWD	FWD (2)	FWD (3)	FWD (4)	FWD	FWD (2)	FWD (3)	FWD (4)
R	L	R	L	R	L	R	L

REPEAT

17-32   Promenade 16 steps counterclockwise with partner (end in original position)

LEAD-UP ACTIVITIES

Practice SLIDE and SKIP and GALLOP (individual tempo).

Practice SLIDE and SKIP with a partner (partner beat).

Practice SLIDE and SKIP using a circle formation (group beat).

Practice the STAR formation.

Move around the room while practicing PROMENADE with a partner (partner beat).

TEACHING SUGGESTIONS

Form square sets and practice the SLIDE (SAY & DO); add the music.

Practice the STAR figure.

Practice the BUZZ TURN for the BASKET with partners holding both hands, then add the BASKET formation.

Practice the fourth figure (SKIP left and PROMENADE right).

Do the entire dance with music.

CHAIR DANCING

May be modified for wheelchairs.

Men use opposite footwork.

Dučec

Yugoslavia

RECORD	*Rhythmically Moving 8*
INTRODUCTION	8 beats
FORMATION	Free formation

PART I

JUMP (FWD STRIDE)	JUMP (2)	JUMP (3)	JUMP (4)	APART / TOG (IN AIR)	APART / TOG (IN AIR)	APART / TOG (IN AIR)	TOG (ON FLOOR)
B	B	B	B	B B	B B	B B	B

REPEAT

Beat 1 Jump to forward stride position, (L foot forward, R foot backward)

2 Jump to R foot forward, L foot backward

3-4 Repeat beats 1-2

5 Jump to sideward stride (feet apart)

& Jump into air clicking heels—legs straight

6-7 Repeat beats 5 &, two times

8 Land with feet together

9-16 Repeat Part I, beats 1-8

PART I SIMPLIFIED

JUMP (FWD STRIDE)	JUMP (2)	JUMP (3)	JUMP (4)	JUMP (SWD)	JUMP (SWD)	JUMP (SWD)	TOG
B	B	B	B	B	B	B	B

REPEAT

PART II

JUMP	JUMP	JUMP / JUMP	JUMP	JUMP	JUMP	JUMP / JUMP	JUMP
B	B	B B	B	B	B	B B	B

REPEAT

Beat 1	Jump to forward stride position (L foot forward, R foot backward)
2	Jump to R foot forward, L foot backward
3	Jump in place
&	Jump in place
4	Jump in place
5-16	Repeat Part II, beats 1-4, three more times

LEAD-UP ACTIVITIES

Practice forward stride JUMPS (one foot forward and one foot backward) alternating feet (individual tempo).

Practice sideward stride JUMPS, feet apart sideward (individual tempo).

Practice 3 sideward stride JUMPS followed by a JUMP with feet together (individual tempo).

Practice moving from forward stride to sideward stride JUMPS.

Practice JUMPS in a rhythmic pattern of 1, 2, 3 &, 4 (individual tempo).

Practice bringing the feet together in the air between sideward stride JUMPS (individual tempo).

TEACHING SUGGESTIONS

Practice 4 forward stride JUMPS followed by 3 sideward stride JUMPS and end with a JUMP, feet together; JUMP, JUMP; JUMP, JUMP; SIDE; SIDE, SIDE, TOGETHER; (SAY & DO).

Practice JUMP, JUMP; JUMP/JUMP, JUMP with SAY & DO.

Put the dance together with SAY & DO and then add the music.

After the dance has been executed successfully, add the APART/TOGETHER pattern of Part I.

CHAIR DANCING

Do as described.

Körtanc

Hungary

RECORD	*Rhythmically Moving 3*
INTRODUCTION	4 beats
FORMATION	Single circle or hands joined in front basket with L hand under (move clockwise throughout the dance)

PART I   *CW*

FWD	FWD	SIDE	TOUCH (CLICK)	SIDE	TOUCH (CLICK)
L	R	L	(R)	R	(L)

4X

Beat 1   Step L foot forward clockwise

2   Step R foot forward and turn to face center

3   Step L foot sideward left

4   Bring R foot to L foot clicking heels and straightening legs or substitute a touch

5   Step R foot sideward right

6   Bring L foot to R foot as in beat 4, or substitute a touch

7-24   Repeat Part I, beats 1-6, three more times

NOTE   In Part I, a slight bend of the knee occurs before each step: BEND-STEP.

PART II   *CW*

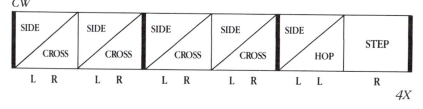

SIDE / CROSS	SIDE / CROSS	SIDE / CROSS	SIDE / CROSS	SIDE / HOP	STEP
L R	L R	L R	L R	L L	R

4X

Beat 1   Step L foot sideward left

&   Step R foot crossing in front of L foot

2-4   Repeat beats 1-2, three more times

5   Step L foot sideward left

&   Hop L foot

6   Step R foot next to L foot

7-24   Repeat Part II, beats 1-6, three more times

TO SIMPLIFY   RUN 8 steps clockwise for the 4 SIDE/CROSS steps.

LEAD-UP ACTIVITIES   Practice SIDE, TOUCH, SIDE, TOUCH, then change the TOUCH to a HEEL CLICK (individual tempo).

Practice SIDE/CROSS (individual tempo).

TEACHING SUGGESTIONS   Practice SIDE, TOUCH, SIDE, TOUCH or substitute a CLICK for the TOUCH beginning L foot and using SAY & DO.

Precede the first SIDE, TOUCH with a FORWARD, FORWARD beginning L foot (individual tempo, then SAY & DO).

Practice SIDE/CROSS to the left (individual tempo, then SAY & DO). Add on SIDE/HOP, STEP to 4 SIDE/CROSS steps.

Practice Part II with SAY & DO.

SAY & DO the entire dance and then add the music.

CHAIR DANCING   Substitute steps in place for those moving left.

La Raspa

The Rasp (Mexican Shuffle)
Mexico

RECORD	*Rhythmically Moving 3*
INTRODUCTION	8 beats
FORMATION	Partners facing each other, both hands joined
FORMATION (SIMPLIFIED)	Single circle, no partners

PART I

LEAP	LEAP (2)	LEAP (3)		LEAP	LEAP (2)	LEAP (3)	
R	L	R		L	R	L	

4X

Beat 1	Leap on R foot, extending L foot forward, heel touching floor
2	Change feet, extending R foot
3	Repeat beat 1 step
4	Rest (2 quick claps may be added)

— Bleking Step

5-8	Repeat beats 1-4 with opposite footwork and beginning leap on L foot
9-32	Repeat Part I, beats 1-8, three more times
NOTE	Using partner formation, thrust arm forward opposite to the foot that is extended forward.

PART II

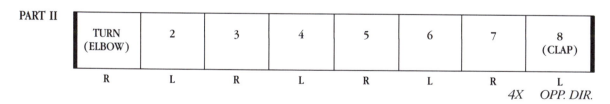

TURN (ELBOW)	2	3	4	5	6	7	8 (CLAP)
R	L	R	L	R	L	R	L

4X   OPP. DIR.

Beat 1-8	R elbow swing, L hand high; release elbows and clap on beat 8
9-16	Repeat, using L elbow (R hand high)
17-32	Repeat R and L elbow
NOTE	Part II may be used as a mixer, changing partners with each 8 beats or after 16 beats; men advance counterclockwise, women advance clockwise.

**PART II
(SIMPLIFIED)**

Beat 1-16   Walk right (or use any other locomotor step)

17-32   Walk left

**LEAD-UP
ACTIVITIES**

Practice the LEAP, LEAP, LEAP, REST (Bleking Step) at individual tempo.

Practice 8-beat ELBOW SWINGS with partner (partner beat).

Practice locomotor movements to the music (RUN and HOP) if using the circle dance.

**TEACHING
SUGGESTIONS**

Practice Part I with SAY & DO.

When teaching the partner dance, work on Parts I and II with SAY & DO before adding the music.

**CHAIR
DANCING**

Do steps in place.

May be adapted for wheelchairs.

Limbo Rock*

Novelty Dance
U.S.A.

RECORD   *Rhythmically Moving 2*

INTRODUCTION   6 beats

FORMATION   Circle, no hands held

PART I

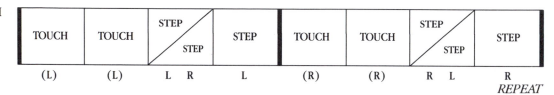

TOUCH	TOUCH	STEP / STEP	STEP	TOUCH	TOUCH	STEP / STEP	STEP
(L)	(L)	L R	L	(R)	(R)	R L	R *REPEAT*

Beat 1   Touch L foot in

2   Touch L foot out

3-4   Three steps in place L, R, L foot (3 &, 4)

5-8   Repeat beats 1-4 with opposite footwork, beginning R foot

9-16   Repeat Part I, beats 1-8

NOTE   No right or left foot needs to be specified.

PART II

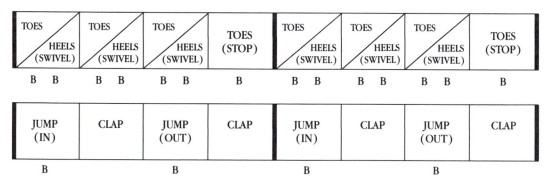

TOES / HEELS (SWIVEL)	TOES / HEELS (SWIVEL)	TOES / HEELS (SWIVEL)	TOES (STOP)	TOES / HEELS (SWIVEL)	TOES / HEELS (SWIVEL)	TOES / HEELS (SWIVEL)	TOES (STOP)
B B	B B	B B	B	B B	B B	B B	B

JUMP (IN)	CLAP	JUMP (OUT)	CLAP	JUMP (IN)	CLAP	JUMP (OUT)	CLAP
B		B		B		B	

Beat 1	Swivel toes right
&	Swivel heels right
2-3	Repeat beat 1 &, two more times
4	Straighten feet
5-8	Repeat beats 1-4 beginning with swivel toes left
9	Jump toward center
10	Clap
11	Jump away from center
12	Clap
13-16	Repeat beats 9-12

TO SIMPLIFY   Part II, beats 1-8, WALK either 8 steps right or 4 steps right and 4 steps left.

LEAD-UP ACTIVITIES   Practice STEP/STEP, STEP in place, changing feet with each repetition (individual tempo).

Practice moving sideward with SWIVEL FEET, moving toes then heels (individual tempo).

Practice 4-beat sequences of JUMP, CLAP, JUMP, CLAP, moving in and out.

TEACHING SUGGESTIONS   Practice TOUCH, TOUCH, STEP/STEP, STEP (SAY & DO). SAY & DO Part I, 4 times.

Practice SWIVEL FEET to the divided beat (individual tempo), then SAY & DO Part II, beats 1-8.

JUMP IN, CLAP, JUMP OUT, CLAP twice with SAY & DO. SAY & DO all of Part II.

Practice the entire dance with SAY & DO and add the music.

CHAIR DANCING   STEP in place.

Choreographed by Phyllis Weikart.

Man in the Hay

Germany

RECORD	*Rhythmically Moving 3*
INTRODUCTION	8 beats
FORMATION	Square sets

DANCE INTRODUCTION

Beat 1-16   Join hands in circle; swing arms up (bent elbow) on odd beats and down on even beats

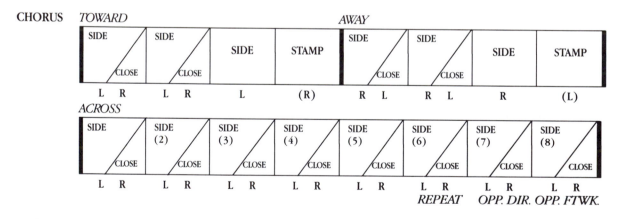

PART I
SKIP

CW

Beat 1-16   Skip (16 times) once around clockwise; continue arm swings as in Introduction

CHORUS

Beat 1-4   Head couples slide 3 times toward one another and stamp on beat 4; men begin with L foot, women, R foot

5-8   Slide back to place 3 times and stamp on beat 4

9-24   Slide across the set and back, 8 slides each way; men (L hand partner) pass back to back going over; women (R hand partner) pass back to back returning to place

25-48   Side couples repeat Chorus

PART II   *CW*
SKIP

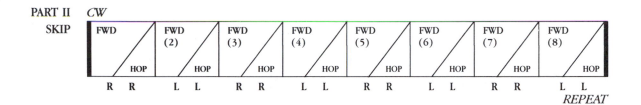

Beat 1-16   Women join hands and skip 16 times once around clockwise

CHORUS   Repeat Chorus, beats 1-48

PART III   *CW*
SKIP

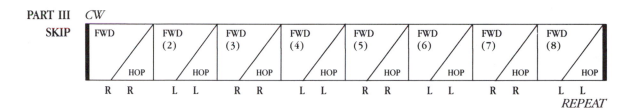

Beat 1-16   Men join hands and skip 16 times twice around clockwise

CHORUS   Repeat Chorus, beats 1-48

PART IV   *CW*
BASKET

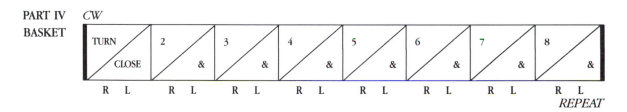

Beat 1-16   Head couples do a basket (men join hands behind women's backs and women join hands behind men's shoulders)

CHORUS   Repeat Chorus, beats 1-48

PART V   *CW*
BASKET

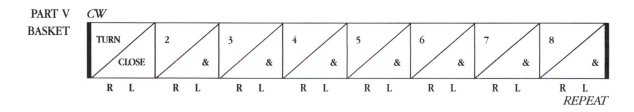

Beat 1-16   Side couples basket

CHORUS   Repeat Chorus, beats 1-48

PART VI
SKIP

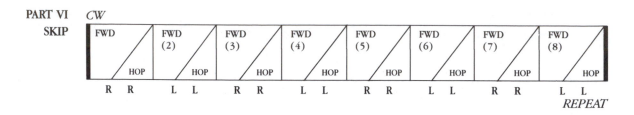

Beat 1-16   Repeat Part I (16 skips) and end dance on last note

LEAD-UP
ACTIVITIES

Practice SLIDE with a partner one way and then the other way.

Practice SKIP.

TEACHING
SUGGESTIONS

Divide the students into sets of 2 couples (sides and heads) and have each group practice the parts of the dance that are executed with 4 people.

Form square sets and practice the Chorus, then practice each of the verses.

Do the entire dance and then add the music.

CHAIR
DANCING

May be adapted for wheelchairs.

Plješkavac Kolo

Clap Hands Kolo
Yugoslavia

RECORD *Rhythmically Moving 3*

INTRODUCTION 8 beats

FORMATION Broken circle, hands joined in "V" position

PART I *CCW-DIAG*

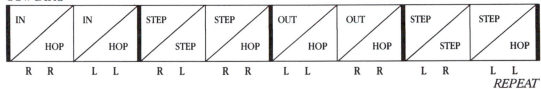

Beat 1 Step R foot in diagonally right and hop R foot

2 Step L foot in diagonally right and hop L foot

3-4 Step R, L, R in place (3 &, 4) and hop R foot

5 Step L foot out diagonally right and hop L foot

6 Step R foot out diagonally right and hop R foot

7-8 Step L, R, L in place (7 &, 8) and hop L foot

9-16 Repeat Part I, beats 1-8

TO SIMPLIFY Leave out the hops

PART II

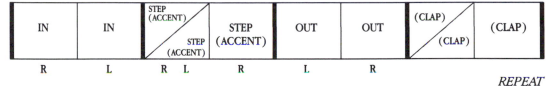

Beat 1-2 Step R foot, L foot toward center

3-4 Step R, L, R foot in place (3 &, 4), accent steps

5-6 Step L foot, R foot out

7-8 Clap hands 3 times (7 &, 8)

9-16 Repeat Part II, beats 1-8

LEAD-UP ACTIVITIES WALK in a rhythmic pattern of 1, 2, 3 &, 4 (individual tempo), then change the direction to 2 steps IN followed by 3 steps in place, then 2 steps OUT and 3 steps in place (individual tempo).

Practice 2 WALKS, 3 ACCENTS (3 &, 4) and 2 WALKS, 3 CLAPS (3 &, 4), then change to IN and OUT.

TEACHING SUGGESTIONS WALK 4 steps IN diagonally right and 4 steps OUT diagonally right with SAY & DO, then change the walking pattern to Part I using SAY & DO.

SAY & DO Part II.

SAY & DO the entire dance and then add the music.

CHAIR DANCING Do the steps away from and toward the chair.

Tant' Hessie

Aunt Hessie
South Africa

RECORD	*Rhythmically Moving 7*
INTRODUCTION	8 beats
FORMATION	Double circle, partners
ALTERNATE FORMATION	Circle, no partners

PART I

TWD	TWD (2)	TWD (3)	TOUCH (NOD)	AWAY	AWAY (2)	AWAY (3)	TOUCH
R	L	R	(L)	L	R	L	(R) *REPEAT*

Beat 1-3 Step R, L, R foot toward each other until R shoulders adjacent

4 Touch L foot next to R foot and nod to partner

5-8 Step L, R, L foot back to place and touch R foot next to L foot

9-16 Repeat beats 1-8 with L shoulders adjacent

NOTE The walking steps may be changed to STEP-BENDS and simplified to 4 WALKS without the TOUCH.

PART II

AROUND (DO-SA-DO)	2	3	4	5	6	7	8
R	L	R	L	R	L	R	L *REPEAT*

Beat 1-8 Do-sa-do 8 step-bends with your partner passing R shoulders first

9-16 Do-sa-do 8 step-bends while passing L shoulders first

PART III   *CW*

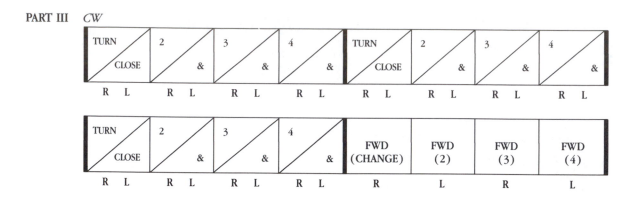

TURN / CLOSE	2 / &	3 / &	4 / &	TURN / CLOSE	2 / &	3 / &	4 / &
R L	R L	R L	R L	R L	R L	R L	R L

TURN / CLOSE	2 / &	3 / &	4 / &	FWD (CHANGE)	FWD (2)	FWD (3)	FWD (4)
R L	R L	R L	R L	R	L	R	L

Beat 1-12   Buzz turn with 12 buzz steps (using shoulder-waist position—double arm-hold, if two women)

13-16   Step R, L, R, L foot forward to new partner. Outside partner moves clockwise, inside partner, counterclockwise.

TO SIMPLIFY   Use an elbow turn with 12 steps.

CIRCLE DANCE

PART I   WALK forward counterclockwise right, ending with a TOUCH then backward clockwise

PART II   WALK IN 8 steps and OUT 8 steps

PART III   WALK in own circle 8 steps right and 8 steps left

LEAD-UP ACTIVITIES   Practice DO-SA-DO with a partner (partner beat).

Practice a slow BUZZ TURN with a partner (partner beat).

TEACHING SUGGESTIONS   Practice Part I with a partner (SAY & DO).

Practice Part II with a partner (SAY & DO).

Practice Part III with a partner and practice the transition to a new partner.

SAY & DO the entire dance and then add the music.

Use the circle formation with no partners for young children or very inexperienced dancers.

CHAIR DANCING   May be adapted for wheelchairs.

Ve David

Israel

RECORD	*Rhythmically Moving 3*
INTRODUCTION	8 beats
FORMATION	Partners in a double circle facing counterclockwise, inside hands joined

PART I *CCW*

FWD	FWD (2)	FWD (3)	FWD (4)	TURN (SINGLE)	TURN (CIRCLE)	TURN (3)	TURN (4)
R	L	R	L	R	L	R	L

IN	IN (2)	IN (3)	IN (4)	OUT	OUT (2)	OUT (3)	OUT (4)
R	L	R	L	R	L	R	L

3X

CW

TURN / CLOSE	2 / &	3 / &	4 / &	TURN / CLOSE	2 / &	3 / &	4 / &
R L	R L	R L	R L	R L	R L	R L	R L

Beat 1-4	Step R, L, R, L foot forward counterclockwise
5-8	Step R, L, R, L foot forming a single circle (right-hand partner steps in, while left-hand partner steps out)
9-12	Step R, L, R, L foot in (hands are joined and arms are raised)
13-16	Step R, L, R, L foot out (arms are lowered)
17-20	Women (partner on right) step R, L, R, L foot in while men clap 4 times
21-24	Women step R, L, R, L foot out; men continue 4 claps
25-28	Men step R, L, R, L foot in; (clapping continues), turn right 180° to face out
29-32	Men step R, L, R, L foot out to new partner
33-40	Israeli turn with new partner (8 buzz steps)
NOTE	No R foot or L foot is necessary. Refer to outside and inside (or R and L) person in groups without equal numbers of men and women.

LEAD-UP ACTIVITIES

Practice walking IN 4 steps, OUT 4 steps (individual tempo).

Practice walking with a partner (partner beat).

Practice walking to the music, changing direction after each 4 steps.

Practice a GALLOP with the R foot leading (individual tempo).

Practice a GALLOP turning right in a fairly large circle then narrow the circle—be certain students are leading with the R foot (individual tempo).

TEACHING SUGGESTIONS

Practice walking with a partner to the music.

Practice the first 16 beats of the dance with SAY & DO.

Add on the next 8 beats for the outside partner then the 8 beats for the inside partner. (Be certain to identify the person to whom the inside partner will be walking before adding on those 8 beats.)

Practice the final 8 beats using a WALK and a R elbow hold. (Change to the BUZZ TURN when the dance is reviewed.)

SAY & DO the entire dance and then add the music.

CHAIR DANCING

Beat 1-16	Move feet away from and back to the chair
17-24	Clap hands
25-32	Pat thighs
33-40	Pat thighs and clap hands in an alternating pattern
NOTE	May be adapted for wheelchairs.

Zemer Atik

Israel

RECORD	*Rhythmically Moving 4*	
INTRODUCTION	16 beats	
FORMATION	Broken circle facing counterclockwise, L hand at shoulder, R arm straight, hands joined	

PART I *CCW*

FWD	FWD (2)	FWD (3)	FWD (4)	FWD	CLAP	FWD	CLAP
R	L	R	L	R		L	

4X

Beat 1-4	Step R, L, R, L foot forward counterclockwise and release handhold
5-6	Step R foot forward then clap over R shoulder
7-8	Step L foot forward then clap over L shoulder
9-32	Repeat Part I, beats 1-4, three more times

PART II

IN	SNAP	IN	SNAP	OUT	OUT (2)	OUT (3)	OUT (4)
R		L		R	L	R	L

4X

Beat 1-2	Step R foot in, sway arms overhead to right (snap fingers after the step)
3-4	Step L foot in, sway arms left (snap fingers after the step)
5-8	Step R, L, R, L foot out while lowering the arms slowly in front of body
9-32	Repeat Part II, beats 1-4, three more times

NOTE	This is the circle version of *Zemer Atik*; there is also a couple dance. No R foot or L foot is necessary.
LEAD-UP ACTIVITIES	WALK, combining 4 quick steps with 2 slow steps: FORWARD, 2, 3, 4; FORWARD, REST, FORWARD, REST (individual tempo).
	Repeat the above with 2 slow steps IN and 4 quick steps OUT (individual tempo).
	Practice STEP, CLAP several times and STEP, SNAP several times.

TEACHING SUGGESTIONS Practice Part I without adding a CLAP—FORWARD, 2, 3, 4; FORWARD, REST, FORWARD, REST (SAY & DO).

Practice Part II without the SNAPS (SAY & DO).

Practice the transitions between the parts.

Do the dance with the music and add on the CLAPS and SNAPS if the group is not having any difficulty—otherwise add on during the review of the dance.

CHAIR DANCING

PART I   STEP in place then lean right, CLAP, lean left, CLAP.

PART II   STEP away from the chair and toward the chair.

*Locomotor Movement II:
The following dances use recurring 4-beat movements (the second sequence of four beats begins on the same foot).*

Good Old Days

**Novelty Dance
U.S.A.**

RECORD	*Rhythmically Moving 6*
INTRODUCTION	8 beats
FORMATION	Partners in double circle facing counterclockwise, inside hands joined. Directions given for person on left, opposite footwork for right-hand person.

PART I

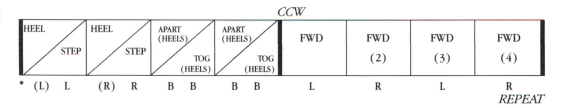

CCW

HEEL / STEP	HEEL / STEP	APART (HEELS) / TOG (HEELS)	APART (HEELS) / TOG (HEELS)	FWD	FWD (2)	FWD (3)	FWD (4)
* (L) L	(R) R	B B	B B	L	R	L	R

REPEAT

Beat 1	Extend L heel forward keeping weight on R foot
&	Step L foot next to R foot
2	Extend R heel forward keeping weight on L foot
&	Step R foot next to L foot
3	Weight on both feet—turn heels out
&	Turn heels in (feet are straight)
4 &	Repeat beats 3 &
5	Step L foot forward counterclockwise
6-8	Step R, L, R foot forward counterclockwise
9-16	Repeat Part I, beats 1-8

PART II

FWD	KICK	BWD	TOUCH	FWD	KICK	BWD	TOUCH
L	(R)	R	(L)	L	(R)	R	(L)

HEEL / STEP	HEEL / STEP	APART (HEELS) / TOG (HEELS)	APART (HEELS) / TOG (HEELS)	TURN (CHANGE)	TURN (2)	TURN (3)	TURN (4)
(L) L	(R) R	B B	B B	L	R	L	R

Beat 1   Step L foot forward counterclockwise

2   Kick R foot forward counterclockwise

3   Step R foot backward

4   Touch L foot backward

5-8   Repeat beats 1-4

9-12   Repeat Part I, beats 1-4

13-16   Step L, R, L, R foot turning ½ circle to the left and return to new partner; right-hand partner step R, L, R, L foot forward to meet new partner

CIRCLE DANCE   Dance left-hand person's part; specifying R or L foot is not necessary.

LEAD-UP ACTIVITIES   Practice HEEL/STEP (individual tempo).

Practice turning heels APART/TOGETHER in a steady tempo (individual tempo).

Practice STEP, KICK, STEP, TOUCH (individual tempo).

TEACHING SUGGESTIONS   Teach the dance without reference to R or L foot, using a circle formation.

Practice HEEL/STEP, HEEL/STEP, APART/TOGETHER, APART/TOGETHER with SAY & DO.

Add on FORWARD, 2, 3, 4 taking a full beat as contrasted with the divided beat in the preceding section.

SAY & DO Part I.

Practice Part II (FORWARD, KICK, BACKWARD, TOUCH) in the same tempo as the walking steps (SAY & DO).

Practice the transition from FORWARD, 2, 3, 4 to the FORWARD, KICK, BACKWARD, TOUCH.

SAY & DO the transition from the STEP, TOUCH to the HEEL/STEP, HEEL/STEP.

SAY & DO the TURN, 2, 3, 4 and go back to the beginning HEEL/STEP, HEEL/STEP.

SAY & DO the circle version, then add the music.

Add the partner dance when the dance has been reviewed.

CHAIR DANCING   Do as described; substitute steps in place for WALK.

Footwork for person left. Person on right uses opposite footwork.

Popcorn*

Novelty Dance
U.S.A.

RECORD	*Rhythmically Moving 7*
INTRODUCTION	24 beats
FORMATION	Individual

PART I

HEEL	STEP	HEEL	STEP	KICK	STEP	KICK	STEP
(R)	R	(L)	L	(R)	R	(L)	L

SIDE	BOUNCE	SIDE	BOUNCE	RUN	RUN (2)	RUN (3)	RUN (4)
R	(R)	L	(L)	R	L	R	L

REPEAT PART I

Beat 1	Extend R heel
2	Step R foot next to L foot
3	Extend L heel
4	Step L foot next to R foot
5	Kick R foot
6	Step R foot next to L foot
7	Kick L foot
8	Step L foot next to R foot
9-10	Step R foot sideward right and bounce
11-12	Step L foot sideward left and bounce
13-16	Run R, L, R, L foot kicking out
17-32	Repeat Part I, beats 1-16

PART II

UP	STEP	UP	STEP	DOWN (KNEES)		UP (KNEES)	
(R)	R	(L)	L	B		B	

IN	BOUNCE	OUT	BOUNCE	IN	BOUNCE	OUT	BOUNCE
R	(R)	L	(L)	R	(R)	L	(L)

REPEAT PART II

Beat 1	Raise R knee
2	Step R foot in place
3	Raise L knee
4	Step L foot in place
5-8	Circle knees in bent knee position or substitute down, up
9-10	Step R foot in, then bounce
11-12	Step L foot out, then bounce
13-14	Step R foot in, then bounce
15-16	Step L foot out, then bounce
17-32	Repeat Part II, beats 1-16

NOTE   Repeat entire dance 3 more times, then do Part I the fourth time and add the ending.

ENDING

UP	STEP	UP	STEP	DOWN (KNEES)		UP (KNEES)	
(R)	R	(L)	L	B		B	

REPEAT

IN	OUT	SIDE	TOG	DOWN / UP (POP)
R	L	R	B	B

Beat 1-16	Do Part II, beats 1-8, two times
17	Step R foot in
18	Step L foot out
19	Step R foot sideward right
20	Step L foot next to R foot
21	Circle knees for final "pop"

TO SIMPLIFY   Do only one section, or do only 2 motions per section rather than 4. No R foot or L foot is necessary.

LEAD-UP ACTIVITIES   Practice the following 2-beat sequences (individual tempo): HEEL, STEP; KICK, STEP; UP, STEP; SIDE, BOUNCE; IN, BOUNCE; OUT, BOUNCE.

TEACHING SUGGESTIONS   Practice HEEL, STEP, HEEL, STEP; KICK, STEP, KICK, STEP (individual tempo, then SAY & DO); add on SIDE, BOUNCE, SIDE, BOUNCE; RUN, 2, 3, 4.

Practice Part I with SAY & DO.

Practice Part II UP, STEP, UP, STEP; DOWN, REST, UP, REST (individual tempo, then SAY & DO); add on IN, BOUNCE, OUT, BOUNCE; IN, BOUNCE, OUT, BOUNCE.

Practice Part II with SAY & DO.

SAY & DO the entire dance and then add the music.

CHAIR DANCING PART I   Substitute steps in place for RUN.

Choreographed by Phyllis Weikart.

Twelfth St. Rag

Novelty Dance
U.S.A.

RECORD	*Rhythmically Moving 5*
INTRODUCTION	8 beats
FORMATION	Free formation or circle or lines

PART I *CCW*

FWD	FWD (2)	FWD (3)	FWD (4)	TOUCH	TOUCH	BACK / OUT	CROSS
L	R	L	R	(L)	(L)	L R	L

REPEAT OPP. FTWK.

Beat 1 Step L foot forward counterclockwise

2 Step R foot forward counterclockwise

3-4 Repeat beats 1-2

5 Touch L foot forward

6 Touch L foot sideward in

7 Step L foot crossing in back of R foot

& Step R foot sideward right

8 Step L foot crossing in front of R foot

9-16 Repeat Part I, beats 1-8, with opposite footwork, using back/in, cross for beats 15-16

PART I (SIMPLIFIED) *CCW*

FWD	FWD (2)	FWD (3)	FWD (4)	TOUCH	TOUCH	STEP / STEP	STEP
L	R	L	R	(L)	(L)	L R	L

REPEAT OPP. FTWK.

Beat 7-8 Step L, R, L foot in place

PART II

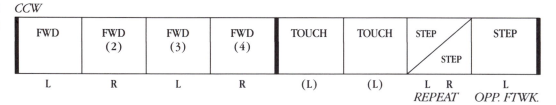

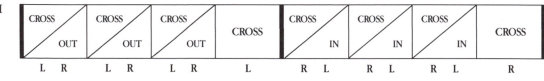

Beat 1 &   Cross L foot in front of R foot, then step sideward right with R foot

2-3   Repeat beat 1 &, two more times

4   Repeat the cross of beat 1

5-8   Repeat beats 1-4 with opposite footwork and cross toward the center

PART II
(SIMPLIFIED)

OUT	OUT (2)	OUT (3)	TURN	IN	IN (2)	IN (3)	IN (4)
L	R	L	R	L	R	L	R

Beat 1-4   Step L, R, L, R foot moving right out of the circle

5-8   Step L, R, L, R foot moving left toward the center of the circle

PART III

IN	KICK	OUT	TOUCH	IN	KICK	OUT	TOUCH
L	(R)	R	(L)	L	(R)	R	(L)

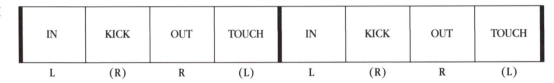

Beat 1   Step L foot in

2   Kick R foot in

3   Step R foot out   CHARLESTON

4   Touch L toe out

5-8   Repeat Part III, beats 1-4

BRIDGE

JUMP (IN)	CLAP	JUMP (OUT)	CLAP	TURN	TURN (2)	TURN (3)	TURN (4)
B		B		L	R	L	R

Beat 1-2   Jump in

3-4   Jump out

5-8   Step L, R, L, R foot while turning 360° in place counterclockwise

NOTE   The Bridge is executed after each second repetition of the dance.

TO SIMPLIFY   No R or L foot is necessary.

LEAD-UP
ACTIVITIES

Practice TOUCH, TOUCH, STEP/STEP, STEP (individual tempo).

Practice walking OUT 4 steps and IN 4 steps.

Practice IN, KICK, OUT, TOUCH (individual tempo).

TEACHING SUGGESTIONS   Practice TOUCH, TOUCH, STEP/STEP, STEP with SAY & DO. Precede with FORWARD, 2, 3, 4 and SAY & DO Part I.

Practice OUT, 2, 3, 4; IN, 2, 3, 4 with SAY & DO and link to Part I.

Practice IN, KICK, OUT, TOUCH with SAY & DO and add on to Part II.

SAY & DO the entire dance and then add the music. After two repetitions add on the Bridge.

CHAIR DANCING

PART I   Do the WALKS in place.

PART II   Move feet away from and toward the chair.

PART III   Do as described.

BRIDGE   Do the JUMPS and substitute steps in place for the TURN.

Locomotor Movement II:
The following dances use alternating 4-beat movements (the second sequence of four beats begins on the opposite foot).

Instant Success*

Novelty Dance
U.S.A.

RECORD	"Sun Flower Slow Drag," *Rhythmically Moving 9*
INTRODUCTION	8 beats
FORMATION	Circle, no hands held

PART I *CCW*

FWD	FWD (2)	FWD (3)	FWD (4)	FWD	FWD (2)	FWD (3)	FWD (4)
R	L	R	L	R	L	R	L
						4X CCW	4X CW

Beat 1-32   Walk 32 steps forward counterclockwise

33-64   Walk 32 steps forward clockwise

PART II *CCW*

SIDE	CLOSE	SIDE	CLOSE	SIDE	CLOSE	SIDE	CLOSE
R	L	R	L	R	L	R	L
					4X CCW	4X CW	OPP. FTWK.

Beat 1   Step R foot sideward right

2   Step L foot next to R foot

3-32   Repeat beats 1-2, fifteen more times; touch on beat 32

33-64   Repeat Part II, beats 1-32, moving sideward left, beginning L foot

PART III

HEEL	STEP	HEEL	STEP	HEEL	STEP	HEEL	STEP
(R)	R	(L)	L	(R)	R	(L)	L

4X

TOE	STEP	TOE	STEP	TOE	STEP	TOE	STEP
(R)	R	(L)	L	(R)	R	(L)	L

4X

Beat 1	Extend R heel diagonally right
2	Step R foot next to L foot
3	Extend L heel diagonally left
4	Step L foot next to R foot
5-32	Repeat Part III, beats 1-4, seven more times
33	Extend R toe behind
34	Step R foot next to L foot
35	Extend L toe behind
36	Step L foot next to R foot
37-64	Repeat Part III, beats 33-36, seven more times

PART IV   *CCW*   *CW*

SIDE	CLOSE	SIDE	TOUCH	SIDE	CLOSE	SIDE	TOUCH
R	L	R	(L)	L	R	L	(R)

5X

Beat 1	Step R foot sideward right
2	Step L foot next to R foot
3	Step R foot sideward right
4	Touch L foot next to R foot
5-8	Repeat beats 1-4 sideward left, beginning L foot
9-40	Repeat Part IV, beats 1-8, four more times

PART V *CCW*

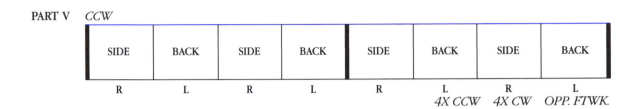

SIDE	BACK	SIDE	BACK	SIDE	BACK	SIDE	BACK
R	L	R	L	R	L	R	L

4X CCW   4X CW   OPP. FTWK.

Beat 1   Step R foot sideward right

2   Step L foot crossing in back of R foot

3-32   Repeat beats 1-2 fifteen more times; touch on beat 32

33-64   Repeat Part V, beats 1-32, sideward left, beginning L foot

PART VI

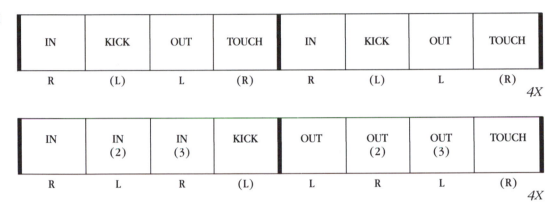

IN	KICK	OUT	TOUCH	IN	KICK	OUT	TOUCH
R	(L)	L	(R)	R	(L)	L	(R)

4X

IN	IN (2)	IN (3)	KICK	OUT	OUT (2)	OUT (3)	TOUCH
R	L	R	(L)	L	R	L	(R)

4X

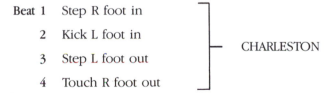

Beat 1   Step R foot in ⎤
2   Kick L foot in   ⎥
                            ⎬ CHARLESTON
3   Step L foot out   ⎥
4   Touch R foot out ⎦

5-32   Repeat Part VI, beats 1-4, seven more times

33-35   Step R, L, R foot toward center of circle

36   Kick L foot in

37-39   Step L, R, L foot out

40   Touch R foot out

41-64   Repeat Part VI, beats 33-40, three more times

NOTE   This is designed as a follow-the-leader warm-up, and the specific use of R or L foot is not necessary.

LEAD-UP ACTIVITIES   Do 2-beat movements with the arms in an alternating pattern.

Practice the various movement sequences found in the dance (individual tempo).

TEACHING
SUGGESTIONS
Have the students practice each movement sequence to be used with SAY & DO. Practice any difficult transitions.

CHAIR
DANCING
Substitute steps in place.

Choreographed by Phyllis Weikart.

Irish Mixer

Novelty Dance
U.S.A.

RECORD	"O'Keefe Slide/Kerry Slide,"*Rhythmically Moving 1*
INTRODUCTION	8 beats
FORMATION	Partners in a double circle facing each other

PART I

SIDE	BACK	SIDE	KICK	SIDE	BACK	SIDE	KICK
R	L	R	(L)	L	R	L	(R)

CLAP	CLAP	HIT	HIT	CLAP	CLAP	PAT / PAT	PAT

REPEAT PART I

Beat 1	Step R foot sideward right (partners move sideward away from each other)
2	Step L foot crossing in back of R foot
3	Step R foot sideward right
4	Kick L foot diagonally in front of R foot
5-8	Repeat beats 1-4 moving sideward left, beginning L foot
9-10	Clap hands 2 times
11-12	Hit partner's hands 2 times
13-14	Clap hands 2 times
15-16	Pat thighs 3 times in a "HON-ey Bee" rhythm
17-32	Repeat Part I, beats 1-16

PART II

AWAY	AWAY (2)	AWAY (3)	TOUCH (CLAP)	TWD	TWD (2)	TWD (3)	TOUCH (HIT)
R	L	R	(L)	L	R	L	(R)

AROUND (DO-SA-DO)	2	3	4	5	6	7	8
R	L	R	L	R	L	R	L

REPEAT PART II

Beat 1-3 Step R, L, R foot away from your partner (inside person moves toward the center and outside person away from the center)

4 Clap hands

5-7 Step R, L, R foot toward your partner

8 Hit partner's hands with your hands

9-16 Partners DO-SA-DO

17-20 Repeat beats 1-4

21-24 Repeat beats 5-8, moving diagonally forward left to a new partner

25-32 DO-SA-DO new partner

LEAD-UP ACTIVITIES Practice SIDE, BACK, SIDE, KICK both directions (individual tempo) then with partner (partner beat).

Practice clapping and hitting pattern with partner. Practice moving away and toward partner, and DO-SA-DO.

TEACHING SUGGESTIONS Practice SIDE, BACK, SIDE, KICK; SIDE, BACK, SIDE, KICK with a partner (SAY & DO); and add on the claps and hits. SAY & DO Part I.

Practice Part II with partner (SAY & DO).

Add on moving to a new partner when the group is ready.

CHAIR DANCING Face a partner. Substitute steps in place for the steps away and toward. Do a "hand jive" for the DO-SA-DO, such as CLAP, HIT R, CLAP, HIT L; CLAP, HIT, HIT, SNAP.

Choreographed by Phyllis Weikart.

Spanish Coffee*

Novelty Dance
U.S.A.

RECORD *Rhythmically Moving 4*

INTRODUCTION 8 beats

FORMATION Circle, hands joined in "W" position

PART I *CCW*

FWD	FWD	TOUCH	TOUCH	FWD	FWD	TOUCH	TOUCH
R	L	(R)	(R)	R	L	(R)	(R)

FWD	FWD	TOUCH	TOUCH	FWD	FWD	SIDE	TOUCH
R	L	(R)	(R)	R	L	R	(L)

REPEAT   OPP. DIR. OPP. FTWK.

Beat 1 Step R foot forward counterclockwise (facing diagonally right)

2 Step L foot forward counterclockwise

3 Touch R toe forward counterclockwise

4 Touch R toe backward behind and to left of L foot (sweeping motion)

5-12 Repeat beats 1-4, two more times

13-14 Step R foot, L foot forward counterclockwise and turn to face center

15 Step R foot sideward right facing center

16 Touch L foot next to R foot

17-32 Repeat Part I, beats 1-16, clockwise beginning L foot

PART II

IN	IN (2)	IN (3)	SWING	OUT	OUT (2)	OUT (3)	SWING
R	L	R	(L)	L	R	L	(R)

REPEAT

Beat 1-3   Step R, L, R foot toward center

4   Swing L foot in while raising heel of R foot

5-7   Step L, R, L foot out

8   Swing R foot out while raising heel of L foot

9-16   Repeat Part II, beats 1-8

PART III

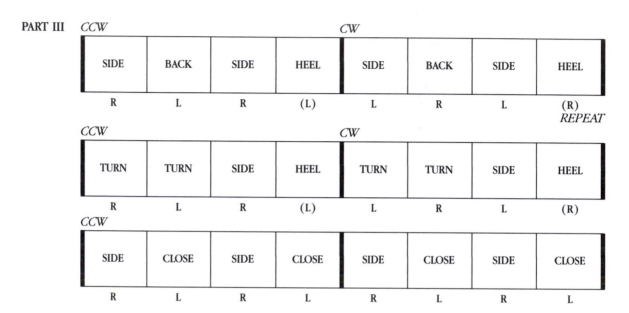

CCW				CW			
SIDE	BACK	SIDE	HEEL	SIDE	BACK	SIDE	HEEL
R	L	R	(L)	L	R	L	(R)

REPEAT

CCW				CW			
TURN	TURN	SIDE	HEEL	TURN	TURN	SIDE	HEEL
R	L	R	(L)	L	R	L	(R)

CCW							
SIDE	CLOSE	SIDE	CLOSE	SIDE	CLOSE	SIDE	CLOSE
R	L	R	L	R	L	R	L

Beat 1   Step R foot sideward right (facing center)

2   Step L foot crossing in back of R foot

3   Step R foot sideward right

4   Extend L heel diagonally left

5-16   Repeat beats 1-4 three more times, using opposite footwork and direction

17-19   Turn right clockwise beginning R foot (3-step turn)

20   Extend L heel

21-24   Repeat beats 17-20 clockwise beginning L foot

25   Step R foot sideward right (raise R hip)

26   Step L foot next to R foot

27-32   Repeat beats 25-26, three more times

LEAD-UP ACTIVITIES   Practice FORWARD, FORWARD, TOUCH, TOUCH (individual tempo), then FORWARD, FORWARD, SIDE, TOUCH (individual tempo).

Practice STEP, STEP, STEP, SWING (IN and OUT using individual tempo).

Practice SIDE, BACK, SIDE, HEEL (individual tempo).

Practice 3-step turns followed by HEEL (individual tempo).

TEACHING SUGGESTIONS Practice FORWARD, FORWARD, TOUCH, TOUCH (3 times) with SAY & DO, then add on FORWARD, FORWARD, SIDE, TOUCH beginning R foot. Repeat in other direction.

SAY & DO all of Part I.

Practice Part II with SAY & DO and then use the music for Parts I and II.

Practice Part III, beats 1-16 (SAY & DO), then add on the TURN, 2, 3, HEEL executed twice and add on the SIDE, CLOSE 4 times.

Practice Part III, beats 1-16 (SAY & DO), then add on the TURN, 2, 3, HEEL executed twice and add on the SIDE, CLOSE 4 times.

Practice the transitions.

Practice the entire dance with SAY & DO and then add the music.

CHAIR DANCING

PART I Substitute steps in place.

PART III Substitute steps in place.

Choreographed by Phyllis Weikart.

Ugros
Hungary

RECORD	*Rhythmically Moving 3*
INTRODUCTION	4 beats
FORMATION	Open circle, no hands held

PART I   *CCW*

DOWN	UP	DOWN	UP
B	B	B	B

8X

Beat 1   Bend knees

2   Straighten knees

3-32   Repeat Part I, beats 1-2, fifteen more times

PART II

SIDE	TOUCH (CLICK)	SIDE	TOUCH (CLICK)
R	(L)	L	(R)

8X

Beat 1   Step R sideward right

2   Touch L foot next to R foot, or heel click

3   Step L foot sideward left

4   Touch R foot next to L foot, or heel click

5-32   Repeat Part II, beats 1-4, seven more times

PART III

SIDE	CLOSE	SIDE	TOUCH	SIDE	CLOSE	SIDE	TOUCH
R	L	R	(L)	L	R	L	(R)

4X

Beat 1 Step R foot sideward right

    2 Step L foot next to R foot

    3 Step R foot sideward right

    4 Touch R foot next to L foot, or heel click

   5-8 Repeat beats 1-4 sideward left beginning L foot

  9-32 Repeat Part III, beats 1-8, three more times

PART IV

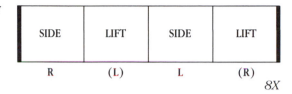

SIDE	LIFT	SIDE	LIFT
R	(L)	L	(R)

8X

Beat 1 Step R foot sideward right

    2 Lift L foot in front of R leg

    3 Step L foot sideward left

    4 Lift R foot in front of L leg

  5-32 Repeat Part IV, beats 1-4, seven more times

PART V

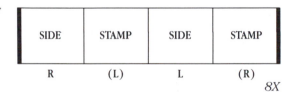

SIDE	STAMP	SIDE	STAMP
R	(L)	L	(R)

8X

Beat 1 Step R foot sideward right

    2 Stamp L foot next to R foot

    3 Step L foot sideward left

    4 Stamp R foot next to L foot

  5-32 Repeat Part V, beats 1-4, seven more times

PART VI

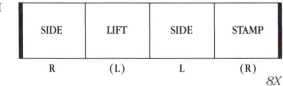

SIDE	LIFT	SIDE	STAMP
R	(L)	L	(R)

8X

Beat 1   Step R foot sideward right

  2   Lift L foot in front of R leg

  3   Step L foot sideward left

  4   Stamp R foot next to L foot

5-32   Repeat Part VI, beats 1-4, seven more times

PART VII

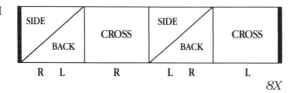

Beat 1   Leap R foot sideward right

  &   Step L foot slightly behind R foot

  2   Step R foot crossing in front of L foot

  3   Leap L foot sideward left

  &   Step R foot slightly behind L foot

  4   Step L foot crossing in front of R foot

5-32   Repeat Part VII, beats 1-4, seven more times

TO SIMPLIFY   LEAP in place, then TOUCH foot behind.

PART VIII

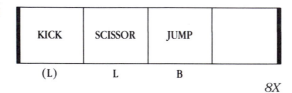

Beat 1   Kick L foot in

  2   Scissor R foot in, leaping on L foot

3-4   Jump in place with feet together

5-32   Repeat Part VIII, beats 1-4, seven more times

NOTE   First sequence, beat 1: scissor L foot in while leaping on R foot.

PART IX

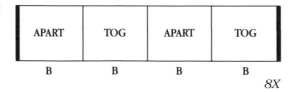

Beat 1	Jump with feet apart, knees bent
2	Jump with feet together straightening knees (add heel click if desired)
3-32	Repeat Part IX, beats 1-2, fifteen more times
NOTE	Part IX may be done with 2 beats for each JUMP.

LEAD-UP ACTIVITIES Practice each of the following sequences several times in succession (individual tempo): SIDE, TOUCH; SIDE, LIFT; SIDE, STAMP; STEP/STEP, STEP; SIDE, CLOSE, SIDE, TOUCH.

TEACHING SUGGESTIONS Practice each part of the dance with SAY & DO.

Start the music and PAT the dancing beat.

Do the dance with the music (WHISPER & DO for the first 2-3 sequences of each new part).

CHAIR DANCING
PART I Substitute raising and lowering the heels.

Do the remaining parts as described.

Locomotor Movement III

Characteristics:

1. Quicker footwork may be demanded because the tempo of music is faster.

2. There may be several parts to the dance.

3. The dances may require complex changes of direction.

4. The music may have a more ethnic sound with a less easily defined beat.

5. There are groupings of beats other than twos and fours. Movement sequences grouped in threes and fives are introduced.

NOTE: Locomotor Movement III dances are similar in level of difficulty to the Even and Uneven dances.

> *Locomotor Movement III:*
> *The following dances use two different 2-beat sequences*
> *performed once.*

Bulgarian Dance #1*

Bulgarian Music

RECORD	*Rhythmically Moving 8*
INTRODUCTION	8 beats
FORMATION	Circle or broken circle, hands held in "W" position

PART I *CCW*

FWD	FWD	SIDE	LIFT	OUT	LIFT
R	L	R	(L)	L	(R)

8X

Beat 1	Step R foot forward counterclockwise
2	Step L foot forward counterclockwise
3	Step R foot sideward right facing center
4	Lift L foot in front of R leg
5	Step L foot out (away from center)
6	Lift R foot in front of L leg
7-48	Repeat Part I, beats 1-6, seven more times

PART II

IN	IN (2)	IN (3)	LIFT	OUT	OUT (2)	OUT (3)	LIFT
R	L	R	(L)	L	R	L	(R)

CCW

SIDE	CROSS	SIDE	CROSS	SIDE	STAMP	SIDE	STAMP
R	L	R	L	R	(L)	L	(R)

3X

Beat 1-3   Step R, L, R foot toward center

4   Lift L foot in front of R leg

5-7   Step L, R, L foot out (away from center)

8   Lift R foot in front of L leg

9   Step R foot sideward right

10   Step L foot crossing in front of R foot

11-12   Repeat beats 9-10

13   Step R foot sideward right

14   Stamp L foot next to R foot

15   Step L foot sideward left

16   Stamp R foot next to L foot

17-48   Repeat Part II, beats 1-16, two more times

LEAD-UP ACTIVITIES   Teach the *Hasapikos* (Locomotor Movement II dance) with the basic step before introducing this dance.

Review the *Hasapikos* basic step (individual tempo).

Review STEP, STAMP using one foot and then the other (individual tempo).

Practice or review SIDE, CROSS in each direction (individual tempo).

Practice moving in a pattern of WALK, WALK, WALK, LIFT—use a forward as well as a backward direction (individual tempo).

TEACHING SUGGESTIONS   Practice the basic step of the *Hasapikos* changing the second SIDE, LIFT to OUT, LIFT (SAY & DO). Add the music and do several repetitions.

Practice IN, IN, IN, LIFT; OUT, 2, 3, LIFT (SAY & DO).

Add on SIDE, CROSS, SIDE, CROSS to the OUT, OUT, OUT, LIFT then add on SIDE, STAMP; SIDE, STAMP (SAY & DO).

Do all of Part II, 3 times and practice the transition to Part I, then SAY & DO.

Do the entire dance to the music.

CHAIR DANCING

PART I   Do the walking steps in place and the SIDE, LIFT, OUT, LIFT in place.

PART II   Change the SIDE, CROSS to SIDE, CLOSE.

Choreographed by Phyllis Weikart.

Pata Pata

South Africa

RECORD	*Rhythmically Moving 6*
INTRODUCTION	16 beats
FORMATION	Individual

PART I

TOUCH	STEP	TOUCH	TOG	TOES (OUT)	HEELS (OUT)	HEELS (IN)	TOES (IN)
(R)	R	(L)	B	B	B	B	B

CCW

UP	TOUCH	UP	STEP	KICK	TURN	TURN	TURN
(R)	(R)	(R)	R	(L)	L	R	L

Beat 1	Touch R foot sideward right (arms sideward with snap)
2	Step R foot next to L foot (clap)
3	Touch L foot sideward left (arms sideward with snap)
4	Step L foot next to R foot (clap) and transfer weight to both feet
5	Turn toes out (raise arms, elbows in)
6	Turn heels out (lower arms)
7	Turn heels in (arms as in beat 5)
8	Turn toes in (arms as in beat 6)
9	Raise R knee in front of body
10	Touch R foot sideward right
11	Raise R knee
12	Step R foot next to L foot
13	Kick L foot in
14-16	Step L, R, L foot turning left (body turns counterclockwise)

LEAD-UP ACTIVITIES

Practice TOUCH, STEP, TOUCH, TOGETHER (individual tempo).

Practice moving toes apart, heels apart, heels together, toes together (TOES, HEELS, HEELS, TOES—individual tempo). Practice 3-step TURNS (individual tempo).

TEACHING SUGGESTIONS

Do not use any hand motions when teaching the dance the first time. Add motions when dance is secure.

Practice TOUCH, STEP, TOUCH, TOGETHER beginning R foot with SAY & DO; add on TOES, HEELS, HEELS, TOES.

SAY & DO the first 8 beats then add on UP, TOUCH, UP, STEP—(R foot).

SAY & DO the first 12 beats and add on KICK, TURN, 2, 3 or execute the TURN, 2, 3 with 3 steps in place. SAY & DO the entire dance and then add the music.

CHAIR DANCING

Substitute steps in place for the TURN.

Locomotor Movement III:
The following dances use uneven timing of movements (rests
and divided beats).

Hot Pretzels

Novelty Dance
U.S.A.

RECORD   *Rhythmically Moving 8*

INTRODUCTION   8 beats

FORMATION   Individual or short lines

PART I

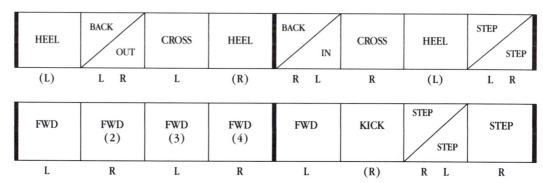

Beat 1	Extend L heel diagonally left (weight on R foot)
2	Step L foot crossing in back of R foot
&	Step R foot sideward right
3	Step L foot crossing in front of R foot
4	Extend R heel diagonally right (weight on L foot)
5	Step R foot crossing in back of L foot
&	Step L foot sideward left
6	Step R foot crossing in front of L foot
7	Extend L heel diagonally left
8	Step L foot next to R foot
&	Step R foot next to L foot
9-12	Step L, R, L, R, foot forward
13	Step L foot forward
14	Kick R foot (pedal backward)
15-16	Step R, L, R foot in place

LEAD-UP ACTIVITIES

Practice BACK/OUT, CROSS and BACK/IN, CROSS (individual tempo).

Practice HEEL, BACK/OUT, CROSS and HEEL, BACK/IN, CROSS (individual tempo).

TEACHING SUGGESTIONS

Practice the first 8 beats (individual tempo), then SAY & DO.

Practice beats 9-16 (individual tempo), then SAY & DO.

SAY & DO the entire sequence and then add the music.

CHAIR DANCING

Do walking steps in place.

Sham Hareh Golan

There They Are the Mountains of Golan
Israel

RECORD	*Rhythmically Moving 9*
INTRODUCTION	8 beats
FORMATION	Line facing counterclockwise, hands joined

PART I *CCW*

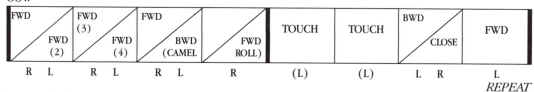

Beat 1-2	Step R, L, R, L foot forward counterclockwise
3-4	Camel roll backward; step forward on R foot, raise up on R foot and begin to sway backward onto L foot; bend both knees and come forward on R foot again (during the roll the hips make a backward circle)
5-6	Touch L foot forward twice (heel or toe may be touched)
7	Step L foot backward
&	Step R foot next to L foot
8	Step L foot forward counterclockwise
9-16	Repeat Part I, beats 1-8 and turn to face center

PART II

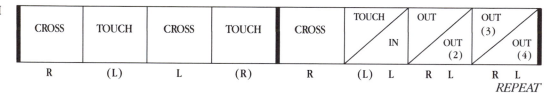

Beat 1	Step R foot crossing in front of L foot (bend both knees)
2	Touch L foot sideward (straighten legs)
3	Step L foot crossing in front of R foot (bend both knees)
4	Touch R foot sideward (straighten legs)
5	Repeat beat 1
6	Touch L foot sideward
&	Step L foot toward center bending knee
7-8	Step R, L, R, L foot out with small steps
9-16	Repeat Part II, beats 1-8

LEAD-UP ACTIVITIES

Practice or learn the CAMEL ROLL (individual tempo).

Practice BACKWARD/CLOSE, FORWARD (individual tempo).

Practice CROSS, TOUCH (individual tempo).

TEACHING SUGGESTIONS

Practice TOUCH, TOUCH; BACKWARD/CLOSE, FORWARD beginning L foot (individual tempo then SAY & DO); precede with the CAMEL ROLL and then with the 4 FORWARD steps.

SAY & DO Part I.

Practice CROSS, TOUCH, CROSS, TOUCH (individual tempo, then SAY & DO) and add on CROSS, TOUCH/IN; OUT/2, 3/4.

SAY & DO Part II.

Practice the transitions between the parts.

SAY & DO the entire dance and then add the music.

CHAIR DANCING

PART I   Do steps in place and simulate CAMEL ROLL with upper body.

PART II   Do as described.

Tanko Bushi

Coal Miner's Dance
Japan

RECORD   *Rhythmically Moving 9*

INTRODUCTION   9 beats

FORMATION   Individual dance often done in an open circle

PART I   *CCW*

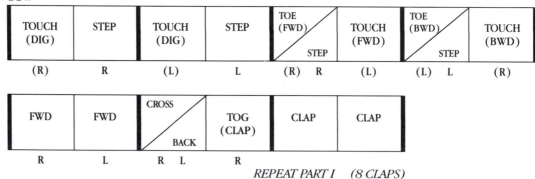

TOUCH (DIG)	STEP	TOUCH (DIG)	STEP	TOE (FWD) / STEP	TOUCH (FWD)	TOE (BWD) / STEP	TOUCH (BWD)
(R)	R	(L)	L	(R) R	(L)	(L) L	(R)

FWD	FWD	CROSS / BACK	TOG (CLAP)	CLAP	CLAP
R	L	R L	R		

REPEAT PART I   (8 CLAPS)

Beat 1   Weight on L foot, lift R foot in front of L foot (pointed diagonally right); thrust R foot to floor in digging motion (hands apart as if holding a shovel—R hand low)

2   Repeat beat 1 and step on R foot

3-4   Repeat beats 1-2 with weight on R (dig left and step L foot)

5   Touch R toe forward (bring both hands over R shoulder—throwing bag of coal over shoulder)

&   Lower R heel transferring weight to R foot

6   Touch L foot forward (bring hands over L shoulder)

7   Touch L toe backward (bring L arm in back of body with it bent and R arm up to forehead—shielding eyes)

&   Lower L heel to floor transferring weight to L foot

8   Touch R foot backward (switch arms in beat 7)

9   Step R foot forward (push both arms forward—pushing coal car)

10   Step L foot forward (push again)

11   Step R foot crossing in front of L foot (bring arms down and out)

&   Step L foot crossing in back of R foot

12   Step R foot next to L foot (weight on both feet); clap hands in front

13-14   Clap hands 2 more times

Repeat dance and add 5 claps

LEAD-UP ACTIVITIES

Practice the different arm motions (individual tempo).

Practice the 2-beat foot patterns (individual tempo).

TEACHING SUGGESTIONS

First teach only the foot pattern with SAY & DO beginning with the TOE/STEP, TOUCH; TOE/STEP, TOUCH in a forward and backward direction.

Precede the above with DIG, STEP, DIG, STEP and SAY & DO beats 1-8; add on the FORWARD, FORWARD, CROSS/BACK, TOGETHER.

SAY & DO the entire dance (feet only) and then add the music.

The second time the dance is presented review the foot movements first, then the arm movements. Demonstrate the arm movements with very few directions then DO the arm sequence while SAYING the foot patterns (be certain to stand still). When this has been mastered, combine the two.

Do the entire dance with the arm motions to the music.

CHAIR DANCING

Do the arm motions only or add the feet in place.

Toi Nergis

Armenia

RECORD	*Rhythmically Moving 4*
INTRODUCTION	8 beats
FORMATION	Broken circle, men outside; men—shoulder hold; women—"W" position with little fingers joined

PART I   *CCW (Men)*

FWD	FWD	SIDE	LIFT	SIDE	TOUCH	STAMP / STAMP	STAMP
R	L	R	(L)	L	(R)	(R) (R)	(R)

Beat 1 Step R foot forward counterclockwise

2 Step L foot forward counterclockwise and turn to face center

3 Step R foot sideward right

4 Lift L foot in front of R leg

5 Step L foot sideward left

6 Touch R foot in

7-8 Stamp R foot next to L foot 3 times (7 &, 8)

CCW (Women)

SIDE	CLOSE	SIDE	TOUCH	SIDE	TOUCH	STAMP / STAMP	STAMP
R	L	R	(L)	L	(R)	(R) (R)	(R)

1 Step R foot sideward right (hands move to right)

2 Step L foot next to R foot (hands move to left)

3 Step R foot sideward right (hands move to right)

4 Touch L foot next to R foot (hands move to left)

5 Step L foot sideward left (hands move to right)

6-8 Same as men above (hands move to left on beat 6 and arms move up and down on stamps)

LEAD-UP ACTIVITIES   Practice STAMP/STAMP, STAMP while standing on one foot (individual tempo).

Practice SIDE, TOUCH (individual tempo).

TEACHING
SUGGESTIONS
Either teach one part and then the other to everyone or separate the men and women and teach each group its own part.

Men—Practice FORWARD, FORWARD, SIDE, LIFT with SAY & DO and add on SIDE, TOUCH and then STAMP/STAMP, STAMP.

SAY & DO the entire sequence.

Women—Practice SIDE, CLOSE, SIDE, TOUCH with SAY & DO and then add on SIDE, TOUCH and then STAMP/STAMP, STAMP.

SAY & DO the entire arm sequence but do not move the feet.

Do the entire sequence and add the music.

CHAIR
DANCING
Step in place for moving steps.

Locomotor Movement III:
The following dances use alternating 4-beat movements (the second sequence of four beats begins on the opposite foot).

Alunelul

Little Hazelnuts
Romania

RECORD	*Rhythmically Moving 6*
INTRODUCTION	8 beats
FORMATION	Circle, "T" position (shoulder hold)

PART I

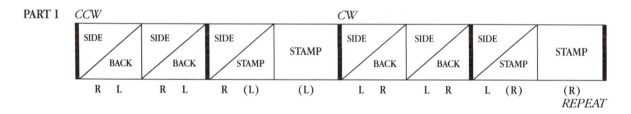

Beat 1	Step R foot slightly sideward right (weight on ball of foot)
&	Step L foot crossing in back of R foot
2 &	Repeat beat 1 &
3	Step R foot slightly sideward right
&	Stamp L foot next to R foot
4	Stamp L foot next to R foot
5-8	Repeat beats 1-4, moving left
9-16	Repeat Part I, beats 1-8, moving right then left

PART II

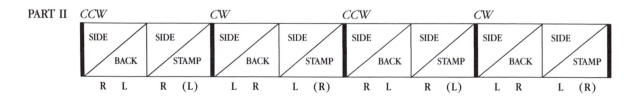

Beat 1   Step R foot slightly sideward

&   Step L foot in back of R foot

2   Step on R foot sideward right

&   Stamp L foot

3-4   Repeat to left

5-8   Repeat Part II, beats 1-4

PART III

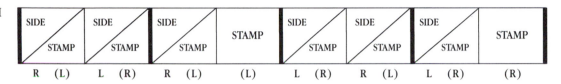

Beat 1   Step R foot slightly sideward right

&   Stamp L foot next to R foot

2   Step L foot slightly sideward left

&   Stamp R foot next to L foot

3   Step R foot slightly sideward right

&   Stamp L foot next to R foot

4   Stamp L foot next to R foot

5-8   Repeat Part III, beats 1-4, beginning L foot

LEAD-UP   Practice moving SIDE/BACK first one way and then the other—slowly at first, then faster
ACTIVITIES   (individual tempo).

Practice SIDE/BACK, SIDE/REST each direction (individual tempo).

Practice STAMPS without changing weight to the stamping foot (individual tempo).

TEACHING   Practice SIDE/STAMP with each foot (SAY & DO).
SUGGESTIONS
Practice SIDE/STAMP, STAMP/REST with each foot (SAY & DO).

Practice SIDE/BACK, SIDE/STAMP with each foot (SAY & DO).

SAY & DO each part of the dance, including the transitions from one part to the other.

CHAIR   Place the feet one in front of the other for the SIDE/BACK or substitute SIDE/CLOSE.
DANCING

Bossa Nova

Novelty Dance
U.S.A.

RECORD	*Rhythmically Moving 7*
INTRODUCTION	6 beats
FORMATION	Double circle, partners facing each other (directions given for person on inside, outside person uses opposite footwork)

PART I

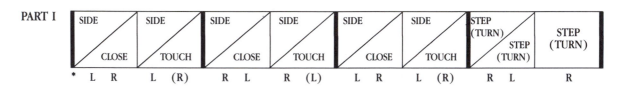

Beat 1	Step L foot sideward left
&	Step R foot next to L foot
2	Step L foot sideward left
&	Touch R foot next to L foot
3-4	Repeat beats 1-2 sideward right beginning R foot
5-6	Repeat beats 1-2
7-8	Step in place 3 steps while turning to face clockwise (partner is now facing counterclockwise)

PART II

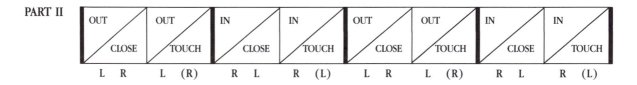

Beat 1-2	Repeat Part I, beats 1-2, sideward away from center of circle beginning L foot
3-4	Repeat Part I, beats 1-2, sideward toward center of circle beginning R foot
5-8	Repeat Part II, beats 1-4

PART III

FWD	KICK	BWD	TOUCH	FWD	KICK	BWD	TOUCH
L	(R)	R	(L)	L	(R)	R	(L)

Beat 1   Step L foot forward ⎤

2   Kick R foot forward ⎥

3   Step R foot backward ⎥ — CHARLESTON

4   Touch L foot backward ⎦

5-8   Repeat Part III, beats 1-4

PART IV

CROSS	TOUCH	CROSS	TOUCH	CROSS	TOUCH	FWD / FWD	FWD / FWD
L	(R)	R	(L)	L	(R)	R L	R (R)

Beat 1   Step L foot crossing in front of R foot (in)

2   Touch R foot sideward right (in)

3-4   Step R foot crossing in front of L foot and touch L foot sideward left (out)

5-6   Repeat beats 1-2

7-8   Step R, L, R foot forward counterclockwise

&   Pivot to face new partner (keep weight on R foot)

LEAD-UP ACTIVITIES   Practice SIDE/CLOSE, SIDE/TOUCH both directions (individual tempo).

Practice the CHARLESTON (STEP, KICK, STEP, TOUCH) (individual tempo).

WALK, crossing the feet in front with each step (individual tempo).

Practice a pattern of CROSS, TOUCH, crossing the foot in front and touching to the side (individual tempo).

TEACHING SUGGESTIONS   Use a circle formation and practice 4 SIDE/CLOSE, SIDE/TOUCH steps (OUT and IN) followed by 2 slow CHARLESTON steps in which each beat takes twice the amount of time to execute as the beats in the SIDE/CLOSE, SIDE/TOUCH. Alternate starting foot during the practice (SAY & DO).

In a circle, practice 2 CHARLESTON steps and continue with CROSS, TOUCH steps. Alternate starting foot during the practice (SAY & DO).

Using partner formation practice Part I, adding the ¼ TURN (partner beat).

Link Part II to Part I and practice both parts (partner beat).

Link Part III to Part II and put the first 3 parts together (SAY & DO).

Link Part IV to Part III and put all 4 parts together (SAY & DO).

Practice transition from Part IV to Part I.

Be sure students understand that each part begins with the same foot.

CHAIR DANCING   Omit the TURNS and STEP in place.

Footwork for inside person. Outside person uses opposite footwork.

Jamaican Holiday*

Novelty Mixer
U.S.A.

RECORD	*Rhythmically Moving 5*
INTRODUCTION	16 beats
FORMATION	Partners side by side facing counterclockwise; no hands held, inside person's footwork given for Part I (outside person use opposite footwork and direction)
ALTERNATE FORMATION	Circle

PART I   *CCW*

FWD	FWD (2)	FWD (3)	LIFT (HIT)	FWD	FWD (2)	FWD (3)	LIFT (HIT)
R	L	R	(L)	L	R	L	(R)

TOUCH	TOUCH	TOUCH	STEP	TOUCH	TOUCH	TOUCH	STEP
(R)	(R)	(R)	R	(L)	(L)	(L)	L

TURN	TURN	OUT	CLAP	TURN	TURN	IN	CLAP
R	L	R		L	R	L	

CCW

BUMP	BUMP	HIT	HIT	FWD (CHANGE)	FWD (2)	FWD (3)	FWD (4)
				R	L	R	L

Beat 1-3	Step R, L, R foot forward counterclockwise
4	Lift L foot and hit inside of L foot with R hand
5-8	Repeat beats 1-4 beginning L foot, on beat 8 hit inside of R foot with L hand
9	Touch R foot sideward right
10	Touch R foot next to L foot
11	Touch R foot sideward right
12	Step R foot next to L foot
13-16	Repeat beats 9-12 beginning L foot (outside persons do a fourth touch rather than step)
17-19	Inside person: 3-step turn to the right beginning R foot crossing behind partner
20	Clap over R shoulder
NOTE	Outside person: 3-step turn to the left beginning L foot in front of partner, then clap.
21-24	Repeat beats 17-20 in opposite direction with opposite footwork
25-26	Bump partner twice and turn to face partner
27	Inside person hits partner's hands with a downward motion; outside person hits up
28	Reverse beat 27
29-32	Inside person walks R, L, R, L foot forward to new partner; outside person steps in place or turns in 4 steps

NOTE	Dance may be done without reference to R or L feet. Beats 17-24 may be modified to moving sideward rather than turning.
CIRCLE DANCE	Follow directions for inside person and change beats 25-32 to combinations of thigh PATS, CLAPS, and SNAPS.
LEAD-UP ACTIVITIES	Practice STEP, STEP, STEP, HIT (individual tempo).
	Practice TOUCH, TOUCH, TOUCH, STEP (individual tempo).
	Practice 3-step TURN adding a CLAP on the fourth beat (individual tempo).
TEACHING SUGGESTIONS	Practice beats 1-16 using individual tempo and then SAY & DO.
	Practice TURN, TURN, OUT, CLAP; TURN, TURN, IN, CLAP first with inside person moving and outside person standing still, then with only outside person moving, and finally with both people moving.
	Practice BUMP, BUMP, HIT, HIT with partner.
	Practice sequence with partner (partner beat, then SAY & DO).
CHAIR DANCING	TURNS—substitute SIDE, CLOSE, SIDE, CLAP.
	BUMP, BUMP, HIT, HIT—substitute thigh PATS and CLAPS or SNAPS.

Choreographed by Phyllis Weikart.

Joe Clark Mixer*

Novelty Dance
U.S.A.

RECORD	*Rhythmically Moving 1*
INTRODUCTION	8 beats
FORMATION	Double circle, partners facing each other, man on inside; directions given for inside person, outside person uses opposite direction and footwork for Part I

PART I   *CCW*   *CW*

SIDE	CLOSE	SIDE	TOUCH	SIDE	CLOSE	SIDE	TOUCH
L	R	L	(R)	R	L	R	(L)

AROUND (DO-SA-DO)	2	3	4	5	6	7	8
L	R	L	R	L	R	L	R

REPEAT PART I

Beat 1	Step L foot sideward left (partners hold both hands)
2	Step R foot next to L foot
3	Step L foot sideward left
4	Touch R foot next to L foot
5-8	Repeat beats 1-4 sideward right beginning R foot
9-16	Do-sa-do partner
17-32	Repeat Part I, beats 1-16 and turn ¼ right to face clockwise (partner facing counterclockwise), inside person touch R foot on beat 32

PART II *CW*   *CCW*

FWD	FWD (2)	FWD (3)	TOUCH (HIT)	BWD	BWD (2)	BWD (3)	TOUCH (HIT)
R	L	R	(L)	L	R	L	(R)

CW

FWD	FWD (2)	FWD (3)	TOUCH (HIT)	FWD	FWD (2)	FWD (3)	FWD (4)
R	L	R	(L)	L	R	L	R

JUMP	KICK	JUMP	KICK	JUMP	KICK	JUMP	KICK
B	(L)	B	(R)	B	(L)	B	(R)

PAT	CLAP	HIT (R)	CLAP	HIT (L)	CLAP	HIT (BOTH)	PAT

Beat 1-3 Step R, L, R foot forward clockwise

4 Touch L foot next to R foot (hit both hands with the next outside person)

5-7 Step L, R, L foot backward counterclockwise

8 Touch R foot next to L foot (hit both hands with your original partner)

9-12 Repeat beats 1-4

13-16 Step L, R, L, R foot forward clockwise to next outside person (you have moved 2 people beyond your partner)

17 Jump facing new partner (join hands)

18 Hop R foot, kicking L foot across (both persons use same footwork)

19-20 Jump, then hop L foot kicking R foot across

21-24 Repeat beats 17-20

25-26 Pat thighs with both hands, clap own hands

27-28 Hit partner's R hand with your R hand, clap own hands

29-30 Hit partner's L hand with your L hand, clap own hands

31-32 Hit partner's hands with yours, pat thighs

LEAD-UP ACTIVITIES

Practice SIDE, CLOSE; SIDE, TOUCH (individual tempo), then with partner (partner beat).

Practice DO-SA-DO with partner (partner beat).

Practice walking FORWARD 4 steps, BACKWARD 4 steps, and FORWARD 8 steps (individual tempo).

Practice JUMP, KICK (individual tempo).

Practice "hand-jive" patterns with a partner (partner beat).

TEACHING SUGGESTIONS

Practice SIDE, CLOSE, SIDE, TOUCH; SIDE, CLOSE, SIDE, TOUCH with a partner (SAY & DO) then add on the DO-SA-DO and SAY & DO Part I.

Practice the FORWARD, BACKWARD walking pattern of Part II with SAY & DO then add on the HIT while doing the walking pattern.

Practice the JUMP, KICK with SAY & DO.

Practice the "hand-jive" pattern of the final 8 beats with SAY & DO. SAY & DO Part II.

Practice the transition from the DO-SA-DO into Part II and from the end to the beginning.

SAY & DO the entire dance and add the music.

CHAIR DANCING

PART I Do the SIDE, CLOSE, SIDE, TOUCH as described and substitute walking the feet away from and toward the chair for the DO-SA-DO.

PART II WALK the feet in place and PAT the thighs for the HIT. Simulate the "hand-jive" by hitting the air for R hand, L hand, both hands.

NOTE This dance may be done in wheelchairs.

Choreographed by Phyllis Weikart.

Locomotor Movement III:
The following dances involve complex use of space.

Hole in the Wall

Contradance
England

RECORD	*Rhythmically Moving 4*
INTRODUCTION	12 beats
FORMATION	Longways set; couple #1 dances with couple #2

PART I   *COUPLE #1*

TURN	TURN	FWD	FWD	FWD	FWD	TURN	TURN

FWD	FWD	FWD	FWD

REPEAT   *COUPLE #2*

#1 MAN #2 WOMAN

ACROSS	2	3	4	5	6

REPEAT   *#2 MAN #1 WOMAN*

COUPLES #1 & 2

CIRCLE CW	2	3	4	5	6

COUPLE #1

TURN	TURN	FWD	FWD	FWD	FWD

Beat 1-12	#1 couples turn away from partners and walk behind #2 couples; proceed around #2 couples to center of set, join hands and walk back to place
13-24	#2 couples turn away from partners and walk behind #1 couples; proceed around #1 couples, join hands, and walk back to place
25-30	#1 men change places with #2 women, passing R shoulders
31-36	#1 women change places with #2 men, passing R shoulders
37-42	#1 and #2 couples join hands and circle left to starting position
43-48	#1 couples turn away from partners and walk behind #2 couples, change places with #2 couples; #2 couples walk up the inside of the set to #1 couples' places

LEAD-UP ACTIVITIES

Do progressive circle dances.

Do other contradances so students gain experience in moving up and down the set.

TEACHING SUGGESTIONS

Beats 1-12, 13-24, and 43-48 should be learned without turning away from partner (WALK straight down or up the set).

After the parts are learned, put together the contra sets and be certain that the students understand the #1 couples' transition from the end of the dance to the beginning. Students also must understand what happens at each end of the set.

CHAIR DANCING

Dance may be executed in wheelchairs.

Mexican Mixer

Mexico

RECORD	*Rhythmically Moving 3*
INTRODUCTION	4 beats
FORMATION	Partners in a double circle facing counterclockwise, skater's hold; directions given for inside person

PART I   *CCW*

FWD	FWD (2)	FWD (3)	TURN (1/2)	BWD	BWD (2)	BWD (3)	BWD (4)
L	R	L	R	L	R	L	R
						REPEAT	*OPP. DIR.*

Beat 1-4	Walk 4 steps forward counterclockwise (on fourth step turn 180° to face clockwise)
5-8	Walk 4 steps backward counterclockwise
9-16	Repeat Part I, beats 1-8, moving clockwise
	Keep R handhold with partner, release L hand with partner and take neighbor's hand; men are facing out of circle; women are facing into circle (Alamo position)
NOTE	Part I is a simplification; the actual Part I follows.
Beat 1-4	Men walk L, R, L, R foot
5	Step L foot sideward left (counterclockwise)
6	Step R foot crossing in back of L foot
7	Step L foot sideward left
8	Touch R foot next to L foot
9-16	Repeat beats 1-8 in opposite direction beginning R foot (women use opposite footwork on beats 1-16)

PART II

IN (IN TO THE	TOUCH SPACE	OUT OUT OF THE	TOUCH SPACE	TURN TURN	TURN WITH YOUR	TURN PART-	TURN NER)
L	(R)	R	(L)	L	R	L	R

IN (IN TO THE	TOUCH SPACE	OUT OUT OF THE	TOUCH SPACE YOUR	TURN NEIGHBOR	TURN IS YOUR	TURN PART-	TURN NER)
L	(R)	R	(L)	L	R	L	R

Beat 1-2	Step R foot into the space and touch L foot next to R foot
3-4	Step L foot out of the space and touch R foot next to L foot
5-8	Turn ½ using 4 steps, keeping R handhold with partner (you are now facing the opposite direction)
9-12	Repeat beats 1-4
13-16	Keep holding neighbor's L hand and release partner's R hand; move in 4 steps to a position side by side with neighbor; start dance from beginning with new partner

LEAD-UP ACTIVITIES

Walk 4 steps FORWARD, turn 180° and walk BACKWARD 4 steps (individual tempo)—first move counterclockwise, then move clockwise.

Practice the above with a partner using skater's hold (partner beat).

TEACHING SUGGESTIONS

Practice Part I with a partner (partner beat, then SAY & DO)—teach the simplification before attempting the actual dance.

Have the students move into the formation for Part II and execute beats 1-8—SAY "IN to the space, OUT of the space, TURN with your partner" (partners now have changed places)—continue with "IN to the space, OUT of the space, your neighbor is your partner."

Return to original partner and practice Part II until executed successfully.

Practice the transition from Part I to Part II.

SAY & DO the entire dance and then add the music.

CHAIR DANCING

May be adapted for wheelchairs.

Locomotor Movement III:
The following dances use uncommon meter ($^3/_4$ and $^5/_4$).

Tsakonikos

Tsakonia, Peloponnesos
Greece

RECORD   *Rhythmically Moving 9*

INTRODUCTION   2 measures (10 beats)

FORMATION   Broken circle, leader at right; escort hold with R under

PART I   *CCW*

FWD	FWD (2)	FWD (3)	FWD	DRAW
R	L	R	L	(R)

8X

Beat 1   Step R foot forward moving counterclockwise

2   Step L foot forward moving counterclockwise

3-4   Repeat beats 1-2

5   Draw the R foot up to the L foot without a change of weight

6-40   Repeat Part I seven more times

PART II   *CCW*

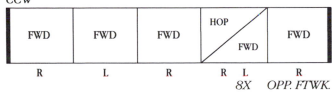

FWD	FWD	FWD	HOP / FWD	FWD
R	L	R	R L	R

8X   OPP. FTWK.

Beat 1   Step R foot forward counterclockwise

2   Step L foot forward counterclockwise

3   Step R foot forward counterclockwise

4   Hop R foot (foot barely leaves the floor)

&   Step L foot forward

5   Step R foot forward

6-10   Repeat beats 1-5 with opposite footwork beginning L foot

11-40   Repeat Part II, beats 1-10, three more times

LEAD-UP ACTIVITIES   Practice walking in grouping of 5 beats. Accent beat 1 of each 5 beats (individual tempo).

Practice 4 steps followed by a TOUCH beginning R foot (individual tempo).

PAT the rhythm of Part II on the legs.

Practice a pattern of STEP, HOP/STEP, STEP (individual tempo).

TEACHING SUGGESTIONS   Listen to Part I of the music and identify the grouping of 5 beats using a PAT on the legs.

Practice Part I with SAY then with SAY & DO.

Practice Part II with SAY, then practice pattern at individual tempo, then SAY & DO.

Practice the transitions and add the music.

CHAIR DANCING
PART I   Move feet away from and toward the chair for each 5-beat sequence.
PART II   Do in place.

Vranjanka (Sano Duso)

Sana, Sweetheart
Yugoslavia (Macedonia)

RECORD	*Rhythmically Moving 8*
INTRODUCTION	4 measures (12 beats)
FORMATION	Broken circle, hands held in "W" position

PART I

SIDE	BOUNCE	CROSS	SIDE	BOUNCE	BOUNCE
R	(R)	L	R	(R)	(R)

SIDE	BOUNCE	BOUNCE	SIDE	BOUNCE	BOUNCE
L	(L)	(L)	R	(R)	(R)

SIDE	SIDE	CROSS
L	R	L

MEASURE I
Beat 1   Step R foot sideward right

2   Bounce slightly on R foot, carrying L foot across in front of R foot

3   Step L foot crossing in front of R foot

MEASURE II
Beat 4   Step R foot sideward right

5-6   Touch L foot sideward left while bouncing twice on R foot

MEASURE III
Beat 7   Step L foot sideward left

8-9   Touch R foot sideward right while bouncing twice on L foot

MEASURE IV
Beat 10-12   Repeat Measure II

MEASURE V
Beat 13   Step L foot sideward left

14   Step R foot sideward right

15   Step L foot crossing in front of R foot

LEAD-UP ACTIVITIES

Practice a SIDE, BOUNCE pattern (individual tempo).

Practice SIDE, BOUNCE, CROSS (individual tempo).

Practice SIDE, SIDE, CROSS (individual tempo).

WALK in different groupings of 3 beats—WALK all the beats, WALK only the first of each 3 beats, WALK the first and third beats (individual tempo).

TEACHING SUGGESTIONS

PAT the legs to the music, accenting the first PAT of each 3 PATS; PAT only the first beat; PAT beats 1 and 3.

WALK to the music, using the same patterns as in the Lead-Up Activities.

Practice SIDE, BOUNCE, BOUNCE with SAY & DO.

Precede 3 patterns of SIDE, BOUNCE, BOUNCE with SIDE, BOUNCE, CROSS (SAY & DO).

Add on the last measure of SIDE, SIDE, CROSS (SAY & DO).

Practice the transition of measure 5 to measure 1.

Practice the entire dance with SAY & DO and then add the music.

CHAIR DANCING

Do steps in place.

Even
Dance Steps

Characteristic:

Each movement in the sequence takes the same amount of time to execute.

Cherkessiya

Israel

RECORD	*Rhythmically Moving 2*
INTRODUCTION	8 beats
FORMATION	Single circle, facing center

CHORUS

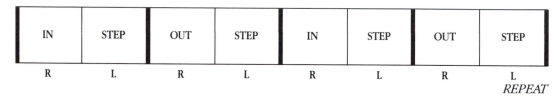

IN	STEP	OUT	STEP	IN	STEP	OUT	STEP
R	L	R	L	R	L	R	L
							REPEAT

Beat 1-16   Do 4 Cherkessiya steps beginning R foot

TO SIMPLIFY   Substitute 4 steps in place (body low) and 4 steps in place (body tall) for the CHERKESSIYA steps. This sequence is done twice. No R or L foot is necessary. Further simplification: 8 steps (body low), 8 steps (body tall).

PART I

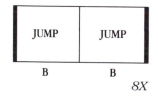

JUMP	JUMP
B	B
	8X

Beat 1-16   Jump 16 times in place

CHORUS   Repeat Chorus, beats 1-16

PART II
SKIP   *CCW*

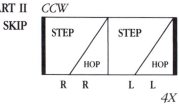

STEP		STEP	
	HOP		HOP
R	R	L	L
			4X

Beat 1-16   Skip 8 times forward counterclockwise beginning R foot

CHORUS   Repeat Chorus, beats 1-16

PART III
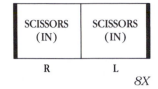
8X

Beat 1-16   Scissors kicks toward the center (16 leg kicks)

CHORUS   Repeat Chorus, beats 1-16

PART IV   *CCW*
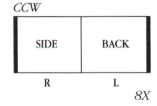
8X

Beat 1   Step R foot sideward right

2   Step L foot crossing in back of R foot (bending knees)

3-16   Repeat beats 1-2, seven more times

CHORUS   Repeat Chorus, beats 1-16

PART V
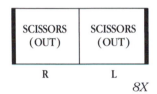
8X

Beat 1-16   Scissors kicks away from the center (16 leg kicks)

CHORUS   Repeat Chorus, beats 1-16

PART VI   *CCW*
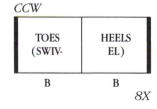
8X

Beat 1-16   Move toes right, then move heels right; keep feet together; repeat seven more times

CHORUS   Repeat Chorus, beats 1-16

PART VII   *(HORSE TROT) CCW*

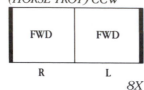

R   L
8X

Beat 1-16   Horse trot 16 times forward counterclockwise beginning R foot

CHORUS   Repeat Chorus, beats 1-16

PART VIII   *(LOCOMOTIVE) CCW*

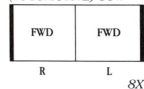

R   L
8X

Beat 1-16   Walk 16 steps forward counterclockwise (4 steps with body low and knees bent, 4 steps with body tall and legs straight; repeat 4 low and 4 tall)

LEAD-UP
ACTIVITIES   STEP in place with the body low then with the body tall—do 4 low and 4 tall (individual tempo).

SKIP, HORSE TROT, JUMP (individual tempo).

KICK the legs IN, KICK the legs OUT (individual tempo).

Move in a SIDE, BACK pattern (individual tempo).

Move with SWIVEL STEPS (individual tempo).

TEACHING
SUGGESTIONS   Practice the CHERKESSIYA step beginning with 4 steps in place and accenting the first of each 4 steps, then STEP IN on the first of each 4 steps (SAY & DO).

If simplifying the CHERKESSIYA, move in a pattern of 4 steps in place with the body bent over and 4 steps with the arms overhead.

Practice the verses or use other movement ideas.

Do the dance with the music.

CHAIR
DANCING   Change the verses to include arm movements.

Ciocarlanul

The Lark
Romania

RECORD   *Rhythmically Moving 8*

INTRODUCTION   8 beats

FORMATION   Circle, hands joined, face center

PART I

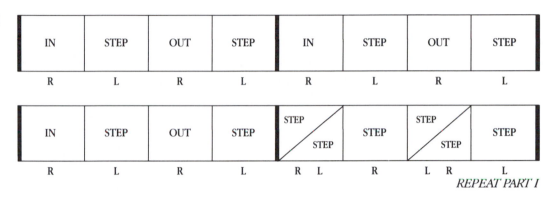

REPEAT PART I

Beat 1-4   Cherkessiya beginning R foot (cross R foot in front of L foot, lifting L foot behind, beat 1)

5-12   Repeat Cherkessiya beginning R foot, two more times

13   Step R foot next to L foot

&   Step L foot next to R foot or cross slightly in front of R foot

14   Step R foot next to L foot or cross in back of L foot

15-16   Repeat beats 13-14 beginning L foot

17-32   Repeat Part I, beats 1-16

PART II   *CCW*

SIDE	BACK	SIDE	BACK	SIDE	STAMP	STAMP	
R	L	R	L	R	(L)	(L)	

4X   OPP. FTWK. OPP. DIR.

Beat 1	Step R foot sideward right (ball of foot)
2	Step L foot crossing in back of R foot
3	Step R foot sideward right
4	Step L foot crossing in back of R foot
5	Step R foot sideward right
6-7	Stamp L foot next to R foot, 2 times
8	Rest
9-16	Repeat Part II, beats 1-8, sideward clockwise beginning L foot
17-32	Repeat Part II, beats 1-16

LEAD-UP ACTIVITIES

Review CHERKESSIYA step (individual tempo).

PAT the legs in an even beat and say "Bumble Bee" for each 2 pats then do "Bumble Bee" with the feet (STEP/STEP, STEP) in place (individual tempo).

Practice SIDE, BACK steps in each direction (individual tempo).

Practice stamps without changing weight, then SIDE, STAMP, STAMP, REST in each direction (individual tempo).

TEACHING SUGGESTIONS

PAT the rhythm of Part I, then add the language of Part I (IN, STEP, OUT, STEP; IN, STEP, OUT, STEP; IN, STEP, OUT, STEP; STEP/STEP, STEP, STEP/STEP, STEP).

SAY & DO Part I.

SAY the language of Part II, then SAY & DO.

Practice the transitions from Part I to Part II and back to the beginning.

CHAIR DANCING

Substitute SIDE, CLOSE for SIDE, BACK in Part II.

Mechol Hagat

Dance of the Winepressers
Israel

RECORD	*Rhythmically Moving 4*
INTRODUCTION	8 beats
FORMATION	Broken circle, L hand carried at L shoulder, R arm straight
CHORUS	*CCW*

FWD	FWD (2)	FWD (3)	FWD (4)	FWD	FWD (2)	FWD (3)	FWD (4)
R	L	R	L	R	L	R	L

4X

Beat 1-32 Shuffle 32 steps forward counterclockwise beginning R foot, body leans slightly backward

PART I

IN	STEP	OUT	STEP	IN	STEP	OUT	STEP
R	L	R	L	R	L	R	L

REPEAT

IN	STEP	OUT	STEP	TURN	TURN (2)	TURN (3)	TURN (4)
R	L	R	L	R	L	R	L

REPEAT

Beat 1-16	Cherkessiya 4 times beginning R foot (facing center)
17-20	Cherkessiya beginning R foot
21-24	Turn right with 4 steps beginning R foot (full turn)
25-28	Cherkessiya beginning R foot
29-32	Turn right with 4 steps beginning R foot
CHORUS	Repeat Chorus, beats 1-32

PART II

IN	STEP	OUT	STEP	STEP (ACCENT)	STEP (2)	STEP (3)	STEP (4)
R	L	R	L	R	L	R	L

4X

Beat 1-4   Cherkessiya beginning R foot

5-8   Accent R, L, R, L foot, body low

9-32   Repeat Part II, beats 1-8, three more times

CHORUS   Repeat Chorus, beats 1-32

PART III

IN	STEP	OUT	STEP	IN	STEP	OUT	STEP
R	L	R	L	R	L	R	L

REPEAT

STEP (DOWN)	STEP (2)	STEP (3)	STEP (4)	STEP (UP)	STEP (2)	STEP (3)	STEP (4)
R	L	R	L	R	L	R	L

REPEAT

Beat 1-16   Cherkessiya 4 times beginning R foot

17-20   Accent R, L, R, L foot, body low and arms down

21-24   Accent R, L, R, L foot, body high and arms up

25-32   Repeat beats 17-24

Repeat dance from the beginning.

LEAD-UP
ACTIVITIES
Practice the SHUFFLE step (individual tempo).

Practice the CHERKESSIYA (individual tempo).

Practice turning in 4 steps (individual tempo).

TEACHING
SUGGESTIONS
Start the music and identify the beat, then SHUFFLE to it.

Practice Part I (SAY & DO).

Practice Part II (SAY & DO), then do Part I again.

Practice Part III (SAY & DO), then do Parts I and II again.

Help students understand the format of the dance with the Chorus repeated in between the parts (rondo).

CHAIR
DANCING
PART I   SHUFFLE feet in place.

PART II   Use steps in place for the TURN.

Armenian Misirlou

Armenia

RECORD	*Rhythmically Moving 9*
INTRODUCTION	8 beats
FORMATION	Broken circle, little fingers joined

PART I   *CCW*

TOUCH	TOUCH	TOUCH	TOUCH	CROSS	CROSS	CROSS / SIDE	BACK / SIDE
(L)	(L)	(L)	(L)	L	R	L R	L R

Beat 1   Touch L foot across in front of R foot

2   Touch L foot to the left side

3   Touch L foot as in beat 1

4   Touch L foot to the left side

5   Step L foot crossing in front of R foot

6   Step R foot crossing in front of L foot

7   Step L foot crossing in front of R foot

&   Step R foot sideward right

8   Step L foot crossing in back of R foot

&   Step R foot sideward right

LEAD-UP ACTIVITIES   Practice standing on one foot and touching the free foot 4 times (individual tempo).
Practice stepping several times using a CROSS (individual tempo).
Practice a GRAPEVINE beginning L foot.

TEACHING SUGGESTIONS   Practice CROSS/SIDE, BACK/SIDE beginning L foot with SAY & DO then precede with CROSS, CROSS.

Practice beats 5-8 with individual tempo then SAY & DO.

Precede beats 5-8 with TOUCH, TOUCH, TOUCH, TOUCH and SAY & DO the entire dance.

Add the music.

CHAIR DANCING   Do steps in place substituting a CHERKESSIYA for the GRAPEVINE (CROSS/SIDE, BACK/SIDE).

Corrido

Mexico

RECORD   *Rhythmically Moving 5*

INTRODUCTION   8 beats

FORMATION   Couples in a double circle, men with backs to center, closed dance position; footwork given for men, women use opposite footwork

ALTERNATE
FORMATION   Circle

PART I   *CW*

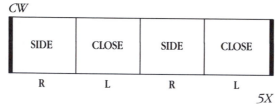

Beat 1   Step R foot sideward right

2   Step L foot next to R foot

3-20   Repeat Part I, beats 1-2, nine more times

PART II   *CCW*

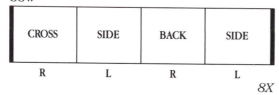

Beat 1-4   Grapevine counterclockwise, begin crossing R foot in front of L foot

5-32   Repeat Part II, beats 1-4, seven more times

BRIDGE   *CW*

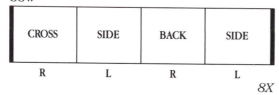

Beat 1-4   Repeat Part I, beats 1-2, two times

PART III

IN	IN (2)	IN (3)	IN (4)	OUT	OUT (2)	OUT (3)	OUT (4)
R	L	R	L	R	L	R	L

4X

Beat 1-4   Step R, L, R, L foot diagonally toward center

5-8   Step R, L, R, L foot diagonally away from center

9-32   Repeat Part III, beats 1-8, three more times

NOTE   Double circle is moving counterclockwise in Part III.

PART IV   *CCW*

CROSS	SIDE	BACK	SIDE
R	L	R	L

8X

Beat 1-32   Repeat Part II, beats 1-32, seven more times

NOTE   Handhold may be substituted for closed dance position.

CIRCLE DANCE   Dance women's part beginning L foot.

LEAD-UP ACTIVITIES   Practice SIDE, CLOSE both directions (individual tempo).

Practice GRAPEVINE starting with one foot for several repetitions and then the other foot (individual tempo).

Practice walking diagonally IN 4 steps and diagonally OUT 4 steps (individual tempo).

TEACHING SUGGESTIONS   Partners practice SIDE, CLOSE (partner beat)—while moving in the same direction.

Partners practice GRAPEVINE while moving in the same direction (partner beat).

Partners move IN and OUT of the circle with 4 steps each and then execute on the proper diagonal (partner beat).

SAY & DO the entire dance and then add the music.

CHAIR DANCING   Substitute CHERKESSIYA steps for GRAPEVINE steps.

Substitute steps in place for SIDE, CLOSE or use a SIDE, TOUCH; SIDE, TOUCH pattern.

Move feet away from and toward the chair for IN, 2, 3, 4; OUT, 2, 3, 4.

Debka Le Adama

Debka of the Soil
Israel

RECORD	*Rhythmically Moving 9*
INTRODUCTION	8 beats
FORMATION	Line facing right, hands joined with L arm behind back

PART I   *CCW*

FWD	FWD (2)	FWD (3)	FWD (4)	FWD	FWD (2)	FWD (3)	FWD (4)
L	R	L	R	L	R	L	R

CW

BWD	BWD (2)	BWD (3)	BWD (4)	BWD	BWD (2)	BWD (3)	BWD (4)
L	R	L	R	L	R	L	R

Beat 1-8   Walk 8 steps forward counterclockwise beginning L foot

9-16   Walk 8 steps backward beginning L foot (move clockwise)

PART II

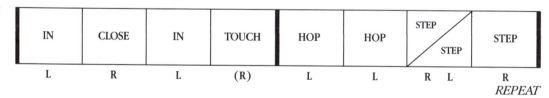

IN	CLOSE	IN	TOUCH	HOP	HOP	STEP / STEP	STEP
L	R	L	(R)	L	L	R L	R

REPEAT

Beat 1   Step L foot sideward (toward the center) with accent

2   Step R foot next to L foot

3   Step L foot sideward with accent

4   Touch R foot next to L foot

5   Hop L foot sideward right (away from center)

6   Hop L foot sideward right

7-8   Step R, L, R foot in place (substitute Yemenite beginning R foot for more experienced dancers)

9-16   Repeat Part II, beats 1-8

PART III   *CCW*

FWD	FWD (2)	FWD (3)	FWD (4)	CROSS	SIDE	BACK	SIDE
L	R	L	R	L	R	L	R

CROSS	SIDE	BACK	SIDE	CROSS	SIDE	BACK	SIDE
L	R	L	R	L	R	L	R

3X

Beat 1-4	Step L, R, L, R foot forward counterclockwise
5-8	Grapevine counterclockwise beginning L foot crossing in front of R foot
9-32	Repeat Grapevine 6 more times; accelerate slightly and turn steps of Grapevine into leaping steps

LEAD-UP ACTIVITIES

Walk FORWARD 8 steps and BACKWARD 8 steps. Use different starting foot (individual tempo).

Practice hopping on one foot SIDEWARD, moving in the direction opposite to the hopping foot (individual tempo).

Practice SIDE, CLOSE; SIDE, TOUCH in each direction (individual tempo).

Practice GRAPEVINES in one direction then the other (individual tempo).

TEACHING SUGGESTIONS

Walk FORWARD 8 steps and BACKWARD 8 steps beginning L foot. Add IN, CLOSE; IN, TOUCH sideward left beginning L foot (SAY & DO).

Practice HOP, HOP; STEP/STEP, STEP moving sideward right hopping on the L foot. Put this sequence together with the IN, CLOSE; IN, TOUCH (SAY & DO).

Practice Part III moving from the WALK to the GRAPEVINE (SAY & DO).

Practice the transition from Part II to Part III and from Part III to Part I.

Practice the entire dance with SAY & DO and then add music.

CHAIR DANCING

PART I   Substitute steps in place or away from and toward the chair.

PART II   Move to the left and to the right.

PART III   Substitute CHERKESSIYA steps for the GRAPEVINE steps.

Dimna Juda Mamo

Macedonia

RECORD   *Rhythmically Moving 6*

INTRODUCTION   8 beats

FORMATION   Broken circle, leader at right. Hands joined in front basket with R hand under.

PART I   *CCW*

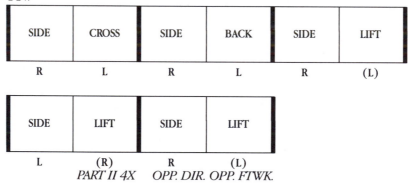

Beat 1-40   Walk 40 steps forward counterclockwise beginning R foot. Turn to face center on beat 40

PART II   *CCW*

SIDE	CROSS	SIDE	BACK	SIDE	LIFT
R	L	R	L	R	(L)

SIDE	LIFT	SIDE	LIFT
L	(R)	R	(L)

PART II 4X   OPP. DIR. OPP. FTWK.

Beat 1   Step R foot sideward right

2   Step L foot crossing in front of R foot

3   Step R foot sideward right

4   Step L foot crossing in back of R foot

5   Step R foot sideward right

6   Lift L foot in front of R leg (keep lift low to floor)

7-10   Repeat beats 5-6 two more times alternating footwork

11-20   Repeat beats 1-10 to the left beginning L foot

21-40   Repeat Part II, beats 1-20

LEAD-UP ACTIVITIES	Practice SIDE, LIFT (individual tempo).
	Practice SIDE, CROSS, SIDE, BACK (individual tempo).

TEACHING SUGGESTIONS	WALK to the music.
	Practice SIDE, CROSS, SIDE, BACK several times each direction (SAY & DO).
	Do 1 pattern of SIDE, CROSS, SIDE, BACK and add on 3 SIDE, LIFT patterns. Practice each direction with SAY & DO.

CHAIR DANCING	
PART I	WALK in place.
PART II	Do as described, keeping steps small.

Dirlada

Greece

RECORD	*Rhythmically Moving 5*	
INTRODUCTION	8 beats	
FORMATION	Free formation	

PART I *CCW*

SIDE	BACK	SIDE	CROSS	SIDE	LIFT	SIDE	LIFT (HIT)
R	L	R	L	R	(L)	L	(R)

SIDE	LIFT (HIT)	TURN (¼ L)	KICK (CLAP)
R	(L)	L	(R)

Beat 1 Step R foot sideward right

2 Step L foot crossing in back of R foot

3 Step R foot sideward right

4 Step L foot crossing in front of R foot

5 Step R foot sideward right

6 Lift L foot in front of R leg

7 Step L foot sideward left

8 Raise R foot, knee bent, in back of L foot, hit R shoe with L hand

9 Step R foot sideward right

10 Lift L foot in front of R leg and hit inside of L shoe with L hand

11 Step L foot turning ¼ left

12 Kick R leg and clap under R leg

LEAD-UP ACTIVITIES Practice GRAPEVINE patterns each direction (individual tempo).

Practice STEP, HIT hitting free foot in back, then practice hitting free foot in front, then practice clapping under free leg (individual tempo).

TEACHING SUGGESTIONS Practice SIDE, LIFT; SIDE, LIFT (in back) beginning R foot (SAY & DO), add on SIDE, LIFT and practice beats 5-10, then add on TURN, KICK (SAY & DO).

Precede sequence with beats 1-4 (SAY & DO).

Do entire dance and add music.

CHAIR DANCING Omit TURN and STEP in place. Do other beats as described.

Hora Medura

Hora Around the Campfire
Israel

RECORD	*Rhythmically Moving 3*
INTRODUCTION	4 beats
FORMATION	Single circle facing center, hands joined

PART I   *CCW*

SIDE	CLOSE	SIDE	CLOSE	SIDE	CLOSE	SIDE	CLOSE
R	L	R	L	R	L	R	L

IN	IN (2)	IN (3)	IN (4)	OUT	OUT (2)	OUT (3)	OUT (4)
R	L	R	L	R	L	R	L

REPEAT PART I

Beat 1	Step R foot sideward right
2	Step L foot next to R foot
3-8	Repeat beats 1-2, three more times
9-12	Step R, L, R, L foot toward center of circle, raise arms
13-16	Step R, L, R, L foot out, lower arms
17-32	Repeat Part I, beats 1-16

TO SIMPLIFY   RUN 8 steps forward counterclockwise on beats 1-8.

PART II   *CW*

CROSS	SIDE	BACK	SIDE	FWD (RUN)	FWD (2)	FWD (3)	FWD (4)
R	L	R	L	R	L	R	L

CROSS	SIDE	BACK	SIDE	HEEL		HEEL	
R	L	R	L	(R)		(R)	

REPEAT PART II

Beat 1-4	Grapevine beginning R foot crossing in front of L foot
5-8	Run R, L, R, L foot forward clockwise
9-12	Grapevine beginning R foot and turn to face center
13	Stamp R heel (raise arms overhead)
14	Rest (lower arms)
15-16	Repeat beats 13-14
17-32	Repeat Part II, beats 1-16

TO SIMPLIFY
FORWARD, 2, 3, 4 (3 times); HEEL, REST, HEEL, REST.
Beat 1-12   Run 12 steps forward clockwise.

LEAD-UP ACTIVITIES
Practice SIDE, CLOSE (individual tempo).

Practice GRAPEVINES if teaching actual dance rather than simplification.

Practice IN, 2, 3, 4; OUT, 2, 3, 4, followed by a running STEP or GRAPEVINE clockwise.

TEACHING SUGGESTIONS
SAY & DO Part I.

SAY & DO simplification of Part II.

If using actual Part II, practice sequence of GRAPEVINE, RUN 4; GRAPEVINE with individual tempo before SAY & DO, adding on the HEEL, REST, HEEL, REST.

Practice the transitions from Part I to Part II and back to Part I, and then add the music.

CHAIR DANCING PART II   STEP in place.

Mayim

Water
Israel

RECORD	*Rhythmically Moving 5*
INTRODUCTION	8 beats
FORMATION	Single circle facing center, hands joined

PART I *CW*

CROSS	SIDE	BACK	SIDE	CROSS	SIDE	BACK	SIDE
R	L	R	L	R	L	R	L *REPEAT*

Beat 1-16   Grapevine 4 times moving clockwise, beginning R foot crossing in front of L foot

PART II

IN (RUN)	IN (2)	IN (3)	IN (4)	OUT (CLAP)	OUT (2)	OUT (3)	OUT (4)
R	L	R	L	R	L	R	L *REPEAT*

Beat 1-4   Run R, L, R, L foot in to center of circle (raise arms)

5-8   Run R, L, R, L foot out backing up (lower arms); a clap may be added on beat 5

9-16   Repeat Part II, beats 1-8

BRIDGE *CW*

FWD	FWD	FWD	HOP
R	L	R	R

Beat 1-3   Run R, L, R foot forward clockwise

4   Hop R foot turning to face center, bringing L foot in toward the center

PART III

HOP	HOP (2)	HOP (3)	HOP (4)	HOP	HOP (2)	HOP (3)	HOP (4)
R	R	R	R	R	R	R	R
						REPEAT	*OPP. FTWK.*

Beat 1	Hop on R foot touching L foot in front of R foot
2	Hop on R foot touching L foot to left side
3-8	Repeat beats 1-2, three more times
9	Hop on L foot and touch R foot in front
10	Hop on L foot touching R foot to right side
11-16	Repeat beats 9-10, three more times
NOTE	If desired, release hands on Part III, beats 9-16, and clap hands in front of body each time foot touches in front.

LEAD-UP ACTIVITIES

Practice GRAPEVINE (individual tempo).

Practice touching the free foot forward and sideward while hopping (individual tempo).

Practice combining GRAPEVINES with IN 4 steps and OUT 4 steps (individual tempo).

TEACHING SUGGESTIONS

Practice 4 GRAPEVINE steps moving clockwise (SAY & DO).

SAY & DO Parts I and II.

Practice FORWARD, 2, 3, HOP, moving clockwise, beginning R foot and bringing the L foot toward the center on the HOP. Add on 8 HOPS on the R foot followed by 8 HOPS on the L foot— add the TOUCH after the sequence has been learned without it (SAY & DO).

SAY & DO Part III.

SAY & DO the entire dance and then add the music.

CHAIR DANCING

PART I	Do as described with small steps using CHERKESSIYA.
PART II	WALK feet away from and toward the chair.
PART III	Do in place.

Romanian Hora

Triple Hora
Romania

RECORD   *Rhythmically Moving 7*

INTRODUCTION   8 beats

FORMATION   Circle facing center, arms in "T" position

PART I   *CCW*

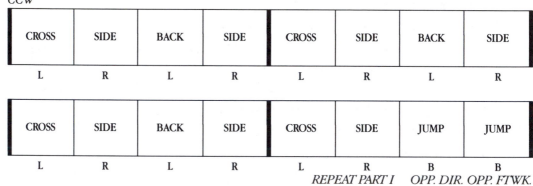

CROSS	SIDE	BACK	SIDE	CROSS	SIDE	BACK	SIDE
L	R	L	R	L	R	L	R

CROSS	SIDE	BACK	SIDE	CROSS	SIDE	JUMP	JUMP
L	R	L	R	L	R	B	B

REPEAT PART I   OPP. DIR. OPP. FTWK.

Beat 1-4   Grapevine moving counterclockwise beginning L foot

5-12   Repeat beats 1-4, two more times

13   Step L foot crossing in front of R foot

14   Step R foot sideward right

15-16   Jump 2 times

17-32   Repeat Part I, beats 1-16, beginning R foot moving clockwise

TO SIMPLIFY   RUN 14 steps followed by 2 JUMPS counterclockwise then clockwise.

PART II   *CCW*   *CW*

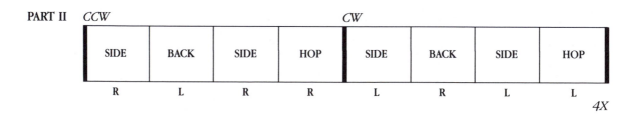

SIDE	BACK	SIDE	HOP	SIDE	BACK	SIDE	HOP
R	L	R	R	L	R	L	L

4X

Beat 1	Step R foot sideward right
2	Step L foot crossing in back of R foot
3	Step R foot sideward right
4	Hop R foot swinging L foot in front of R leg
5-8	Repeat beats 1-4 beginning L foot sideward left
9-32	Repeat Part II, beats 1-8, three more times

PART III

SCISSORS		SCISSORS		SCISSORS	SCISSORS (2)	SCISSORS (3)	SCISSORS (4)
R		L		R	L	R	L

3X

SCISSORS		SCISSORS		SCISSORS	SCISSORS	SCISSORS	
R		L		R	L	R	

Beat 1-2	Leap on R foot in place extending L heel in
3-4	Leap on L foot in place extending R heel in
5-8	Leap on R, L, R, L foot in place (scissors)
9-24	Repeat Part III, beats 1-8, two more times
25-28	Repeat beats 1-4
29-32	Leap on R, L, R foot in place, rest on beat 32

LEAD-UP ACTIVITIES

Practice 14 RUNS followed by 2 JUMPS in place (SAY & DO).

Practice GRAPEVINES each direction (individual tempo).

Practice SIDE, BACK, SIDE, HOP each direction (individual tempo).

Practice SCISSORS KICKS.

TEACHING SUGGESTIONS

Practice GRAPEVINES with SAY & DO.

Practice CROSS, SIDE, JUMP, JUMP with SAY & DO.

SAY & DO Part I and add music before teaching Parts II and III.

Practice Part II with SAY & DO.

Practice LEAP, REST, LEAP, REST with SAY & DO and add on 4 SCISSORS IN.

SAY & DO Part III.

Practice the transitions between parts.

SAY & DO the entire dance and then add the music.

**CHAIR
DANCING**

PART I   Substitute CHERKESSIYA steps for GRAPEVINE steps.

PART II   Do as described.

PART III   Do as described.

Sweet Girl

Armenia

RECORD	*Rhythmically Moving* 7
INTRODUCTION	Pick-up plus 7 beats
FORMATION	Line, little fingers joined in "W" position

PART I   *CCW*

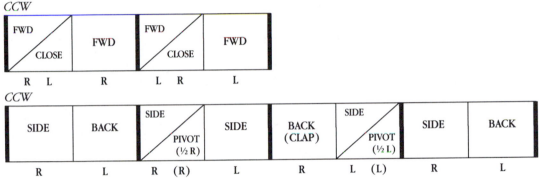

Beat 1-4	Two-step beginning R foot, L foot
5	Step R foot sideward right (facing center)
6	Step L foot crossing in back of right (lean body out)
7	Step R foot sideward with ½ turn to the right
8	Step L foot sideward left (facing out)
9	Step R foot crossing in back of L foot (clap and lean forward)
10	Step L foot sideward with ½ turn to left
11	Step R foot sideward right (facing in)
12	Step L foot crossing in back of R foot

TO SIMPLIFY
Beats 1-4   Walk R, L, R, L foot

LEAD-UP ACTIVITIES   Practice stepping R foot with a ½ TURN right then L foot with a ½ TURN left. The movement is counterclockwise (individual tempo). Encourage students to take large steps.

Practice moving counterclockwise with a series of SIDE, BACK, ½ TURN patterns. Make sure students balance themselves on the TURN and do not step down on the free foot until the next SIDE step (individual tempo).

Practice quick TWO-STEPS before the change from the simplified 4 WALKS to the 2 TWO-STEPS (individual tempo).

TEACHING SUGGESTIONS	Practice FORWARD, 2, 3, 4; SIDE, BACK beginning R foot and moving counterclockwise (individual tempo, then SAY & DO).

Add on the ½ TURN following the SIDE, BACK, then add on another SIDE, BACK, ½ TURN. Note for the students that they have their backs to the center of the circle on this second SIDE, BACK, ½ TURN. Finally, add on the SIDE, BACK of beats 11-12.

Do not add the CLAP until the students are comfortable with the dance.

SAY & DO the entire dance and then add the music.

CHAIR DANCING

Beat 1-4	Do the four WALKS or the 2 TWO-STEPS in place.
Beat 5-10	Substitute a side-to-side stepping pattern. (SIDE, BACK, SIDE—SIDE, BACK, SIDE—SIDE, BACK).

Branle Normand

France

RECORD	*Rhythmically Moving 6*
INTRODUCTION	4 beats
FORMATION	Circle, hands held at shoulder level, "W" position

PART I *CCW*

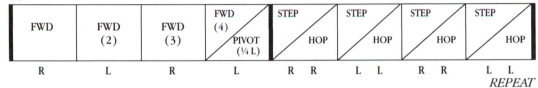

FWD	FWD (2)	FWD (3)	FWD (4) PIVOT (¼ L)	STEP / HOP	STEP / HOP	STEP / HOP	STEP / HOP
R	L	R	L	R R	L L	R R	L L

REPEAT

Beat 1	Step-bend R foot forward counterclockwise
2	Step-bend L foot forward counterclockwise
3-4	Repeat beats 1-2 and turn to face center
5	Step Hop R foot in place, kicking L foot in
6	Step Hop L foot in place, kicking R foot out
7-8	Repeat beats 5-6
9-16	Repeat beats 1-8

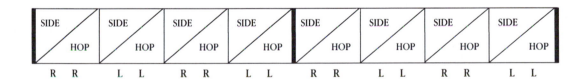

SIDE / HOP	SIDE / HOP	SIDE / HOP	SIDE / HOP	SIDE / HOP	SIDE / HOP	SIDE / HOP	SIDE / HOP
R R	L L	R R	L L	R R	L L	R R	L L

17	Side Hop R foot sideward right (bring L foot to R calf with knee turned out)
18	Side Hop L foot sideward left (bring R foot to L calf with knee turned out)
19-24	Repeat beats 17-18, three more times

LEAD-UP ACTIVITIES	Practice walking in a STEP/BEND movement pattern (individual tempo).
	Allow the STEP and the BEND to take the same amount of time.
	Practice the STEP HOP, kicking the free leg IN; practice kicking it OUT; practice bringing the free foot to the hopping leg and turning the knee out (individual tempo).

TEACHING SUGGESTIONS

Practice the STEP/BEND to the music.

Practice the STEP HOP to the music.

Practice swinging the L leg IN when the R foot is doing the STEP HOP and the R leg OUT when the L foot is doing the STEP HOP. Add this to music.

Do the side-to-side SIDE HOP, bringing the free foot to the calf of the hopping leg.

Practice the transition of the STEP HOP with the free leg swinging IN, then OUT to the SIDE HOP.

SAY & DO the dance sequence, then add music.

CHAIR DANCING

Substitute lifting the free leg for the BEND of the supporting leg.

Do the STEP HOP with leg swing on the diagonal and the SIDE HOP with the knee turned OUT slightly.

Debka Kurdit

Debka of the Kurds
Israel

RECORD	*Rhythmically Moving 7*	
INTRODUCTION	8 beats	
FORMATION	Short lines in shoulder hold, "T" position	

PART I

IN	BEND	OUT	BEND	IN	BEND	OUT	BEND
L	(L)	R	(R)	L	(L)	R	(R) *REPEAT*

Beat 1	Step L foot in (lift R leg in back with knee bent)
2	Bend L knee
3	Step R foot out (lift L leg in front with knee bent)
4	Bend R knee
5-16	Repeat Part I, beats 1-4, three more times

PART II

IN	HOP	OUT	HOP	IN	HOP	OUT	HOP
L	L	R	R	L	L	R	R *REPEAT*

Beat 1-2	Step Hop L foot in (lift R leg in back—higher, bigger motion)
3-4	Step Hop R foot out (lift L leg in front—higher, bigger motion)
5-16	Repeat Part II, beats 1-4, three more times
NOTE	Stay on R foot to begin Part III.

PART III

BOUNCE	BOUNCE	BOUNCE	IN	BOUNCE	BOUNCE	BOUNCE	IN
(R)	(R)	(R)	L	(L)	(L)	(L)	R *REPEAT*

Beat 1-3   Bounce 3 times on R foot with L leg reaching in front of body

4   Step L foot toward the center with accent

5-8   Repeat beats 1-4, bouncing L foot and stepping R foot toward the center

9-16   Repeat Part III, beats 1-8

PART IV

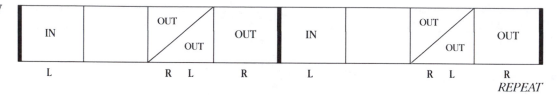

Beat 1-2   Step L foot in, then rest on beat 2

3-4   Step R, L, R foot out (3 &, 4)

5-16   Repeat Part IV, beats 1-4, three more times

PART V

IN	BEND	OUT	BEND	IN	BEND	OUT	BEND
L	(L)	R	(R)	L	(L)	R	(R)

REPEAT

Beat 1-16   Repeat Part I, beats 1-16

PART VI   *CCW*

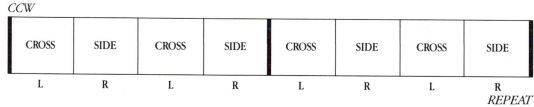

Beat 1   Step L foot crossing in front of R foot

2   Step R foot sideward right

3-16   Repeat Part VI, beats 1-2, seven more times

NOTE   Keep body low with back straight.

LEAD-UP ACTIVITIES	Practice rocking FORWARD and BACKWARD—one foot FORWARD and the other one BACKWARD (individual tempo).
	Practice STEP HOP in place. Practice STEP HOP FORWARD and BACKWARD, then do one FORWARD, one BACKWARD (individual tempo).
	Practice balancing on one foot for 3 beats, then change feet on fourth beat (individual tempo).
	PAT the legs with both hands in a pattern of "1, 2, 3 &, 4" (group beat). WALK pattern (individual tempo).
	Practice a CROSS, SIDE pattern (individual tempo).
TEACHING SUGGESTIONS	Practice IN, BEND, OUT, BEND (rocking pattern).
	Substitute a HOP for the BEND to create IN, HOP, OUT, HOP—begin L foot (SAY & DO).
	Practice balancing on the R foot for 3 beats while extending the L foot IN (BOUNCE, 2, 3, STEP)—change feet on beat 4 and repeat. Do this pattern several times (SAY & DO).
	Practice the transition from OUT, HOP (R foot) to Part III.
	Practice Part IV (IN, REST, OUT/OUT, OUT) several times (SAY & DO).
	Practice the transition from Part III to Part IV.
	Practice Part VI CROSS, SIDE moving right and beginning R foot (SAY & DO).
	Practice the transition from Part VI to Part I.
	Put the dance together with SAY & DO, then add music.
CHAIR DANCING	
PARTS I & II & V	STEP FORWARD and BACKWARD on a diagonal.
PARTS VI	Do in place.
PART IV	STEP in place with one foot in front of the other.

D'Hammerschmiedsgsell'n

The Journeyman Blacksmith
Germany

RECORD	*Rhythmically Moving 7*
INTRODUCTION	4 measures, ¾ meter
FORMATION	Groups of four, two facing two
ALTERNATE FORMATION	Pairs randomly placed

CHORUS

PAT (ME)	CHEST (ME)	CLAP (ME)	HIT R (YOU)	HIT L (YOU)	HIT BOTH (YOU)

8X

Beat 1	Pat thighs (both hands)
2	Hit chest with both hands
3	Clap own hands
4	Hit opposite's R hand with your R hand
5	Hit opposite's L hand with your L hand
6	Hit opposite's two hands with your two hands
7-48	Repeat beats 1-6 seven more times and join hands in circle of 4 dancers

CHORUS (SIMPLIFIED)

CLAP (ME)	CLAP (ME)	CLAP (ME)	HIT (YOU)	HIT (YOU)	HIT (YOU)

8X

CLAP hands or PAT thighs 3 times and HIT partner's hands 3 times.

NOTE   In groups of 4, work diagonally across from partner—1's beginning with beat 1 and 2's beginning with beat 4, simultaneously.

PART I   *CW*
SKIP

FWD		HOP	FWD		HOP
R		R	L		L

4X
REPEAT   OPP. DIR.

Beat 1	Step R foot forward clockwise
2	Rest
3	Hop R foot in place
4	Step L foot forward clockwise
5	Rest
6	Hop L foot in place
7-24	Repeat beats 1-6, three more times
25-48	Repeat Part I, beats 1-24, moving counterclockwise
NOTE	No R foot or L foot is necessary.
CHORUS	Repeat Chorus, beats 1-48

PART II
STAR

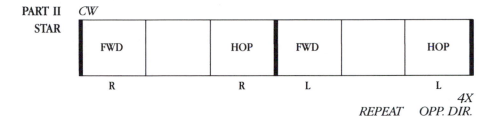

Beat 1-48   Repeat Part II substituting R hand Star and L hand Star

CHORUS   Repeat Chorus, beats 1-48

PART III
SKIP

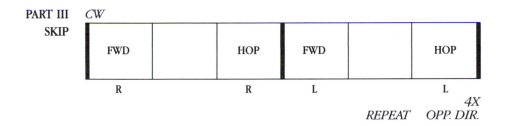

Beat 1-48   Repeat Part I

LEAD-UP ACTIVITIES   Practice using music in ¾ meter—PAT thighs 3 times, then CLAP 3 times.

Practice a sequence of PAT thighs, HIT chest, CLAP hands several times.

Practice a sequence of pushing R hand FORWARD, L hand FORWARD, both hands FORWARD.

Practice walking in this meter, accenting the first WALK (individual tempo).

Practice hopping—3 on one foot and 3 on the other (individual tempo).

Practice skipping slowly (WALK, REST, HOP) (individual tempo).

TEACHING SUGGESTIONS	Have students work in pairs on the Chorus to their own tempo. Do the Chorus to a group beat (SAY & DO).
	Have students work on Part I with their partner. Do Part I to a group beat (SAY & DO).
	Do the dance with SAY & DO and then add music.
	Add groups of 4 the second time the dance is presented.

CHAIR DANCING

PART I	Do facing a partner.
PART II	Do in place while holding hands with the partner or substitute arm motions.

Hora

Israel

RECORD	*Rhythmically Moving 4*
INTRODUCTION	Begin dance with vocal
FORMATION	Single circle facing center, "T" position or hands held down
NOTE	A double circle may be used, with one circle moving in the opposite direction.

PART I　*CW*

SIDE	BACK	SIDE	HOP	SIDE	HOP
L	R	L	L	R	R

Beat 1	Step L foot sideward left
2	Step R foot crossing in back of L foot
3	Step L foot sideward left
4	Hop L foot while swinging R foot toward center
5	Step R foot sideward right
6	Hop R foot and swing L foot

NEW HORA　*CW*

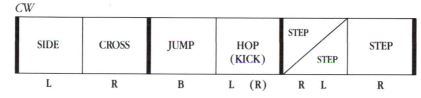

SIDE	CROSS	JUMP	HOP (KICK)	STEP / STEP	STEP
L	R	B	L (R)	R L	R

LEAD-UP ACTIVITIES	Practice STEP HOP in place (individual tempo).
	Practice SIDE, BACK, SIDE, HOP (individual tempo).
TEACHING SUGGESTIONS	Teach the *Hasapikos* first and relate this dance to it.
	Practice the sequence with SAY & DO and add the music.
CHAIR DANCING	Do steps in place.

Machar

Tomorrow
Israel

RECORD	*Rhythmically Moving 5*
INTRODUCTION	16 beats
FORMATION	Groups of 3 side by side, facing counterclockwise

PART I   *CCW*

FWD	FWD (2)	FWD (3)	FWD (4)	CROSS	HOP	CROSS	HOP
R	L	R	L	R	R	L	L

4X

Beat 1-4	Run R, L, R, L foot forward counterclockwise
5-6	Step Hop R foot crossing in front of L foot
7-8	Step Hop L foot crossing in front of R foot
9-32	Repeat Part I, beats 1-8, three more times, then middle dancer and R hand dancer face each other
NOTE	Omit the crossing over STEP HOP when learning the dance.

PART II   *CW*

SIDE	CLAP	SIDE	CLAP	TURN (R ELBOW)	TURN (2)	TURN (3)	TURN (4)
R		L		R	L	R	L

CCW

TURN (L ELBOW)	2	3	4	5	6	7	8
R	L	R	L	R	L	R	L

CW

SIDE	CLAP	SIDE	CLAP	TURN (R ELBOW)	2	3	4
R		L		R	L	R	L

CCW   *CCW*

TURN (L ELBOW)	2	3	4	FWD	2	3	4
R	L	R	L	R	L	R	L

Beat 1-2	Both dancers sway to own right, then clap near R shoulder on beat 2
3-4	Repeat sway to left and clap left (partner on left may do same action)
5-8	Middle dancer and R dancer hook R elbows and turn with 4 steps
9-16	Middle dancer and L dancer hook L elbows and turn with 8 steps; middle dancer ends facing L dancer
17-24	Repeat Part II, beats 1-8, with L dancer
25-28	Middle dancer hooks L elbow with R dancer and turns in 4 steps
29-32	Middle dancer moves forward in 4 steps to join 2 new dancers
NOTE	No R foot or L foot needs to be specified in Part II.

LEAD-UP ACTIVITIES

Practice combinations of running steps and STEP HOPS (individual tempo).

Groups of 3 dancers practice R and L elbow turns with the middle person working with the 2 persons on each side.

TEACHING SUGGESTIONS

Have groups of 3 dancers practice the sequence in Part I at a tempo agreed upon by the 3.

SAY & DO Part I, and then add the music.

Have the groups review the beat structure and movement sequence for Part II and practice in groups of 3.

Do Part II with SAY & DO.

SAY & DO the entire dance, and then add the music.

CHAIR DANCING

| PART I | Do in place. |

PART II

Beat 1-8	Do in place
9-16	Do HEEL, STEP 4 times
17-32	Repeat beats 1-8

Dance may be executed in wheelchairs.

Makazice Kolo

Scissors
Yugoslavia

RECORD	*Rhythmically Moving 7*
INTRODUCTION	8 beats
FORMATION	Broken circle of dancers, hands held in "V" position (kolo hold), face center

PART I

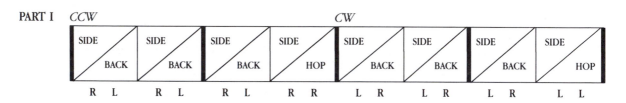

Beat 1 Step R foot sideward right

& Step L foot crossing in back of R foot

2-3 Repeat beat 1 &, two more times

4 & Step Hop R foot

5-8 Repeat Part I, beats 1-4, sideward left beginning L foot

PART II

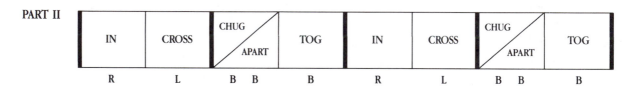

Beat 1 Step R foot in toward center of circle

2 Cross L foot over R foot (weight on both feet)

3 Chug out, keep weight on balls of feet

& Uncross L foot, placing weight on both feet (toes-in, heels-out position)

4 Bring feet together, lowering heels

5-8 Repeat Part II, beats 1-4

STYLE NOTE In Part II a bouncing motion occurs on each beat.

LEAD-UP ACTIVITIES

Practice SIDE/BACK (individual tempo).

Practice jumping with feet slightly apart, toes IN, then bring them together; stand with the L foot crossed over the R foot before jumping to the toes IN position (individual tempo).

Practice chugging backward (individual tempo).

TEACHING SUGGESTIONS

Practice 3 SIDE/BACK steps with SAY & DO then add on the STEP HOP.

SAY & DO Part I.

Practice Part II at individual tempo. SAY & DO beginning with CHUG/APART, TOGETHER and then precede that pattern with IN, CROSS.

SAY & DO the entire dance and then add the music.

CHAIR DANCING

Do as described.

Niguno Shel Yossi

Israel

RECORD   *Rhythmically Moving 6*

INTRODUCTION   8 beats

FORMATION   Partners in a single circle, hands joined

PART I

STEP	HOP	STEP	HOP	IN	IN (2)	IN (3)	IN (4)
R	R	L	L	R	L	R	L

STEP	HOP	STEP	HOP	OUT	OUT (2)	OUT (3)	OUT (4)
R	R	L	L	R	L	R	L

REPEAT PART I

Beat 1-2   Step Hop R foot kicking L foot in

3-4   Step Hop L foot kicking R foot in

5-8   Step R, L, R, L foot toward the center (raise arms)

9-12   Repeat beats 1-4

13-16   Step R, L, R, L foot away from the center (lower arms)

17-32   Repeat Part I, beats 1-16, and turn to face partner

NOTE   Omit the KICK with the STEP HOP when learning the dance.

PART II

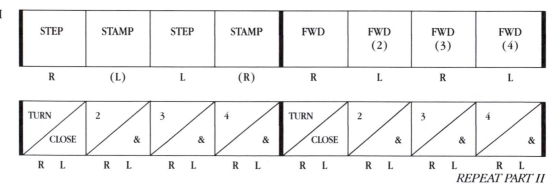

STEP	STAMP	STEP	STAMP	FWD	FWD (2)	FWD (3)	FWD (4)
R	(L)	L	(R)	R	L	R	L

TURN / CLOSE	2 / &	3 / &	4 / &	TURN / CLOSE	2 / &	3 / &	4 / &
R L	R L	R L	R L	R L	R L	R L	R L

REPEAT PART II

Beat 1	Step R foot slightly sideward right
2	Stamp L foot next to R foot (clap hands over R shoulder)
3	Step L foot slightly sideward left
4	Stamp R foot (clap over L shoulder)
5-8	Step R, L, R, L foot forward passing R shoulders with partner
9-16	Israeli turn with new partner, use 8 buzz steps
17-32	Repeat Part II, beats 1-16, progressing to a second new person; end Part II facing center to begin dance again

LEAD-UP ACTIVITIES

Practice STEP HOPS (individual tempo).

Practice combining 2 STEP HOPS with 4 steps IN and with 4 steps OUT (individual tempo).

Practice STEP, STAMP, STEP, STAMP; FORWARD, 2, 3, 4 (individual tempo).

Practice BUZZ TURN with partner (partner beat).

TEACHING SUGGESTIONS

SAY & DO Part I.

SAY & DO Part II up to the BUZZ TURN, then add the TURN.

Practice the transition from Part II to the repeat of Part II to be certain everyone is travelling in the original direction.

Practice the transition from Part II back to the beginning.

SAY & DO the entire dance and then add the music.

CHAIR DANCING PART II

Substitute steps in place for the FORWARD steps and TURN, or further substitute PAT, CLAP for the TURN.

May be adapted for wheelchairs.

Shibolet Basadeh

A Sheaf in the Field
Israel

RECORD	*Rhythmically Moving 5*
INTRODUCTION	12 beats
FORMATION	Circle facing center, hands joined

PART I   *CCW*

SIDE	CLOSE	SIDE	CLOSE	SIDE	CLOSE	SIDE	HOP (½ TURN)
R	L	R	L	R	L	R	R

4X   OPP. FTWK.

Beat 1   Step R foot sideward right moving counterclockwise

2   Step L foot next to R foot

3-6   Repeat beats 1-2, two more times

7   Step R foot sideward right

8   Hop R foot turning ½ clockwise to face out of circle

9-16   Repeat beats 1-8 with opposite footwork, end facing center (continue to move counterclockwise around the circle)

17-32   Repeat beats 1-16

PART II   *CCW*   *CCW*

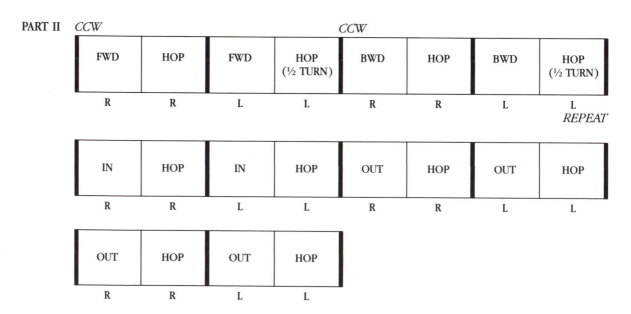

FWD	HOP	FWD	HOP (½ TURN)	BWD	HOP	BWD	HOP (½ TURN)
R	R	L	L	R	R	L	L

REPEAT

IN	HOP	IN	HOP	OUT	HOP	OUT	HOP
R	R	L	L	R	R	L	L

OUT	HOP	OUT	HOP
R	R	L	L

Beat 1	Step R foot forward counterclockwise
2	Hop R foot
3	Step L foot forward counterclockwise
4	Hop L foot turning ½ counterclockwise to face clockwise
5-8	Repeat beats 1-4 backward counterclockwise, end facing counterclockwise
9-16	Repeat beats 1-8
17-20	Step Hop R foot, L foot in (large Step Hops raising arms up)
21-28	Step Hop R, L, R, L foot out (small Step Hops lowering arms)

LEAD-UP ACTIVITIES

Practice sliding, then execute ½ TURNS in the moving direction (individual tempo).

Practice SIDE, CLOSE (individual tempo).

Practice STEP HOP (individual tempo).

Practice STEP HOP and execute a ½ TURN on the HOP (individual tempo).

TEACHING SUGGESTIONS

Practice 3 SIDE, CLOSE steps (use individual tempo then SAY & DO) and add on the SIDE, HOP turning ½ in the moving direction (counterclockwise).

Practice Part I with SAY & DO.

Practice moving FORWARD with 2 STEP HOPS beginning R foot, then moving BACKWARD in the same direction with 2 STEP HOPS, turning ½ after each 2 STEP HOPS (use individual tempo, then SAY & DO). Add on 2 STEP HOPS IN and 4 STEP HOPS OUT.

SAY & DO the entire dance and then add the music.

CHAIR DANCING

PART I   Do in place beginning with feet off to the left and omit TURN (feet move back and forth across in front of the chair).

PART II   Do in place without the TURN, moving feet away from and toward the chair for IN and OUT.

Sicilian Tarantella

Italy

RECORD	*Rhythmically Moving 6*	
INTRODUCTION	8 beats	
FORMATION	Groups of four, two facing two (if couples, men on the same side)	

PART I

STEP	HOP (KICK)	STEP	HOP (KICK)	RUN	RUN (2)	RUN (3)	RUN (4)
R	R	L	L	R	L	R	L

4X

Beat 1-2	Step Hop R foot kicking L foot; clap hands overhead on hop
3-4	Step Hop L foot kicking R foot; clap hands overhead on hop
5-8	Run R, L, R, L foot in place (snap fingers overhead each beat)
9-32	Repeat Part I, beats 1-8, three more times

PART II

IN	IN (2)	IN (3)	IN (4)	OUT	OUT (2)	OUT (3)	OUT (4)
R	L	R	L	R	L	R	L

4X   OPP. DIR.

Beat 1-4	Run R, L, R, L foot right diagonally in (clap on beat 4)
5-8	Run R, L, R, L foot left diagonally out (clap on beat 8)
9-16	Repeat beats 1-8 diagonally left in and right out
17-32	Repeat Part II, beats 1-16

PART III   *CW*

TURN (ELBOW)	2	3	4	5	6	7	8
R	L	R	L	R	L	R	L

4X   OPP. ELBOW

AROUND (DO-SA-DO)	2	3	4	5	6	7	8
R	L	R	L	R	L	R	L

4X   OPP. DIR.

Beat 1-8   Partners on the right do a R elbow turn

9-16   Partners on the left do a R elbow turn

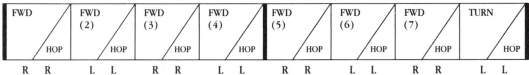

17-32   Repeat with L elbow turns

33-48   Repeat with R shoulder Do-sa-do

49-64   Repeat with L shoulder Do-sa-do

PART IV   *CCW*

SKIP

FWD		FWD (2)		FWD (3)		FWD (4)		FWD (5)		FWD (6)		FWD (7)		TURN	
	HOP		HOP		HOP		HOP		HOP		HOP		HOP		HOP

  R   R   L   L   R   R   L   L   R   R   L   L   R   R   L   L

STAR   *CW*

FWD	FWD (2)	FWD (3)	FWD (4)	FWD	FWD (2)	FWD (3)	FWD (4)
R	L	R	L	R	L	R	L

REPEAT PART IV

Beat 1-8   Skip 8 times counterclockwise in circle of 4 persons, hands on hips

9-16   Walk 8 steps clockwise using R hand Star

17-32   Repeat Part IV, beats 1-16

LEAD-UP ACTIVITIES   Practice the STEP HOP (individual tempo) swinging the free leg IN on the HOP.

Practice running, kicking the feet UP behind (individual tempo).

Practice R and L elbow turns and DO-SA-DO patterns with a partner (partner beat).

TEACHING SUGGESTIONS   Practice Part I with SAY & DO—leave out the CLAP and SNAP while learning.

Practice Part II with SAY & DO, then add the CLAP.

Practice Parts I and II in the dance formation and add music.

Practice Parts III and IV in the dance formation.

SAY & DO the entire dance and add the music.

CHAIR DANCING   Do in place.

May be adapted for wheelchairs.

Bekendorfer Quadrille
Germany

RECORD *Rhythmically Moving 4*

INTRODUCTION 8 beats

FORMATION Square sets

PART I *CW*

FWD	HOP	FWD	HOP	FWD	HOP	FWD	HOP
R	R	L	L	R	R	L	L

2X CW   2X CCW

Beat 1-16 Step Hop 8 times forward clockwise, beginning R foot (hands joined in circle)

17-32 Step Hop 8 times forward counterclockwise, beginning R foot (hands joined in circle)

CHORUS

IN		IN		IN		CLAP	CLAP
R		L		R		B	B

OUT	HOP	OUT	HOP	OUT	HOP	OUT	HOP
R	R	L	L	R	R	L	L

REPEAT CHORUS BEATS 1-16

Beat 1-6 Heads move toward each other with 3 slow steps

7-8 Clap own hands twice

9-16 Heads move back to place with 4 Step Hops

17-32 Sides repeat Chorus, beats 1-16

IN	IN (2)	IN (3)	HOP	FWD	FWD (2)	FWD (3)	HOP
R	L	R	R	L	R	L	L

FWD	FWD (2)	FWD (3)	HOP	OUT	OUT (2)	OUT (3)	HOP
R	L	R	R	L	R	L	L

REPEAT CHORUS BEATS 33-48

33-36   Heads Schottische diagonally left

37-40   Heads Schottische diagonally right, passing back to back with opposite couple

41-44   Heads Schottische diagonally left, passing face to face with opposite couple

45-48   Heads Schottische out to place

49-64   Sides repeat Schottische figure, beats 33-48

GRAND R & L

FWD	HOP	FWD	HOP	FWD	HOP	FWD	HOP
R	R	L	L	R	R	L	L

4X

65-96   All Step Hop 16 times in a Grand Right and Left

PART II STAR   *CW*

FWD	HOP	FWD	HOP	FWD	HOP	FWD	HOP
R	R	L	L	R	R	L	L

2X CW   2X CCW

Beat 1-16   Step Hop 8 times forward clockwise (partners R hand star)

17-32   Step Hop 8 times backward counterclockwise

CHORUS   Repeat Chorus, beats 1-96

PART III PARTNERS

TURN	HOP	TURN	HOP	TURN	HOP	TURN	HOP
R	R	L	L	R	R	L	L

2X CW   2X CCW

Beat 1-16	Step Hop 8 times forward clockwise, partners join hands, R hips adjacent
17-32	Step Hop 8 times forward counterclockwise (L hips adjacent)
CHORUS	Repeat beats 1-96 of Chorus
PART I	Repeat Part I, beats 1-32
LEAD-UP ACTIVITIES	Practice STEP HOP in all directions (individual tempo). Practice SCHOTTISCHE in all directions (individual tempo). Practice Grand Right and Left using a WALK.
TEACHING SUGGESTIONS	Learn the parts of the dance in a full circle of partners so the floor pattern of the partner movements and the floor pattern of the Chorus can be made clear. Form square sets and work on the Chorus. Walk through the sequence before adding the SCHOTTISCHE. Do the Grand Right and Left by walking through the pattern before adding the STEP HOP.
CHAIR DANCING	Do the same steps in place. Move the feet away from and toward the chair on the Chorus.
NOTE	No R foot and L foot is necessary.

Carnavalito

Bolivia

RECORD *Rhythmically Moving 5*

INTRODUCTION 16 beats

FORMATION Broken circle, hands joined in "V" position

PART I *CCW*

FWD	FWD (2)	FWD (3)	HOP	FWD	FWD (2)	FWD (3)	HOP
R	L	R	R	L	R	L	L

4X

Beat 1-4 Schottische R foot forward counterclockwise (body bent over)

5-8 Schottische L foot forward counterclockwise (body straightens)

9-64 Repeat Part I, beats 1-8, seven more times

PART II *CCW*

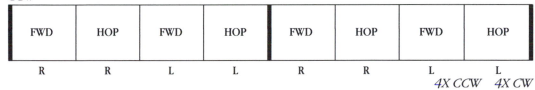

FWD	HOP	FWD	HOP	FWD	HOP	FWD	HOP
R	R	L	L	R	R	L	L

4X CCW   4X CW

Beat 1-2 Step Hop R foot forward counterclockwise (swing arms in)

3-4 Step Hop L foot forward counterclockwise (swing arms out)

5-32 Repeat beats 1-4, seven more times

33-64 Repeat Part II, beats 1-32, forward clockwise 8 times

NOTE On third (last) sequence of the dance do 8 SCHOTTISCHES instead of 16.

LEAD-UP ACTIVITIES Practice walking in sets of 4 steps bending over during one set of 4 and straightening up during another set (individual tempo).

Practice the SCHOTTISCHE, adding the bending and straightening (individual tempo).

Practice the STEP HOP while swinging the arms FORWARD and BACKWARD (individual tempo).

TEACHING SUGGESTIONS

Practice the SCHOTTISCHE to the music, then STEP HOP to the music.

Practice the SCHOTTISCHE to the music, adding bending and straightening.

Practice the STEP HOP, swinging arms IN on the STEP HOP with the R foot and OUT on the STEP HOP with the L foot (SAY & DO).

Put the dance sequence together with SAY & DO, then add music.

CHAIR DANCING

Do as described, executing steps in place.

KICK legs on the diagonal.

Ersko Kolo

Yugoslavia

RECORD	*Rhythmically Moving 4*
INTRODUCTION	8 beats
FORMATION	Broken circle, hands joined in "V" position—face center

PART I   *CCW*

SIDE	BACK	SIDE	BACK	SIDE	BACK	SIDE	BACK
R	L	R	L	R	L	R	L

3X

SIDE	BACK	SIDE	BACK	SIDE		STAMP	
R	L	R	L	R		L	

REPEAT PART I   OPP. FTWK. OPP. DIR.

Beat 1	Extend R heel diagonally sideward with weight on it
2	Step L foot crossing in back of R foot
3-28	Repeat beats 1-2 sideward right 13 more times
29-30	Accent R foot sideward right
31-32	Stamp L foot
33-64	Repeat Part I, beats 1-32, moving sideward left beginning L foot

PART II   *CCW*

FWD	FWD (2)	FWD (3)	HOP	BWD	BWD (2)	BWD (3)	HOP
R	L	R	R	L	R	L	L

IN	IN (2)	IN (3)	HOP	OUT	OUT (2)	OUT (3)	HOP
R	L	R	R	L	R	L	L

REPEAT PART II

Beat 1-4	Schottische forward counterclockwise beginning R foot
5-8	Schottische backward (facing counterclockwise) beginning L foot
9-12	Schottische in to center of circle beginning R foot
13-16	Schottische out from center of circle
17-32	Repeat Part II, beats 1-16

TO SIMPLIFY   Substitute 4 walking steps for each SCHOTTISCHE.

LEAD-UP ACTIVITIES   Practice bringing the heel IN and putting weight on it, then STEP, crossing in back with the opposite foot (individual tempo).

Practice SCHOTTISCHE FORWARD and BACKWARD (individual tempo).

TEACHING SUGGESTIONS   Practice SIDE, BACK in each direction with SAY & DO.

Practice the transitions (beats 29-32 and 60-64).

Practice Part II with SAY & DO.

Put the parts together and add the music.

CHAIR DANCING
PART I   Do in place, bringing heel IN.

Substitute side to side SCHOTTISCHE for FORWARD and BACKWARD.

Fado Blanquita

Brazil-Portugal

RECORD	*Rhythmically Moving 7*
INTRODUCTION	8 beats
FORMATION	Partners in single circle, hands joined

PART I   *CW*

FWD	HOP	FWD	HOP	FWD	HOP	FWD	HOP
R	R	L	L	R	R	L	L

2X CW 2X CCW

Beat 1-2   Step Hop forward clockwise beginning R foot

3-16   Step Hop forward clockwise 7 more times

17-32   Repeat beats 1-16 forward counterclockwise

BRIDGE

SIDE		SIDE		SIDE		SIDE	
R		L		R		L	

Beat 1-2   Sway right

3-8   Repeat sway (left, right, left)—called a Vamp—partners face each other and join R hands (straighten arms)

PART II   *CW*

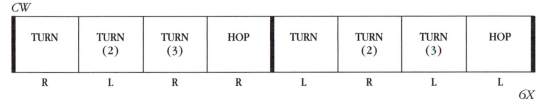

TURN	TURN (2)	TURN (3)	HOP	TURN	TURN (2)	TURN (3)	HOP
R	L	R	R	L	R	L	L

6X

Beat 1-12   Schottische 3 times travelling clockwise in top half of a figure 8 beginning R, L, R foot

13-24   Schottische 3 times holding L hands with corner (travelling counterclockwise in bottom half of figure 8)

25-48   Repeat Part II, beats 1-24, with same two people

BRIDGE

SIDE		SIDE		SIDE		SIDE	
R		L		R		L	

Beat 1-8   Sway right, left, right, left facing center

PART III

JUMP	KICK	JUMP	KICK	JUMP	JUMP (½ TURN)		
B	(R)	B	(L)	B	B		

REPEAT

IN		IN		IN		SWING	
R		L		R		(L)	

OUT		OUT		OUT		TOUCH	
L		R		L		(R)	

REPEAT PART III

Beat 1   Jump

2   Hop R foot kicking L foot in toward center

3   Jump

4   Hop L foot kicking R foot in

5   Jump

6   Jump turning ½ to right

7-8   Rest

9-16   Repeat Part III, beats 1-8, facing away from center

17-22   Step R, L, R foot toward center

23-24   Extend L foot toward center

25-30   Step L, R, L foot away from center

31-32   Touch R foot away from center

33-64   Repeat Part III, beats 1-32

LEAD-UP ACTIVITIES

Practice STEP HOP (individual tempo).

Practice SCHOTTISCHE (individual tempo).

Practice JUMP, KICK alternating feet (individual tempo).

Practice IN, 2, 3, KICK; OUT, 2, 3, TOUCH (individual tempo).

TEACHING SUGGESTIONS

Practice Part I with SAY & DO and add the music.

Face your partners and identify your corners—corners should now be back to back with you. Take partner's hand and WALK the top half of the figure 8 then L hand to corner and WALK the bottom half. Change to SCHOTTISCHE steps with SAY & DO.

SAY & DO Parts I and II, including the Bridge and add the music.

Practice Part III with SAY & DO.

Do the entire dance to the music.

CHAIR DANCING

PARTS I and II   Do in place.

PART III   Do without the TURN.

Dance may be executed in wheelchairs.

Frunza
Romania

RECORD	*Rhythmically Moving 6*
INTRODUCTION	8 beats
FORMATION	Circle, hands joined

PART I   *CCW*

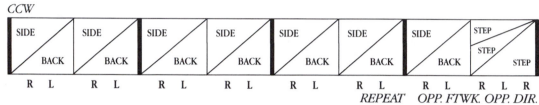

Beat 1	Step R foot slightly sideward right
&	Step L foot crossing in back of R foot
2-7	Repeat beat 1 &, six more times
8	Step R, L, R foot in place on the single beat
9-16	Repeat Part I, beats 1-8, sideward left clockwise beginning L foot

PART II

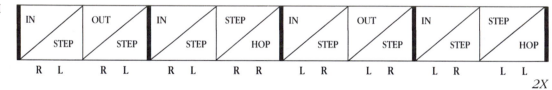

Beat 1-2	Cherkessiya, beginning R foot facing center
3	Step R foot in
&	Step L foot out
4	Step R foot next to L foot
&	Hop R
5-8	Repeat beats 1-4 beginning L foot
9-16	Repeat Part II, beats 1-8

LEAD-UP ACTIVITIES	Practice SIDE/BACK in each direction (individual tempo).
	Practice SCHOTTISCHE in place, alternating feet (individual tempo).
	Practice CHERKESSIYA (individual tempo).
	Practice ACCENT, 2, 3, 4; ACCENT, 2, 3, HOP in place, alternating feet, then change to CHERKESSIYA; SCHOTTISCHE (individual tempo).
TEACHING SUGGESTIONS	Practice SIDE/BACK with SAY & DO.
	Do Part I using the hands in an alternating thigh PAT to practice the sequence and the transition rhythmically. Substitute the feet (SAY & DO).
	Practice Part II with SAY & DO (CHERKESSIYA; IN, STEP, STEP, HOP).
	SAY & DO the entire dance and then add music.
CHAIR DANCING	
PART I	Substitute small steps almost in place.
PART II	Do as in the dance.

Ken Yovdu

Thus Shall They Perish
Israel

RECORD	*Rhythmically Moving 8*
INTRODUCTION	8 beats
FORMATION	Short lines, hands held

PART I *CCW*

SIDE	CLOSE	SIDE		BRUSH	HOP	CLOSE	
R	L	R		(L)	R	L	

SIDE	CLOSE	SIDE		JUMP	HOP	STAMP	
R	L	R		B	L	(R)	

REPEAT PART I

Beat 1	Step R foot sideward right
2	Step L foot next to R foot
3-4	Step R foot sideward right; rest on beat 4
5	Brush L foot forward, accenting heel
6	Hop R foot bringing L knee up
7-8	Step L foot next to R foot with slight accent
9-12	Repeat beats 1-4
13	Jump while turning lower body diagonally left
14	Hop L foot while bringing R knee up (face center)
15-16	Lower R leg with stamp
17-32	Repeat Part I, beats 1-16

PART II   *CCW*

IN	IN (2)	IN (3)	HOP	FWD	FWD (2)	FWD (3)	HOP
R	L	R	R	L	R	L	L

OUT	OUT (2)	OUT (3)	HOP
R	L	R	R

PART II 4X   OPP. FTWK.

Beat 1-4	Schottische in beginning R foot (raise arms)
5-8	Schottische 90° right beginning L foot (line is one behind the other, L hand brought to the shoulder)
9-12	Schottische back to starting point beginning R foot (arms lowered)
13-48	Repeat beats 1-12 (three Schottische sequences) 3 more times

LEAD-UP ACTIVITIES

Practice SCHOTTISCHE, turning in different directions as the HOP is executed (individual tempo).

Practice SIDE, CLOSE, SIDE, REST (individual tempo).

TEACHING SUGGESTIONS

Practice SIDE, CLOSE, SIDE, REST; BRUSH, HOP, CLOSE, REST beginning R foot (individual tempo, then group SAY & DO).

Practice JUMP, HOP, STAMP, REST (individual tempo) and add to SIDE, CLOSE, SIDE, REST beginning R foot (SAY & DO).

Practice Part I with SAY & DO, alternating BRUSH, HOP and JUMP, HOP.

Practice Part II in the correct directions (individual tempo) and then add SAY & DO.

Do the entire dance with SAY & DO and then add the music.

CHAIR DANCING

PART I   Do in place.

PART II   SCHOTTISCHE away from chair, SCHOTTISCHE in place, SCHOTTISCHE back toward the chair.

Korobushka

Peddler's Pack
Russia

RECORD	*Rhythmically Moving 8*
INTRODUCTION	16 beats
FORMATION	Double circle, partners facing each other, man on inside, hands held
ALTERNATE FORMATION	Double line

PART I

OUT*	OUT (2)	OUT (3)	HOP	IN	IN (2)	IN (3)	HOP
L	R	L	L:	R	L	R	R

OUT	OUT (2)	OUT (3)	HOP	TOUCH	APART	TOG	
L	R	L	L	(R)	B	B	

Beat 1-4	Schottische away from center of circle; men begin L foot moving out, women R foot moving out
5-8	Schottische toward center of circle (men R foot moving in, women L foot moving in)
9-12	Repeat beats 1-4
13	Jump (men touching R foot in front of L foot, women touching L foot in front of R foot)
14	Jump feet slightly apart and toes in
15	Jump feet together; men click heels
16	Rest and release hands

PART II

SIDE	BACK	SIDE	HOP	SIDE	BACK	SIDE	HOP
R	L	R	R	L	R	L	L

TOWARD	HOP	AWAY	HOP	TURN	TURN (2)	TURN (3)	TURN (4)
R	R	L	L	R	L	R	L

REPEAT PART II

Beat 1-4	Schottische R foot sideward right (arms are spread diagonally overhead)
5-8	Schottische L foot sideward left
9-10	Step Hop R foot toward partner (R hands held)
11-12	Step Hop L foot away from partner
13-16	Step R, L, R, L foot while changing places with partners
17-32	Repeat Part II, returning to own starting position on beats 29-32
NOTE	Man takes only 3 steps on beats 29-32, resting on beat 32.

LEAD-UP ACTIVITIES   Practice SCHOTTISCHE forward and backward (individual tempo). Practice SCHOTTISCHE with a partner—one moves forward, one backward (partner beat). Practice SCHOTTISCHE side to side (individual tempo).

Practice STEP HOP—forward and backward (individual tempo). Practice STEP HOP with partner—toward and away from partner (partner beat).

TEACHING SUGGESTIONS   Position the students in a double circle with partners facing or a double line with partners facing. Have the students who are facing out do 3 SCHOTTISCHES of Part I moving OUT, IN, OUT with SAY & DO beginning L foot. Then have the students facing in do 3 SCHOTTISCHES OUT, IN, OUT with SAY & DO beginning R foot.

Have the partners do 3 SCHOTTISCHES together with SAY & DO (no handholds). Repeat with hands held, then add on the TOUCH, APART, TOGETHER, REST.

Practice the side-to-side SCHOTTISCHE with a partner using SAY & DO beginning R foot. Add on the 2 STEP HOPS, then add on the 4 steps to change places.

SAY & DO all of Part II. Practice the transition from Part II to Part I, noting the 3 steps instead of 4 steps for the inside person going into the SCHOTTISCHE.

SAY & DO the entire dance and add the music.

CHAIR DANCING   Do as described while facing another person, substitute in-place steps.

Footwork for men; women use opposite footwork.

Kuma Echa

Come Brother, Let's Dance
Israel

RECORD	*Rhythmically Moving 7*
INTRODUCTION	8 beats
FORMATION	Circle facing center, hands joined

PART I

IN	IN (2)	IN (3)	HOP	OUT	OUT (2)	OUT (3)	HOP
R	L	R	R	L	R	L	L

CW

CROSS	SIDE	BACK	SIDE	CROSS	SIDE	BACK	SIDE
R	L	R	L	R	L	R	L

REPEAT PART I

Beat 1-4	Schottische R foot toward center (raise arms)
5-8	Schottische L foot away from center (lower arms)
9-16	Grapevine 2 times moving sideward clockwise
17-32	Repeat Part I, beats 1-16

PART II   *CCW*

FWD	FWD	BWD	BWD	FWD	FWD	BWD	BWD
R	L	R	L	R	L	R	L

REPEAT PART II

Beat 1-2	Run R foot, L foot forward counterclockwise
3-4	Run R foot, L foot backward counterclockwise
5-16	Repeat Part II, beats 1-4, three more times
NOTE	Add a leap onto R foot on beat 3 and raise joined hands overhead.

PART III

IN	IN (2)	IN (3)	IN (4)	IN	OUT	OUT	OUT
R	L	R	L	R	L	R	L

IN	OUT	OUT	OUT	IN	OUT	OUT	OUT
R	L	R	L	R	L	R	L

Beat 1-4	Run R, L, R, L foot toward center
5	Step R foot in with accent (thrust arms in)
6-8	Step L, R, L foot out while lowering arms
9-16	Repeat beats 5-8 two more times

LEAD-UP ACTIVITIES

Practice SCHOTTISCHES moving IN and OUT (individual tempo).

Practice GRAPEVINES moving clockwise (individual tempo).

Practice a running step turning to move FORWARD and BACKWARD every 2 steps (individual tempo).

Practice a sequence of IN, OUT, OUT, OUT (individual tempo).

TEACHING SUGGESTIONS

Practice SCHOTTISCHE IN, SCHOTTISCHE OUT with SAY & DO beginning R foot. Add on 2 GRAPEVINES moving clockwise—practice the transition from the SCHOTTISCHE to the GRAPEVINE—use individual tempo before SAY & DO.

Practice Part II with SAY & DO first as FORWARD running steps then change to the FORWARD, BACKWARD combination (individual tempo, then SAY & DO).

Practice Part III with SAY & DO. Practice the transitions. SAY & DO the entire dance and add the music.

CHAIR DANCING

PART I Do SCHOTTISCHES away from and toward the chair. Substitute CHERKESSIYA for GRAPEVINE.

PART II Do steps in place.

PART III Do steps away from and toward the chair.

Road to the Isles

Scotland

RECORD *Rhythmically Moving 5*

INTRODUCTION 10 beats

FORMATION Couples in Varsovienne position

PART I

TOUCH	BACK / SIDE	CROSS	TOUCH	BACK / SIDE	CROSS	TOUCH	TOUCH
(L)	L R	L	(R)	R L	R	(L)	(L)

Beat 1	Extend L heel diagonally left (women touch toe)
2	Step L foot crossing in back of R foot
&	Step R foot sideward right
3	Step L foot crossing in front of R foot
4	Extend R heel diagonally right (women touch toe)
5	Step R foot crossing in back of L foot
&	Step L foot sideward left
6	Step R foot crossing in front of L foot
7	Extend L heel diagonally left (women touch toe)
8	Extend L toe behind

PART II

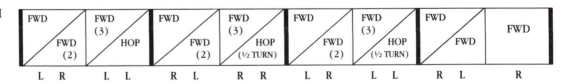

FWD / FWD (2)	FWD (3) / HOP	FWD / FWD (2)	FWD (3) / HOP (½ TURN)	FWD / FWD (2)	FWD (3) / HOP (½ TURN)	FWD / FWD	FWD
L R	L L	R L	R R	L R	L L	R L	R

Beat 1-2	Schottische forward beginning L foot (couples moving side by side)
3-4	Schottische forward beginning R foot; on beat 4 turn ½ to right (clockwise), both turning in the same direction
5-6	Schottische forward beginning L foot; on beat 4 turn ½ to left (counterclockwise)
7-8	Step R, L, R foot

LEAD-UP ACTIVITIES Practice BACK/SIDE, CROSS (individual tempo).

Practice SCHOTTISCHE (individual tempo), then add ½ TURN on the HOP.

TEACHING SUGGESTIONS

Teach without partners until the dance is familiar.

Practice TOUCH, BACK/SIDE; CROSS, TOUCH (SAY & DO) beginning L foot.

Add on BACK/SIDE, CROSS; TOUCH, TOUCH beginning R foot (SAY & DO).

Do Part I with SAY & DO and then with the music.

Practice the SCHOTTISCHES with the ½ TURN and add on the 3 final steps (individual tempo, then SAY & DO).

Do the entire dance with SAY & DO and add the music.

CHAIR DANCING

Do SCHOTTISCHES in place, omitting the ½ TURN.

Salty Dog Rag

U.S.A.

RECORD   *Rhythmically Moving 9*

INTRODUCTION   8 beats

FORMATION   Partners in double circle facing counterclockwise; skater's hold

ALTERNATE
FORMATION   Circle (no partners)

PART I

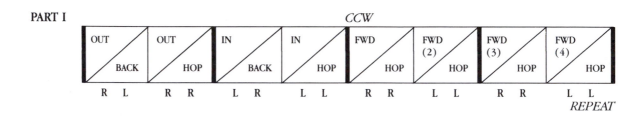

Beat 1-2   Schottische sideward right (OUT) beginning R foot

3-4   Schottische sideward left (IN) beginning L foot

5-8   Step Hop, R, L, R, L foot forward counterclockwise

9-16   Repeat Part I, beats 1-8, and turn to face partner (keep L hands held)

CHORUS

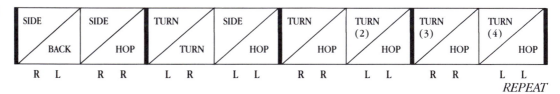

Beat 1-2   Schottische sideward right beginning R foot (facing partner)

3-4   Schottische with full turn left beginning L foot (release handhold)

5-8   Step Hop R, L, R, L foot turning clockwise with partner one full turn (R forearms together)

9-16   Repeat Chorus, beats 1-8

TO SIMPLIFY   Do SCHOTTISCHE beginning L foot without the TURN.

PART II

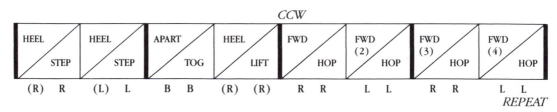

Beat 1	Extend R heel forward
&	Step R foot next to L foot
2	Extend L heel forward
&	Step L foot next to R foot
3	Turn heels out (weight on both feet)
&	Bring heels in
4	Extend R heel forward
&	Raise R foot in front of L foot
5-8	Step Hop R, L, R, L foot forward (counterclockwise)
9-16	Repeat Part II, beats 1-8

CHORUS

Beat 1-16	Repeat Chorus, beats 1-16
	Alternate Part I, Chorus, Part II, Chorus

TO SIMPLIFY   Do Part I and Chorus, omit Part II.

CIRCLE DANCE   Do Parts I and II as described. Face IN on the Chorus and TURN individually.

LEAD-UP ACTIVITIES   Practice SCHOTTISCHE side to side and SCHOTTISCHE TURN (individual tempo).

Practice STEP HOP forward (individual tempo).

TEACHING SUGGESTIONS   Teach Part I in a circle without partners. Put the sequence together with SAY & DO.

Do Part I with the music.

Teach Part II with SAY & DO.

Have students do both parts with a partner (partner beat).

Practice the Chorus leaving out the TURN on the second SCHOTTISCHE (move SIDEWARD right then SIDEWARD left). Use partner beat and then SAY & DO.

Practice the transitions into the Chorus and back to the verse.

Do the entire dance with SAY & DO and then add the music.

CHAIR DANCING   Do the STEP HOPS in place.

Savila Se Bela Loza

A Vine Entwined Itself
Yugoslavia

RECORD	*Rhythmically Moving 6*
INTRODUCTION	8 beats
FORMATION	Broken circle or line, hands joined in "V" position

PART I   *CCW*

FWD	FWD (2)	FWD (3)	FWD (4)	FWD	FWD (2)	FWD (3)	FWD (4)
R	L	R	L	R	L	R	L

2X

FWD	FWD	STEP	HOP (½ TURN)
R	L	R	R

REPEAT PART I   OPP. FTWK. OPP. DIR.

Beat 1-18	Run 18 steps forward right beginning R foot (feet are kicked up behind)
19-20	Step Hop R foot and turn to face left
21-40	Repeat Part I, beats 1-20, beginning L foot and end with a Step Hop L foot; face center

PART II   *CCW*

SIDE	BACK	SIDE	HOP	SIDE	BACK	SIDE	HOP
R	L	R	R	L	R	L	L

3X

Beat 1-4	Schottische sideward right beginning R foot (small steps and no swing of free leg)
5-8	Schottische sideward left beginning L foot
9-24	Repeat Part II, beats 1-8, two more times
NOTE	Kolo steps may be substituted for SCHOTTISCHE steps. Insert a HOP before the SCHOTTISCHE.
LEAD-UP ACTIVITIES	Practice side-to-side SCHOTTISCHE (individual tempo).
	Practice running a designated number of steps then following the RUN with a STEP HOP (individual tempo).

TEACHING
SUGGESTIONS

Identify the underlying beat and do Part I with the music.

Practice the 6 SIDEWARD SCHOTTISCHE steps with SAY & DO.

Do the entire dance with the music.

CHAIR
DANCING
PART I   Do steps in place.

Šetnja

Walking
Yugoslavia

RECORD	*Rhythmically Moving 9*
INTRODUCTION	8 beats
FORMATION	Line, leader at right; escort hold (L hand on hip, R hand takes elbow of person ahead)

PART I   *CCW*

FWD		FWD		FWD	FWD	FWD	
R		L		R	L	R	

OUT		OUT		OUT	SIDE	CROSS	
L		R		L	R	L	

Beat 1-2	Step R foot forward and rest on beat 2
3-4	Step L foot forward and rest on beat 4
5-6	Step R foot, L foot forward
7-8	Step R foot forward then turn to face center so dancers are side by side
9-10	Step L foot out and rest on beat 10
11-12	Step R foot out and rest on beat 12
13	Step L foot out
14	Step R foot sideward right
15-16	Step L foot crossing in front of R foot and rest on beat 16

Continue Part I until music accelerates, then drop arms to "V" position.

STYLE NOTE   The resting beats may be changed to bounces and the steps OUT changed to REEL steps (one foot behind the other).

PART II   *CCW*

FWD	HOP	FWD	HOP	FWD	FWD	FWD	HOP
R	R	L	L	R	L	R	R

OUT	HOP	OUT	HOP	OUT	SIDE	CROSS	HOP
L	L	R	R	L	R	L	L

Beat 1-4   Step Hop R foot, L foot forward

5-8   Schottische beginning R foot

9-12   Step Hop L foot, R foot out

13-16   Schottische beginning L foot (out, side, cross, hop)

NOTE   Repeat Part II to end of music.

LEAD-UP   Practice walking slowly in a rhythmic pattern of 1, 2, 3 &, 4 (individual tempo).
ACTIVITIES
Practice STEP HOPS (individual tempo).

Practice SCHOTTISCHES (individual tempo).

Practice a combination of 2 STEP HOPS and 1 SCHOTTISCHE (individual tempo).

TEACHING   Practice Part I with SAY & DO and then add the music.
SUGGESTIONS
Practice STEP HOP, STEP HOP; SCHOTTISCHE pattern with SAY & DO.

Practice OUT, HOP, OUT, HOP; OUT, SIDE, CROSS, HOP beginning L foot (individual tempo, then SAY & DO).

CHAIR   Do steps in place, moving away from and toward the chair.
DANCING

Uneven Dance Steps

Characteristic:

Movements in the sequence use a resting beat or combine divided beats with single beats.

Bechatzar Harabbi

Israel

RECORD	*Rhythmically Moving 6*
INTRODUCTION	8 beats
FORMATION	Free formation

PART I

SIDE	BACK	SIDE	CLAP	SIDE	BACK	SIDE	CLAP
R	L	R		L	R	L	

TURN	CLOSE	TURN	CLOSE	TURN	CLOSE	TURN	CLOSE
R	L	R	L	R	L	R	L

REPEAT PART I

Beat 1   Step R foot sideward right

2   Step L foot crossing in back of R foot

3   Step R foot sideward right

4   Clap over R shoulder

5-8   Repeat beats 1-4 to left beginning L foot

9   Step R foot on ball of foot while reaching overhead with arms

10   Step L foot next to R foot, bending knee slightly, bringing arms down

11-16   Repeat beats 9-10 three more times while turning full circle right

17-32   Repeat Part I, beats 1-16

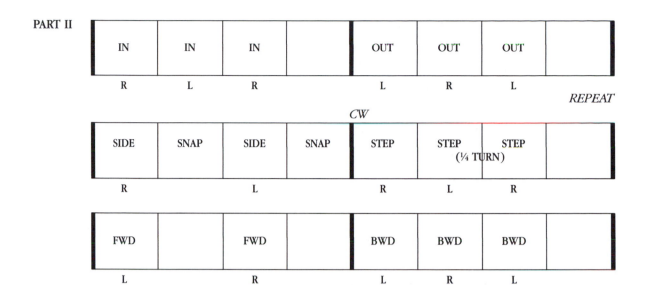

PART II	IN	IN	IN		OUT	OUT	OUT	
	R	L	R		L	R	L	

REPEAT

CW

SIDE	SNAP	SIDE	SNAP	STEP	STEP (¼ TURN)	STEP	
R		L		R	L	R	

FWD		FWD		BWD	BWD	BWD	
L		R		L	R	L	

Beat 1-3 Step R, L, R foot in (toward facing direction)

4 Rest

5-7 Step L, R, L foot out

8 Rest

9-16 Repeat beats 1-8

17-18 Step R foot sideward right, snap fingers on beat 18

19-20 Step L foot sideward left, snap fingers on beat 20

21-23 Step R, L, R foot turning ¼ turn right

24 Rest

25-26 Step L foot forward, rest on beat 26

27-28 Step R foot forward, rest on beat 28

29-31 Step L, R, L foot backward

32 Rest

NOTE Each repeat of the dance begins facing new direction.

LEAD-UP ACTIVITIES Move in a SIDE, BACK, pattern (individual tempo).

Move IN and OUT in a pattern of WALK, 2, 3, REST (individual tempo).

WALK in a rhythmic sequence of WALK, REST, WALK, REST; WALK, WALK, WALK, REST (individual tempo).

Do a slow BUZZ TURN to the right (individual tempo).

TEACHING SUGGESTIONS	Practice SIDE, BACK, SIDE, CLAP in both directions (SAY & DO).

Do 2 patterns of SIDE, BACK, SIDE, CLAP, beginning R foot and add on one slow BUZZ TURN (8 beats). (Do not use arms in BUZZ TURN.)

Practice Part I (SAY & DO).

Do IN, 2, 3, REST; OUT, 2, 3, REST, twice. Add on 2 sequences of SIDE, SNAP, to the IN, OUT pattern (individual tempo).

Do 2 patterns of SIDE, SNAP beginning R foot and add on 3 steps and a hold while turning ¼ right.

Do FORWARD, REST, FORWARD, REST; BACKWARD, 2, 3, REST.

SAY & DO Part II. Practice the transition from Part II to Part I.

SAY & DO entire dance and then add the music.

CHAIR DANCING	Substitute SIDE, CLOSE for SIDE, BACK.

Omit TURNS and STEP in place.

Hora Agadati

Israel

RECORD   *Rhythmically Moving 8*

INTRODUCTION   8 beats

FORMATION   Single circle facing counterclockwise, hands joined

PART I   *CCW*

FWD	FWD (2)	FWD (3)	FWD (4)	JUMP	JUMP	JUMP	JUMP
R	L	R	L	B	B	B	B

4X

Beat 1-4   Run R, L, R, L foot forward counterclockwise

      5   Jump with both knees angled left

      6   Jump (knees straight)

    7-8   Repeat beats 5-6

   9-32   Repeat beats 1-8 three more times and turn to face center

PART II

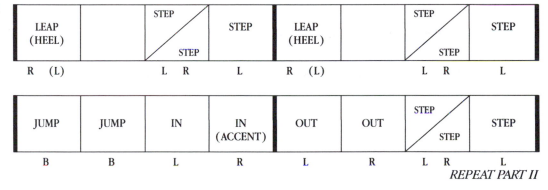

LEAP (HEEL)		STEP / STEP	STEP	LEAP (HEEL)		STEP / STEP	STEP
R (L)		L R	L	R (L)		L R	L

JUMP	JUMP	IN	IN (ACCENT)	OUT	OUT	STEP / STEP	STEP
B	B	L	R	L	R	L R	L

REPEAT PART II

Beat 1	Leap on R foot and extend L heel diagonally left in
2	Rest
3-4	Step L, R, L foot in place (3 &, 4)
5-8	Repeat beats 1-4
9-10	Jump 2 times (knees angled left then straight)
11	Step L foot toward center
12	Step R foot in with accent
13	Step L foot away from center
14	Step R foot out
15-16	Step L, R, L foot in place
17-32	Repeat Part II, beats 1-16

LEAD-UP ACTIVITIES

Practice jumping, angling feet diagonally left and then straight (individual tempo).

Combine 4 RUNS with 4 JUMPS (individual tempo).

Practice LEAP, REST, STEP/STEP, STEP sequences in place (individual tempo).

Practice 2 JUMPS, 2 STEPS IN and 2 STEPS OUT (individual tempo).

TEACHING SUGGESTIONS

Practice Part I with SAY & DO. Practice HEEL, REST, STEP/STEP, STEP with SAY & DO.

Practice JUMP, JUMP, IN, IN, OUT, OUT (STEP L foot, R foot IN). Use SAY & DO then add on the final STEP/STEP, STEP.

SAY & DO Part II.

Practice the transitions, Part I to Part II then back to the beginning. Add the music.

CHAIR DANCING

Do as described except execute running steps in place.

Hora Bialik

Israel

RECORD   *Rhythmically Moving 9*

INTRODUCTION   8 beats

FORMATION   Circle facing center, hands joined

PART I   *CCW*

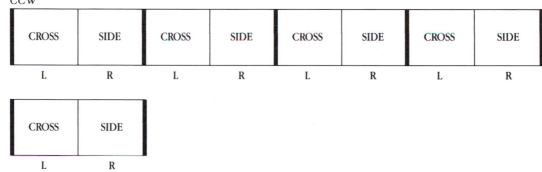

CROSS	SIDE	CROSS	SIDE	CROSS	SIDE	CROSS	SIDE
L	R	L	R	L	R	L	R

CROSS	SIDE
L	R

Beat 1   Step L foot crossing in front of R foot (arms down)

     2   Step R foot sideward right (arms up)

   3-10   Repeat Part I, beats 1-2, four more times

PART II   *CCW*

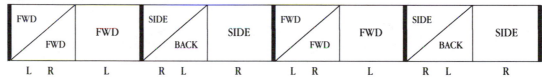

FWD	FWD	FWD	SIDE	SIDE	FWD	FWD	FWD	SIDE	SIDE
FWD			BACK		FWD			BACK	
L R	L	R L	R	L R	L	R L	R		

Beat 1-2   Step L, R, L foot forward counterclockwise and turn to face center

     3   Step R foot sideward right

     &   Step L foot crossing in back of R foot

     4   Step R foot sideward right and turn to face counterclockwise

   5-8   Repeat Part II, beats 1-4

TO SIMPLIFY   Continue to WALK FORWARD instead of SIDE, BACK, SIDE.

PART III

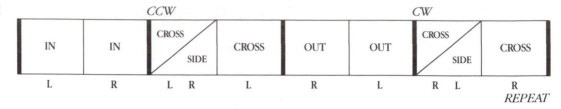

		CCW					CW		
IN	IN	CROSS / SIDE	CROSS	OUT	OUT	CROSS / SIDE	CROSS
L	R	L R	L	R	L	R L	R

REPEAT

Beat 1   Step L foot in toward center

2   Step R foot in

3   Step L foot crossing in front of R foot

&   Step R foot sideward right

4   Step L foot crossing in front of R foot

5   Step R foot out

6   Step L foot out

7   Step R foot crossing in front of L foot

&   Step L foot sideward left

8   Step R foot crossing in front of L foot

9-16   Repeat Part III, beats 1-8

TO SIMPLIFY   TURN body to face in the direction of steps, rather than using crossover steps.

LEAD-UP
ACTIVITIES   Practice CROSS, SIDE (individual tempo).

Practice a sequence of FORWARD, 2, 3, REST (individual tempo).

Practice walking in a pattern of STEP, REST, STEP, REST; STEP, STEP, STEP, REST (individual tempo).

Use the imagery of a "square" and have students WALK around different sized squares using different combinations of movement.

TEACHING
SUGGESTIONS   Practice CROSS, SIDE beginning L foot with SAY & DO. Practice FORWARD, FORWARD, FORWARD, REST around the circle with SAY & DO. Practice SIDE, BACK, SIDE, REST and combine with FORWARD, FORWARD, FORWARD, REST beginning L foot.

SAY & DO Parts I and II and then add the music if desired, omitting Part III.

Practice walking the "square" with IN, REST, IN, REST; CROSS, SIDE, CROSS, REST; OUT, REST, OUT, REST; CROSS, SIDE, CROSS, REST, using individual tempo first and then SAY & DO.

Practice the transitions from Part II to Part III and Part III to Part I.

SAY & DO the entire dance and then add the music.

**CHAIR
DANCING**

    PART I   Substitute L foot in front of R foot in place.

    PART II   STEP in place.

    PART III   Do as described.

Hora Pe Gheaţa

Circle Dance on the Ice
Romania

RECORD	*Rhythmically Moving 4*	
INTRODUCTION	8 beats	
FORMATION	Single circle, hands held in "W" position	

PART I *CCW*

FWD	FWD (2)	FWD (3)	FWD (4)	SIDE		SIDE	
R	L	R	L	R		L	

IN		OUT	OUT (2)	OUT (3)	OUT (4)	OUT	STAMP
R		L	R	L	R	L	(R)

Beat 1-4	Step R, L, R, L foot forward moving counterclockwise and turn to face center
5-6	Gliding step R foot sideward right, lift L leg "skate right"
7-8	Gliding step L foot sideward left, lift R leg "skate left"
9-10	Gliding step R foot toward center of circle, "skate in"
11-15	Step L, R, L, R, L foot out rotating the nonweight-bearing foot outward on each step
16	Stamp R foot

TO SIMPLIFY   Step L, R, L, R, L foot OUT.

PART II *CCW*

IN (DIAG)	IN	IN		OUT (DIAG)	OUT	OUT	
R	L	R		L	R	L	

REPEAT

Beat 1-4	Step R, L, R foot diagonally in right and rest on beat 4
5-8	Step L, R, L foot diagonally out right and rest on beat 8
9-16	Repeat beats 1-8

TO SIMPLIFY   Step R, L, R, L foot IN then OUT. Do not rest on beat 4 and beat 8.

LEAD-UP ACTIVITIES   Use the imagery of a clock and "skate" to various numerals. Each time return to the center of the clock. Use R foot for numerals 1-5, L foot for 7-11.

Move IN and OUT of the circle using 4 steps IN, 4 steps OUT or 3 steps and REST (individual tempo). Change activity to move IN and OUT on a diagonal.

TEACHING SUGGESTIONS   Do a SIDE, REST, SIDE, REST, IN, REST using the clock imagery moving to the numerals 3, 9, 12 beginning R foot (individual tempo, then SAY & DO).

Precede the SIDE, SIDE, IN pattern with 4 walking steps beginning R foot and add on OUT, 2, 3, 4, OUT, STAMP (individual tempo, then SAY & DO).

SAY & DO Part I.

SAY & DO Part II using either 4 steps IN and OUT if group needs the easier pattern or the authentic 3 STEPS and a REST.

Practice the transitions and then add the music.

CHAIR DANCING

PART I   Substitute steps in place for the 4 FORWARD steps.

PART II   Move away from and toward the chair.

Danish Sextur

Dance for Six Couples
Denmark

RECORD	*Rhythmically Moving 5*
INTRODUCTION	8 beats
FORMATION	Six couples in a single circle, numbered 1-6 clockwise around the circle

PART I *CW*

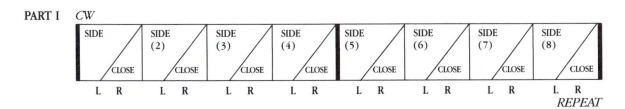

Beat 1-16   Slide 16 times clockwise around the circle (6 couples with hands held)

CHORUS

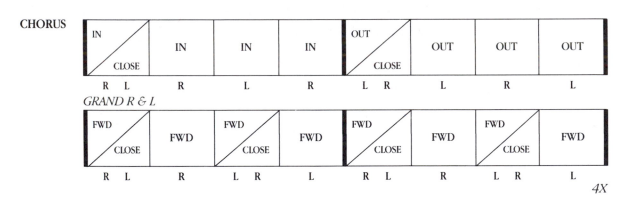

Beat 1-2	Two-Step in beginning R foot (couples 1 and 4)
3-4	Step L foot, R foot in
5-6	Two-Step out beginning L foot
7-8	Step R foot, L foot out
5-12	Couples 2 and 5 begin Chorus on beat 5 as couples 1 and 4 are starting out
9-16	Couples 3 and 6 begin Chorus on beat 9 as couples 2 and 5 are starting out
17-48	Grand right and left all the way around circle using 16 Two-Steps
TO SIMPLIFY	WALK 4 steps IN and 4 steps OUT and use a WALK in the Grand Right and Left.

PART II   *CW*

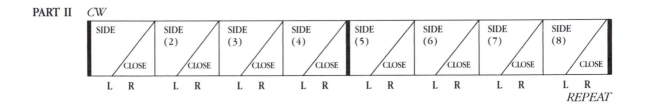

Beat 1-16   Women slide 16 times clockwise once around circle, join hands in center

CHORUS   Repeat Chorus, beats 1-48

PART III
(MEN)
SLIDE   *CW*

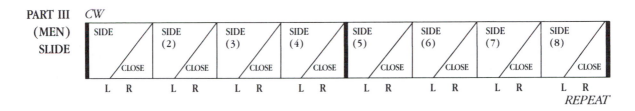

Beat 1-16   Men slide 16 times clockwise twice around circle, join hands in center

CHORUS   Repeat Chorus, beats 1-48

PART IV
(PARTNER)
BUZZ TURN

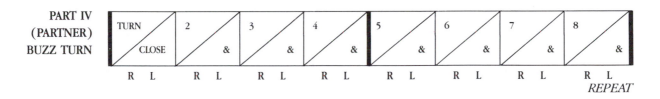

Beat 1-16   Partners buzz turn clockwise (shoulder-waist position)

CHORUS   Repeat Chorus, beats 1-48

PART V
SLIDE   *CW*

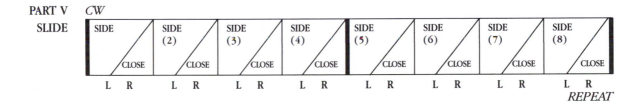

Beat 1-16   Repeat Part I, beats 1-16

LEAD-UP ACTIVITIES

Practice the SLIDE; add a circle formation (individual tempo).

Practice the Grand Right and Left (walk through).

Practice the TWO-STEP IN, OUT, FORWARD (individual tempo).

Practice a TWO-STEP plus 2 WALKS (IN and OUT).

TEACHING SUGGESTIONS

Practice each of the verses in sequence, using circles of 6 couples.

Practice the Chorus with a partner, TWO-STEP (IN) IN, IN; TWO-STEP (OUT), OUT, OUT.

Do the Chorus in circles of 6 couples and add the Grand Right and Left.

Do the entire dance with the music.

CHAIR DANCING

May be modified for wheelchairs.

Hashual

The Fox
Israel

RECORD   *Rhythmically Moving 6*

INTRODUCTION 8 beats

FORMATION   Open circle, no hands held

PART I   *CCW*

FWD	FWD	FWD (CLAP/CLAP)	FWD (CLAP)	FWD	FWD	FWD
R	L	R	L	R	L	R

CROSS	SIDE	BACK	SIDE	CROSS	SIDE	SIDE	BRUSH
L	R	L	R	L	R	L	(R)

REPEAT PART I

Beat 1-4   Step R, L, R, L foot forward counterclockwise, 3 claps with beats 3 & 4

5-7   Step R, L, R foot forward counterclockwise

8-11   Grapevine counterclockwise beginning L foot crossing in front of R foot

12   Step L foot crossing in front of R foot and turn to face center

13   Step R foot sideward right

14   Step L foot sideward left

15   Brush R foot in

16-29   Repeat Part I, beats 1-14 only (omit brush on beat 15)

PART II

IN / CLOSE	IN	IN / CLOSE	IN	IN / CLOSE	IN	IN / CLOSE	IN
R L	R	L R	L	R L	R	L R	L

ACCENT (CLAP)	OUT	OUT	OUT	OUT	OUT (2)	OUT (3)	OUT (4)
R	L	R	L	R	L	R	L

REPEAT PART II

Beat 1-2	Two-Step toward center beginning R foot (R arm in)
3-4	Two-Step in beginning L foot (L arm in)
5-8	Repeat beats 1-4
9	Accent R foot next to L foot (clap hands in front)
10-16	Step L, R, L, R, L, R, L foot out (arms make a circle overhead and down to sides)
17-32	Repeat Part II, beats 1-16

LEAD-UP ACTIVITIES

Practice GRAPEVINE (individual tempo).

Practice moving from walking steps to GRAPEVINES (individual tempo).

Practice quick TWO-STEPS (individual tempo).

TEACHING SUGGESTIONS

Practice CROSS, SIDE, SIDE, BRUSH, beginning L foot first with individual tempo, then with SAY & DO.

Precede CROSS, SIDE, SIDE, BRUSH with a GRAPEVINE, beginning L foot (individual tempo and then SAY & DO).

Precede GRAPEVINE; CROSS, SIDE, SIDE, BRUSH with 7 WALKS (individual tempo and then SAY & DO).

SAY & DO Part I (note the BRUSH is omitted on the repeat). Add the CLAPS later.

Practice 4 TWO-STEPS toward the center with SAY & DO.

Practice an accented step beginning R foot and 7 steps moving OUT backward with SAY & DO.

SAY & DO Part II.

Practice the entire dance with SAY & DO and then add the music.

CHAIR DANCING

Do as described, substituting steps in place for walking steps in Part I.

Hora Hassidit

Israel

RECORD *Rhythmically Moving 5*

INTRODUCTION 8 beats

FORMATION Single circle facing center, hands joined

PART I *CCW*

CROSS	SIDE	BACK	SIDE	CROSS	SIDE	SIDE	SIDE
L	R	L	R	L	R	L	R

CROSS	SIDE	BACK	SIDE	SIDE		SIDE	
L	R	L	R	L		R	

PART I 3X

Beat 1	Step L foot crossing in front of R foot
2	Step R foot sideward right
3	Step L foot crossing in back of R foot
4	Step R foot sideward right
5	Step L foot crossing in front of R foot
6	Step R foot sideward right
7-8	Step L foot, R foot sideward in a Camel Roll (describe small "c" with hips)
9-12	Repeat beats 1-4
13-14	Step L foot sideward left (reach up and to the left with the arms)
15-16	Step R foot sideward right (reach up and to the right with the arms)
17-48	Repeat Part I, beats 1-16, two more times

PART II *CCW*

FWD	FWD (2)	FWD (3)	FWD (4)	STEP / STEP	STEP	STEP / STEP	STEP
L	R	L	R	L R	L	R L	R

4X   OPP. DIR. OPP. FTWK.

IN	IN (2)	IN (3)	IN (4)	STEP / STEP	STEP	STEP / STEP	STEP
L	R	L	R	L R	L	R L	R

OUT	OUT (2)	OUT (3)	OUT (4)	STEP / STEP	STEP	STEP / STEP	STEP
L	R	L	R	L R	L	R L	R

Beat 1-4 Run L, R, L, R foot forward counterclockwise

5-8 Do 2 Two-Steps turning left to face clockwise, beginning L foot

9-12 Run L, R, L, R foot forward clockwise

13-16 Repeat beats 5-8, turning right to face counterclockwise

17-32 Repeat Part II, beats 1-16

33-36 Run L, R, L, R foot toward center

37-40 Do 2 Two-Steps in place; snap fingers on the beat (4 snaps)

41-44 Run L, R, L, R foot out

45-48 Repeat beats 37-40; snap fingers on the beat

LEAD-UP ACTIVITIES Practice GRAPEVINES (individual tempo).

Practice transferring weight side to side (individual tempo).

Practice TWO-STEPS in place turning 180° with each TWO-STEP (individual tempo).

TEACHING SUGGESTIONS Practice CROSS, SIDE; SIDE, SIDE (individual tempo); develop a sideward rolling action.

Practice the above, preceding it with, and adding on, a GRAPEVINE, beginning L foot.

Complete Part I with SIDE, REST; SIDE, REST, then SAY & DO the entire part.

Practice RUN, 2; 3, 4; STEP/STEP, STEP; STEP/STEP, STEP beginning L foot first with individual tempo and then with SAY & DO. Substitute the 180° turn during the 2 TWO-STEPS.

Practice Part II with SAY & DO.

Practice the transition from Part II to Part I and then add the music.

CHAIR DANCING Substitute steps in place where necessary.

Substitute CHERKESSIYA for GRAPEVINE.

Jambo

Hello
Africa (Ghana)

RECORD	*Rhythmically Moving 7*
INTRODUCTION	16 beats
FORMATION	2 circles, individuals facing one another, no handholds
ALTERNATE FORMATION	Circle

INTRODUCTION

LUNGE		NOD		NOD		NOD	

B

4X

Beat 1-2	Lunge diagonally right
3-4	Nod to person diagonally right in other circle
5-6	Nod to person opposite you
7-8	Nod to person diagonally right
9-32	Repeat beats 1-4, three more times, lunging left, right, left

PART I   *CCW**

SIDE		CLOSE		SIDE		CLOSE	
R		L		R		L	

SIDE		CLOSE		SIDE	CLOSE	SIDE	CLOSE
R		L		R	L	R	L

REPEAT PART I

Beat 1-2   Step R foot sideward right (arms raised sideward)

   3-4   Step L foot next to R foot

   5-12   Repeat Part I, beats 1-4, two more times

    13   Step R foot sideward right

    14   Step L foot next to R foot

    15   Step R foot sideward right

    16   Step L foot next to R foot

   17-32   Repeat Part I, beats 1-16

PART II

UP	TOUCH	UP	STEP	UP	TOUCH	UP	STEP
(R)	(R)	(R)	R	(L)	(L)	(L)	L

UP	TOUCH	UP	STEP	JUMP			
(R)	(R)	(R)	R	B			

REPEAT PART II   OPP. FTWK.

Beat 1   Raise R knee (throw head back)

   2   Touch R foot next to L foot

   3   Raise R knee (throw head back)

   4   Step R foot next to L foot

   5-12   Repeat beats 1-4, two more times beginning L foot, R foot

   13-16   Jump (L foot forward, R foot backward)

   17-32   Repeat Part II, beats 1-16, with opposite footwork

PART III

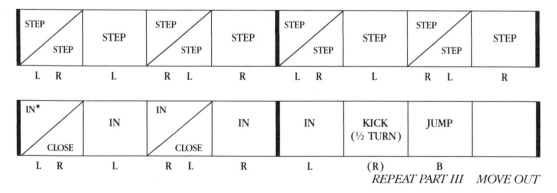

STEP / STEP	STEP	STEP / STEP	STEP	STEP / STEP	STEP	STEP / STEP	STEP
L R	L	R L	R	L R	L	R L	R

IN* / CLOSE	IN	IN / CLOSE	IN	IN	KICK (½ TURN)	JUMP	
L R	L	R L	R	L	(R)	B	

REPEAT PART III   MOVE OUT

Beat 1-2	Two-Step L foot in place, clap beat 2
3-8	Two-Step, R, L, R foot in place, clapping on beat 2 of each Two-Step
9-12	Two-Step L foot, R foot, moving through the other circle, clap beat 2 of each Two-Step
13	Step L foot
14	Kick R foot turning 180° left
15-16	Jump with feet apart
17-32	Repeat Part III, beats 1-16, returning to place

CIRCLE DANCE   Dance as the outside circle.

LEAD-UP ACTIVITIES   Practice SIDE, CLOSE in slow and quick tempo (individual tempo).

Practice UP, TOUCH, UP, STEP (individual tempo).

Practice TWO-STEPS in place and moving (individual tempo).

TEACHING SUGGESTIONS   Teach the dance first as a single circle dance.

Begin with Part I, leaving the Introduction until last. Have students practice 3 SIDE, CLOSE steps at a slow tempo followed by 2 SIDE, CLOSE steps at a quick tempo (SAY & DO).

SAY & DO Part II.

Teach the STEP, KICK, JUMP, REST so students understand the turning direction. Have students practice with individual tempo and then with group SAY & DO.

Precede the STEP, KICK, JUMP, REST with 2 TWO-STEPS IN beginning L foot and then precede with 4 TWO-STEPS in place beginning L foot. Have students practice this sequence moving IN then OUT—first use individual tempo and then SAY & DO.

Learn the Introduction and SAY & DO the entire dance and then add the music.

CHAIR DANCING   Do steps in place.

Omit the TURN, Part III.

Direction given for outer circle, inner circle uses opposite direction.

Makedonikos Horos

Greece (Macedonia)

RECORD	*Rhythmically Moving 9*
INTRODUCTION	8 beats
FORMATION	Open circle or lines, hands joined in "W" position

PART I *CCW*

FWD	FWD (2)	FWD (3)	FWD (4)	SIDE	LIFT	SIDE	LIFT
R	L	R	L	R	(L)	L	(R)

16X

Beat 1-4   Step R, L, R, L foot forward moving counterclockwise and turn to face center

5   Step R foot sideward right

6   Lift L foot in front of R leg

7   Step L foot sideward left

8   Lift R foot in front of L leg

NOTE   Music will change after 16 repetitions of Part I, then Part II should be started.

PART II

OUT	OUT	SIDE / CLOSE	SIDE	IN / CLOSE	IN
R	L	R L	R	L R	L

15X

Beat 1   Step R foot out diagonally right

2   Step L foot out diagonally right

3   Step R foot sideward right

&   Step L foot next to R foot

4   Step R foot sideward right

5   Step L foot in diagonally right

&   Step R foot next to L foot

6   Step L foot in diagonally right

NOTE   Repeat Part II, beats 1–6, 14 more times.

PART III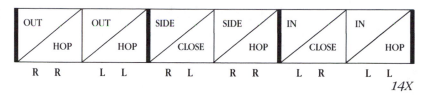

| Beat 1-6 | Repeat Part II, preceding beats 1, 2, 3, 5 with a hop |
| NOTE | Omit the first HOP of Part III. Add it in for the repeats. |

LEAD-UP ACTIVITIES

Practice SIDE, LIFT, SIDE, LIFT (individual tempo).

Practice SIDE/CLOSE, SIDE (individual tempo).

Practice forward TWO-STEP (individual tempo).

TEACHING SUGGESTIONS

Practice 4 WALKS and add on a SIDE, LIFT, SIDE, LIFT pattern (individual tempo then SAY & DO).

Do Part I to the music.

Practice OUT, OUT; SIDE/CLOSE, SIDE beginning R foot. Do only one sequence at a time using individual tempo, then SAY & DO.

Add on IN/CLOSE, IN, then SAY & DO.

Do several sequences of Part II and then add the music.

Practice Part III with the addition of the HOP before trying this to the music.

CHAIR DANCING

| PART I | WALK in place. |
| PART II | Do IN/CLOSE, IN diagonally left away from the chair to permit doing the following pattern—OUT, OUT—toward the chair. |

Misirlou-Kritikos

Greek-American

RECORD *Rhythmically Moving 8*

INTRODUCTION 8 beats

FORMATION "W" position, open circle, leader at right end

PART I

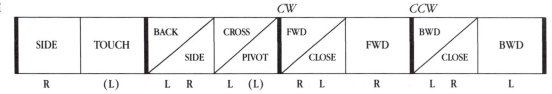

Beat 1 Step R foot sideward right

2 Touch L foot in

NOTE Women may point L foot and men may bring L foot IN while slapping the heel on the floor.

3 Step L foot crossing in back of R foot

& Step R foot sideward right

4 Step L foot crossing in front of R foot and pivot to face clockwise (one behind another)

5-6 Two-Step, beginning R foot forward clockwise (moving one behind another)

NOTE Women may point L foot against R calf on beat 6 while men HOOK L instep behind R knee.

7-8 Two-Step, beginning L foot backward counterclockwise (facing clockwise); end facing center

LEAD-UP ACTIVITIES Practice TWO-STEP FORWARD and BACKWARD (individual tempo).

Practice a sequence of BACK/SIDE, CROSS (individual tempo).

TEACHING SUGGESTIONS Begin with the sequence BACK/SIDE, CROSS beginning L foot with SAY & DO, then precede with TOUCH, BACK/SIDE, CROSS and practice the whole, then precede with SIDE and practice beats 1-4, adding on the ¼ TURN PIVOT at the end.

Practice FORWARD, CLOSE, FORWARD; BACKWARD, CLOSE, BACKWARD, then SAY & DO.

Practice the dance with SAY & DO and then add the music.

CHAIR DANCING Do the TWO-STEP away from and toward the chair.

Nebesko Kolo

Heavenly Circle
Yugoslavia (Serbia)

RECORD	*Rhythmically Moving 9*
INTRODUCTION	8 beats
FORMATION	Broken circle, hands joined in "V"

PART I   *CCW*

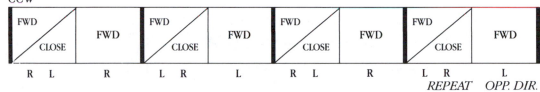

R   L   R   L R   L   R L   R   L R   L

REPEAT   OPP. DIR.

Beat 1-8	Two-Step 4 times forward counterclockwise beginning R foot (each Two-Step takes 2 beats)
9-16	Repeat beats 1-8 forward clockwise and turn to face center

PART II

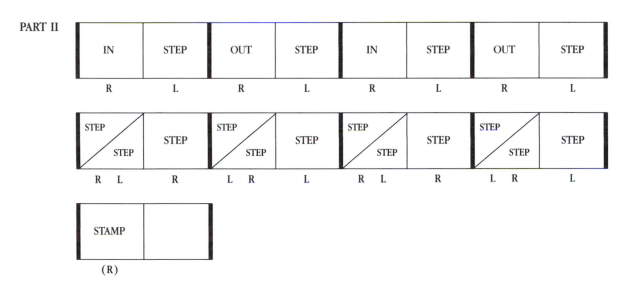

Beat 1	Step R foot in	⌉
2	Step L foot in place	
3	Step R foot out	CHERKESSIYA
4	Step L foot in place	⌋
5-8	Repeat Part II, beats 1-4	
9-10	Step R, L, R foot in place	
11-12	Step L, R, L foot in place	
13-16	Repeat beats 9-12	
17-18	Stamp R foot and rest	

LEAD-UP ACTIVITIES   Practice quick TWO-STEPS (individual tempo).

Practice CHERKESSIYA (individual tempo).

Practice THREES in place—STEP/STEP, STEP (individual tempo).

TEACHING SUGGESTIONS   Practice the 8 TWO-STEPS of Part I while moving counterclockwise, then clockwise (individual tempo, then SAY & DO).

Practice the 2 CHERKESSIYA steps of Part II with SAY & DO and add on to Part I.

Practice the 4 THREES of Part III followed by the STAMP (individual tempo, then SAY & DO).

Practice the transition of Part II to III and back to the beginning.

SAY & DO the entire dance and then add the music.

CHAIR DANCING   Do TWO-STEPS away from and toward the chair with small steps.

Sellenger's Round

England

RECORD   *Rhythmically Moving 7*

INTRODUCTION   8 beats

FORMATION   Partners in a single circle

PART I   *CW*

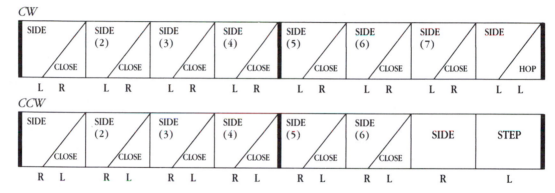

CCW

Beat 1-8   Slide 7 times sideward clockwise followed by a step L foot sideward left and a hop L foot (*Slipping*)

9-16   Slide 6 times sideward counterclockwise followed by a step R foot sideward R and a step L foot in place

CHORUS

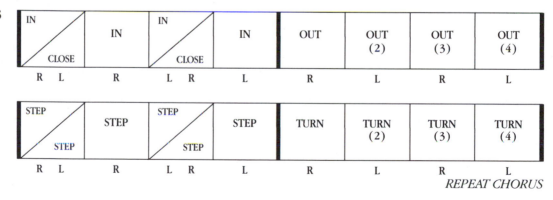

REPEAT CHORUS

Beat 1-2   Two-Step in beginning R foot (*Setting*)

3-4   Two-Step in beginning L foot

5-8   Step R, L, R, L foot out (*Out a double*) and turn to face partner

9-12   Two Threes in place beginning R foot, L foot facing partner (*Setting to partner*), leap onto the first step of each Three

13-16   Full turn R, L, R, L foot to the right (*Turn single*)

17-32   Repeat Chorus, beats 1-16

PART II

IN	IN (2)	IN (3)	IN (4)	OUT	OUT (2)	OUT (3)	OUT (4)
R	L	R	L	R	L	R	L

REPEAT

Beat 1-4   Step R, L, R, L foot in (*In a double*)

5-8   Step R, L, R, L foot out (*Out a double*)

9-16   Repeat Part II, beats 1-8

CHORUS   Repeat Chorus, beats 1-32

PART III

FWD	FWD	FWD	PIVOT	FWD	FWD	FWD	PIVOT
R	L	R	(R)	L	R	L	(L)

REPEAT

Beat 1-3   Step R, L, R foot changing places with partner; women moving inside clockwise and men outside counterclockwise; keep facing partner (*Siding*)

4   Turn ½ while continuing to face partner

5-8   Step L, R, L foot back to face along same path (keep looking at partner)

9-16   Repeat Part III, beats 1-8

CHORUS   Repeat Chorus, beats 1-32

PART IV

TURN (R ELBOW)	TURN (2)	TURN (3)	TURN (4)	TURN	TURN	AWAY	AWAY
R	L	R	L	R	L	R	L

REPEAT   OPP. DIR. (L ELBOW)

Beat 1-8	R elbow turn with partner (*Arming*)—move apart on beats 7-8)
9-16	L elbow turn (move apart on beats 15-16)
CHORUS	Repeat Chorus, beats 1-32
PART V	Repeat Part I, beats 1-16 (*Slipping*)
CHORUS	Repeat Chorus, beats 1-32
LEAD-UP ACTIVITIES	Practice SLIDES (individual tempo).
	Practice TWO-STEPS (individual tempo). Practice STEP/STEP, STEP in place (individual tempo).
	Practice TURNS to the right in 4 steps (individual tempo).
TEACHING SUGGESTIONS	Practice the Chorus, beats 1-8, with a partner (partner beat then SAY & DO). Add on the THREES with partners facing each other and then the full TURN right.
	SAY & DO the entire Chorus.
	Learn each of the verses, repeating the Chorus after each (SAY & DO).
	SAY & DO the entire dance and then add the music.
CHAIR DANCING	Do the verses either in place or away from and toward the chair.
	Substitute steps in place for the TURN in the Chorus.
	May be adapted for wheelchairs.

Hineh Ma Tov

How Good It Is
Israel

RECORD	*Rhythmically Moving 4*
INTRODUCTION	8 beats
FORMATION	Single circle, hands joined, or line with L hand at shoulder and R arm straight

CHORUS *CCW*

FWD	FWD (2)	FWD (3)	FWD (4)	FWD / FWD (&)	FWD (2) / FWD (&)	FWD (3) / FWD (&)	FWD (4) / FWD (&)
R	L	R	L	R L	R L	R L	R L

REPEAT

Beat 1-4 Step R, L, R, L foot forward counterclockwise

5-8 Run 8 steps forward counterclockwise beginning R foot

9-16 Repeat Chorus, beats 1-8, and turn to face center

PART I

SIDE	OUT / CLOSE	IN	STAMP	SIDE / SIDE	CROSS	SIDE / SIDE	CROSS
R	L R	L	(R)	R L	R	L R	L

REPEAT

Beat 1 Step R foot sideward right

2 Step L foot away from center

& Step R foot next to L foot

3 Step L foot toward center

4 Stamp R foot next to L foot

5-6 Yemenite beginning R foot

7-8 Yemenite beginning L foot

9-16 Repeat Part I, beats 1-8

CHORUS
Beat 1-16 Repeat Chorus, beats 1-16

PART II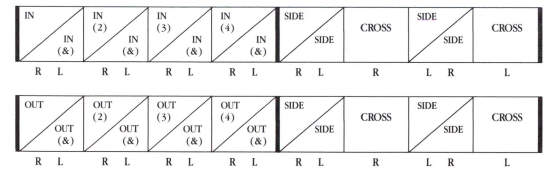

IN / IN (&)	IN (2) / IN (&)	IN (3) / IN (&)	IN (4) / IN (&)	SIDE / SIDE	CROSS	SIDE / SIDE	CROSS
R L	R L	R L	R L	R L	R	L R	L

OUT / OUT (&)	OUT (2) / OUT (&)	OUT (3) / OUT (&)	OUT (4) / OUT (&)	SIDE / SIDE	CROSS	SIDE / SIDE	CROSS
R L	R L	R L	R L	R L	R	L R	L

Beat 1-4   Run 8 steps in beginning R foot

5-8   Repeat Part I, beats 5-8

9-12   Run 8 steps out beginning R foot (backing up)

13-16   Repeat Part I, beats 5-8

LEAD-UP ACTIVITIES   Practice combinations of walking and running with RUNS executed as a divided beat (individual tempo).

Practice YEMENITE steps (individual tempo).

Practice 8 RUNS plus 2 YEMENITE steps.

Practice patterns of OUT/CLOSE, IN (individual tempo).

TEACHING SUGGESTIONS   Practice 4 WALKS, 8 RUNS with SAY & DO.

Practice 8 RUNS IN and 8 RUNS OUT (encourage small steps). Add on 2 YEMENITE steps after the RUNS IN and 2 YEMENITE steps after the RUNS OUT, then SAY & DO.

Practice SIDE, OUT/CLOSE, IN, STAMP with SAY, then SAY & DO.

Practice adding on 2 YEMENITE steps to Part I, beats 1-4 (individual tempo, then SAY & DO).

SAY & DO the dance in sequence and then add the music. Be certain students understand the order of the parts.

NOTE   Part II should be learned before Part I, because it is easier.

CHAIR DANCING

PART I   Substitute steps in place.

PART III   Use small steps away from and toward the chair.

Leor Chiyuchech

To the Light of Your Smile
Israel

RECORD	*Rhythmically Moving 8*
INTRODUCTION	8 beats
FORMATION	Single circle facing center, hands joined

PART I

SIDE	SIDE	CROSS		SIDE	SIDE	CROSS	
L	R	L		R	L	R	

IN	OUT	CLOSE		IN	OUT	CLOSE	
L	R	L		R	L	R	

REPEAT PART I

Beat 1-4	Yemenite beginning L foot
5-8	Yemenite beginning R foot
9	Step L foot in toward center (raise arms)
10	Step R foot out (lower arms)
11-12	Step L foot next to R foot
13-16	Repeat beats 9-12 with opposite footwork beginning R foot
17-32	Repeat Part I, beats 1-16, and turn to face counterclockwise

PART II   *CCW*

FWD	CLOSE	FWD	BRUSH	FWD	CLOSE	FWD	BRUSH
L	R	L	(R)	R	L	R	(L)

FWD		SIDE		BACK		SIDE	
L		R		L		R	

REPEAT PART II

Beat 1-4	Two-Step beginning L foot forward counterclockwise (brush R foot forward on beat 4)
5-8	Two-Step beginning R foot (brush L foot forward on beat 8)
9-10	Step L foot forward and turn to face center
11-12	Step R foot sideward right (raise arms)
13-14	Step L foot crossing in back of R foot (bend knees)
15-16	Step R foot sideward right (lower arms)
17-32	Repeat Part II, beats 1-16

LEAD-UP ACTIVITIES

Learn or practice YEMENITE steps (individual tempo).

Practice slow TWO-STEPS (individual tempo).

Practice the pattern of IN, OUT, CLOSE, REST (individual tempo).

TEACHING SUGGESTIONS

Practice 2 YEMENITE steps in sequence beginning L foot (SAY & DO).

Practice IN, OUT, CLOSE, REST twice in sequence beginning L foot (SAY & DO).

SAY & DO Part I.

Practice 2 slow TWO-STEPS moving counterclockwise beginning L foot (SAY & DO), then add the BRUSH.

Practice the pattern FORWARD, SIDE, BACK, SIDE beginning L foot and moving counterclockwise (SAY & DO).

SAY & DO Part II.

Practice the transition from Part I to Part II remembering to move counterclockwise beginning L foot.

Practice the transition from Part II to Part I with its difficult side-to-side movement pattern.

SAY & DO the entire dance and then add the music.

CHAIR DANCING

Substitute steps in place for moving steps in Part II.

Ma Na'Vu

How Beautiful Upon the Mountains
Israel

RECORD   *Rhythmically Moving 6*

INTRODUCTION 16 beats

FORMATION   Single circle facing center, hands joined

PART I

TOUCH	TOUCH	OUT / CLOSE	IN	OUT	IN	OUT / IN	TOG
(R)	(R)	R L	R	L	R	L R	B
						REPEAT	*OPP. FTWK.*

Beat 1   Touch R toe in, weight on L foot

2   Touch R toe sideward, weight on L foot

3   Step R foot out

&   Step L foot next to R foot

4   Step R foot in

5   Step L foot out

6   Step R foot in

7   Step L foot out

&   Step R foot in

8   Bring both feet together, lowering heels

9-16   Repeat Part I, beats 1-8, with opposite footwork beginning L foot

PART II

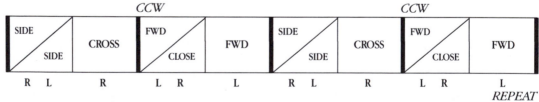

	CCW				*CCW*		
SIDE / SIDE	CROSS	FWD / CLOSE	FWD	SIDE / SIDE	CROSS	FWD / CLOSE	FWD
R L	R	L R	L	R L	R	L R	L
							REPEAT

Beat 1-2   Yemenite beginning R foot, then turn to face counterclockwise

3-4   Two-Step L foot forward, then turn to face center

5-16   Repeat Part II, beats 1-4, three more times

LEAD-UP
ACTIVITIES   Practice YEMENITES (individual tempo).

Practice TWO-STEPS (individual tempo).

Practice combining a YEMENITE with 1 TWO-STEP (individual tempo).

Practice OUT/CLOSE, IN pattern (individual tempo).

TEACHING   Practice TOUCH, TOUCH, OUT/CLOSE, IN (SAY & DO) then add on OUT, IN, OUT/IN,
SUGGESTIONS   TOGETHER. Practice with one foot, then the other.

SAY & DO Part I.

Practice the YEMENITE, TWO-STEP combination (individual tempo, then SAY & DO).

SAY & DO Part II.

Practice the transitions from Part I to Part II and back to the beginning.

SAY & DO the entire dance and then add the music.

CHAIR
DANCING
PART II   Substitute TWO-STEPS in place.

Sapri Tama

Tell Me My Innocent One
Israel

RECORD	*Rhythmically Moving 7*
INTRODUCTION	6 beats
FORMATION	Individuals in lines

PART I

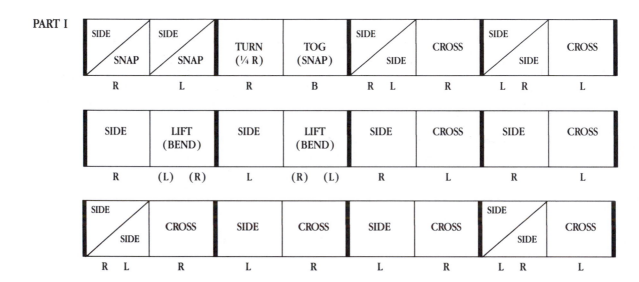

Beat 1	Step R foot sideward right
&	Snap fingers with arms high over right shoulder
2	Step L foot sideward left
&	Snap fingers with arms high over left shoulder
3	Turn ¼ right
4	Bring feet together while bending both knees (snap fingers on the beat as knees are bent)
5-6	Yemenite beginning R foot
7-8	Yemenite beginning L foot
9	Step R foot sideward right
10	Bend R knee while lifting L leg in front (snap fingers—hands close to body), then straighten leg
11	Step L foot sideward left
12	Bend L knee (repeat bend and snap as in beat 10)
13	Step R foot sideward right (spread arms apart)
14	Step L foot crossing in front of R foot (cross arms and snap)
15	Step R foot sideward right, spread arms apart
16	Step L foot crossing in front of R foot (cross arms and snap)
17-18	Yemenite beginning R foot
19-24	Repeat beats 13-18 sideward left beginning L foot

LEAD-UP
ACTIVITIES

Practice YEMENITE steps (individual tempo).

Practice SIDE, CROSS (individual tempo).

TEACHING
SUGGESTIONS

Practice SIDE/SNAP, SIDE/SNAP; TURN, SNAP (individual tempo, then SAY & DO).

Add on the 2 YEMENITE steps.

SAY & DO beats 1-8.

Practice SIDE, LIFT; SIDE, LIFT; SIDE, CROSS; SIDE, CROSS with individual tempo and then SAY & DO.

Add on the YEMENITE and SAY & DO beats 9-18.

Add on the SIDE, CROSS; SIDE, CROSS; YEMENITE sideward left (SAY & DO).

SAY & DO beats 9-24.

Practice the transition from beat 8 to beat 9, from beat 12 to beat 13, and from the end to the beginning.

SAY & DO the entire dance and then add the music.

CHAIR
DANCING

Do the steps in place, omitting the ¼ TURN.

Doudlebska Polka

Double Clap Polka
Czechoslovakia

RECORD	*Rhythmically Moving 2*
INTRODUCTION	8 beats
FORMATION	Partners arranged about the room
ALTERNATE FORMATION	Circle

PART I *CCW*

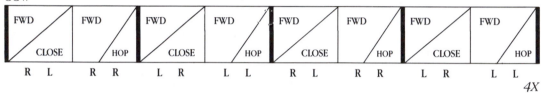

Beat 1-32   Polka 16 times with partner

PART II *CCW*

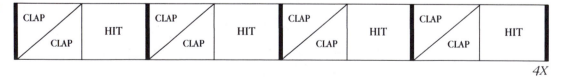

Beat 1-32   Walk 32 steps and form a double circle; persons on left place L hands on L shoulders of persons ahead in the circle and R hands around the waist of partners; all sing "La, La, La" with the music.

PART III

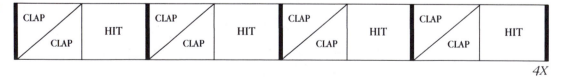

Beat 1-32   Persons on left turn to face center and clap own hands twice, then neighbors hands once, in rhythm of 1 &, 2; the clapping sequence is executed 16 times.

Persons on right turn to face clockwise and dance 16 Polka steps clockwise around the outside of the circle. At the end of the 32 beats begin the dance from the beginning with a new partner.

CIRCLE DANCE   Dance the left-hand person's part; POLKA, WALK into a circle, CLAP.

LEAD-UP ACTIVITIES   Practice GALLOP with each foot leading (individual tempo). Add 4 GALLOPS with one foot, followed by 4 with the other foot. Practice 2 GALLOPS with one foot, then 2 GALLOPS with the other foot (GALLOP POLKA).

If the group is skilled enough to learn the POLKA, review or learn the TWO-STEP and then precede each TWO-STEP with the HOP (individual tempo).

Practice POLKA or GALLOP POLKA with a partner.

Practice having everyone WALK from a scattered free formation to a circle.

Have group stand in a circle and practice the CLAP/CLAP, HIT pattern of PART III (SAY & DO).

TEACHING SUGGESTIONS   It is recommended that the circle dance be taught as a lead-up to the partner dance.

Have everyone POLKA or GALLOP POLKA to the music.

Have everyone do Part I followed by Part II with the music. Add Part III.

CHAIR DANCING   Do as described for Circle Dance.

Substitute steps in place.

Jessie Polka

U.S.A.

RECORD   *Rhythmically Moving 8*

INTRODUCTION   8 beats

FORMATION   Individual, partners, circle, line

PART I

HEEL	STEP	TOE	TOUCH	HEEL	STEP	HEEL	LIFT
(L)	L	(R)	(R)	(R)	R	(L)	(L)

Beat 1   Hop R foot while extending L heel diagonally left

2   Step L foot next to R foot

3   Hop L foot while extending R toe diagonally backward

4   Touch R foot next to L foot

5   Hop L foot while extending R heel diagonally right

6   Step R foot next to L foot

7   Hop R foot while extending L heel diagonally left

8   Hop R foot while lifting L foot in front of R foot (knee bent)

PART II

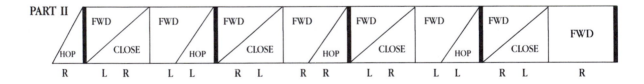

HOP	FWD	CLOSE	FWD	HOP	FWD	CLOSE	FWD	HOP	FWD	CLOSE	FWD	HOP	FWD	CLOSE	FWD
R	L	R	L	L	R	L	R	R	L	R	L	L	R	L	R

Beat 1-8   Polka forward 4 times beginning with hop R foot and Two-Step L foot

TO SIMPLIFY   Change POLKAS to RUNS.

LEAD-UP ACTIVITIES   Practice 2-beat sequences of HEEL, STEP; TOE, TOUCH; HEEL, LIFT (individual tempo).
Practice the POLKA (individual tempo).

**TEACHING
SUGGESTIONS**   Have students work out the language-to-movement patterns of Part I (individual tempo).

Practice Part I without using HOPS.

SAY & DO Part I and add on 4 POLKA steps of Part II.

**CHAIR
DANCING**   Do the sequences in place.

Appendices

The **Rhythmic Competency Analysis Test** is designed to assess an individual's beat competency by testing his/her ability to perform a movement task to the underlying steady beat of music. The test is presented in two levels: nonweight-bearing movement seated and weight-bearing movement, standing and walking. The same musical selection is used for each level of the test. Students are tested individually in a location away from other children or adults, where the tester and the student will be alone and uninterrupted.

Use a tape recorder and two cassette tapes of instrumental musical selections with a strong underlying beat. A number of selections on the *Rhythmically Moving* cassettes are appropriate. One musical selection should have a metronome beat of approximately 130 ($\quad = 130$) and the other selection should have a metronome beat of approximately 120 ($\quad = 120$). Both the student and the tester should be seated for the beginning of the test. The tester should put each student at ease with friendly, relaxed conversation.

Be certain the students understand the movements requested. Play a short follow-the-leader game demonstrating the movements to be done to the music.

Step 1. Use the first musical selection and have the student pat the lap with both hands at the same time. **Avoid providing any visual or auditory assistance to the student**.

Step 2. Continue with the same musical selection and have the student pat the lap, alternating the hands for each pat.

Step 3. Have the student walk the beat while still seated.

Step 4. Have the student stand and walk the beat while remaining in one place.

Step 5. Have the student walk the beat in a forward direction.

Step 6. Have the student walk the beat in a backward direction.

Step 7–12. Use the second musical selection and begin as in Step 1 above.

Scoring. The test is scored as a pass or fail. Give a "1" to the student who is accurate for at least eight beats of each step of the test, matching movement to the underlying steady beat. Give a "0" to the student who is inaccurate or who cannot maintain accuracy for eight beats.

The **Beat Coordination Screening Test** is a follow-the-leader test that is administered without music. This test is designed to predict an individual's **beat competency**—the ability to walk to the steady beat while engaging in a weight-bearing movement—and to assess an individual's **beat coordination** skill level. The test may be administered in a one-to-one testing situation, to small groups (3–4), or to an entire class. It should be noted that persons who are on the borderline of rhythmic competency may not be identified if the entire class is screened at once. No equipment is needed.

If more than one individual is tested at the same time, provide sufficient space for individuals to spread their arms sideward. The tester and students may be seated or standing. The students are instructed to follow the same motions that the tester is doing. Note: If more than one group in the room is to be given the test, steps 3–5 need to incorporate different movements for each group so that no practice takes place by those who are waiting.

Step 1. Pat the thighs with both hands. Do the thigh pat at least eight times until you see that everyone is following your movements.

Step 2. Alternate the movement of your hands as you pat your thighs. Do **not** specify "right" and "left." Repeat this alternating movement until the students seem to be comfortable. Before moving on to Step 3, indicate that you are going to change the movement.

Step 3. Pat the thighs once with both hands followed by one hand clap. Repeat this step a minimum of eight times. Just before going on to the next step, indicate that you are going to change the movement. Do not stop and start again.

Step 4. Snap fingers once with the arms spread sideward, then clap hands. Repeat this step a minimum of eight times and indicate that you are moving to the next step. Do not stop and start again.

Step 5. Pat the thighs once, clap once, snap the fingers once with the arms spread sideward, clap once. Do not stop and start again.

Note: Steps 3–5 may be changed to use other movements, for example, touch knees, touch shoulders for step 3, touch waist, touch head for step 4. Combine steps 3 and 4 for step 5.

Evaluation. Persons who cannot accurately follow the "exact" movements of the tester after several repetitions possess low levels of beat coordination. Students who cannot coordinate step 5 accurately will have difficulty walking to the steady beat of a musical selection. Persons who finally succeed after several repetitions may be able to walk to the steady beat of music but will lack sufficient coordination to succeed with organized movement and dance sequences. Persons who are successful with step 5 on the first or second repetition can be expected to walk to the steady beat of music, as long as they feel beat, and can be expected to perform movement and dance sequences.

Special Directions for the Tester:

- Do not use music with the test.
- Face the students.
- Do not stop once the test has begun. Proceed without interruption from one step to the next.
- Keep the movements slow enough; a metronome beat of 100 is a good testing tempo.
- Assess the students' ability to follow the movements "exactly as executed."

This test has been given to hundreds of individuals ranging in age from 7 to 70. It predicts with 95% accuracy a person's ability to walk to the steady beat of a musical selection.

---

*This test is designed for students in second grade and above.

Locomotor Movement I*

- **Alternate the feet in movement sequences**

  Apat Apat   *Philippines*   118
  Cherkessiya (simplified)   *Israel*   262
  Fjäskern   *Sweden*   120
  Haya Ze Basadeh   *Israel*   122
  Irish Stew   *USA (Novelty)*   124
  La Raspa (simplified)   *Mexico*   194
  Les Saluts   *French Canadian*   126
  Little Shoemaker   *USA (Novelty)*   128
  Sneaky Snake   *USA (Novelty)*   130
  Te Ve Orez   *Israel*   131
  Troika   *Russia*   133
  Two-Part Dance   *USA (Novelty)*   142
  Yankee Doodle   *USA (Novelty)*   135

- **One 2-beat recurring nonweight-transfer sequence**

  Big Circle Dance   *USA (Novelty)*   137
  Count 64   *USA (Novelty)*   138
  Sliding   *USA (Novelty)*   140
  Two-Part Dance   *USA (Novelty)*   142
  Zigeunerpolka   *USA (Novelty)*   143

Locomotor Movement II

- **Three recurring nonweight-transfer movements plus one weight transfer**

  Alley Cat*   *USA (Novelty)*   146
  Djurdjevka Kolo*   *Yugoslavia (Serbia)*   149

- **Three alternating weight transfer movements plus one nonweight-transfer**

  Close Encounters*   *USA (Novelty)*   151
  Hustle   *USA (Novelty)*   153
  Işte Hendek   *Turkey*   155

---

*No right or left foot needs to be specified for any of the **Locomotor Movement I** dances. In addition, dances in **Locomotor Movement II** and **III** that may be taught without reference to right or left foot are marked with an asterisk.

- **Recurring 2-beat sequences moving sideward**

  Bannielou Lambaol   *France (Brittany)*   157
  Erev Shel Shoshanim   *Israel*   159
  Ersko Kolo (simplified)   *Yugoslavia*   311
  Nigun   *USA (Novelty)*   162
  Oh How Lovely   *USA (Novelty)*   164

- **Two different 2-beat sequences performed one time**

  Adje Noga Za Nogama   *Yugoslavia (Croatia)*   165
  Gaelic Waltz   *USA (Novelty)*   167
  Kendimé   *Turkey*   168

- **Alternating 2-beat sequences**

  Áis Giórgis   *Greece*   169
  Amos Moses   *USA (Novelty)*   171
  Bele Kawe (simplified)   *Creole-African (Caribbean Island of Carriacou)*   173
  Debka Daluna (simplified)   *Israel*   176
  Dimna Juda   *Yugoslavia (Macedonia)*   178
  Hasapikos   *Greece*   180
  Pravo Horo   *Bulgaria*   182
  Tipsy*   *USA (Novelty)*   184

- **Uneven timing (divided beat and rest)**

  Chiotikos   *Greece*   186
  Cumberland Square   *England*   188
  Dučec*   *Yugoslavia*   190
  Hora Medura (simplified)   *Israel*   278
  Körtanc   *Hungary*   192
  La Raspa*   *Mexico*   194
  Limbo Rock*   *USA (Novelty)*   196
  Man in the Hay   *Germany*   198
  Pljeskavac Kolo   *Yugoslavia*   201
  Tant' Hessie   *South Africa*   203
  Ve David*   *Israel*   205
  Zemer Atik*   *Israel*   207

- **Recurring 4-beat sequences**

  Good Old Days*   *USA (Novelty)*   209
  Popcorn*   *USA (Novelty)*   211
  Twelfth St. Rag*   *USA (Novelty)*   214

**Locomotor Movement III dances are similar in level of difficulty to Even and Uneven Dances.

Age: Grades 3–6, junior or senior high school to adult (including senior citizens)

Length of class: 45 minutes to 1 hour

Prerequisite Experiences:

• Students possess **basic comfort with movement** (see Chapter 3).

• Students possess a **basic level of rhythmic competency** (see Chapter 4).

• Students have had opportunities to participate successfully in rhythmic movement sequences (see Chapter 5).

This lesson sequence is based on my firm belief that beginning students (including older students) must experience a broad base of locomotor movement experiences before moving on to more difficult folk dance steps and patterns. Therefore, the lesson sequence includes **Locomotor Movement I, II, and III** activities but does not include **Even** and **Uneven Folk Dance Steps**. The lesson sequence covers ten class periods. Upon completion of the sequence, students will be ready for **Even** and **Uneven Folk Dance Steps**. Those teachers who have time for more lessons can refer to the section in Chapter 5 on introducing **Even** and **Uneven Dance Steps** to beginners, as well as to Appendix C, Dances by Level of Difficulty, for specific dances.

Each dance mentioned here is described in Part Two of this book. Since each of those descriptions includes lead-up activities and teaching suggestions, I will not repeat that information here.

*Although the teaching sequence I outline in Chapter 5 can be used with any age group (age seven on), I offer the suggestions here especially for those teachers who are working with adolescents and adults.

Lesson 1

• Exercise warm-up (students standing): Use movements that will determine the rhythmic competency of your students (see Chapter 4).

• *Two-Part Dance (Blackberry Quadrille)*:
Part I: Walk (use a different movement for each repeat).
Part II: Ask students to execute stationary non-locomotor arm movements with the beat (use a different one each time). Examples include pushing arms in different directions, alternating arms, and patting beat. (Note: This dance should be done without an organized formation, unless you need to exert control over the group by using a circle.)

• *Big Circle Dance (Cobbler's Reel/Gaspé Reel)*: Have the group copy you in a visual follow-the-leader sequence. If the students experience difficulty, add aural cues.

• *Sliding*

• *Zigeunerpolka*

• *Doudlebska Polka* (modify to circle variation using the GALLOP in **Part I**)

• *Count 64*

• *Troika*

Lesson 2

• Exercise warm-up: Use rhythmic coordination sequences with the arms. Use different music than used in the first lesson, such as *Rakes of Mallow*.

• *Two-Part Dance*:
Part I: Suggest locomotor movements (WALK different ways, JUMP, HOP)
Part II: Suggest nonlocomotor movements (arm sequences)

• *Big Circle Dance*: Use different music than in first lesson, such as *Little Shoemaker*

• Review: *Count 64*, *Troika*

• New: *Fjäskern* (circle modification version); *Djurdjevka Kolo*; teach the TOUCH, TOUCH, TOUCH, STEP to be used

• *Te Ve Orez* (use the circle variation or the authentic formation and dance)

• Review: *Doudlebska Polka*, *Zigeunerpolka*

Lesson 3

• Rhythmic warm-up: *Big Circle Dance* (add sequences found in dances such as the TOUCH, TOUCH, TOUCH, STEP)

• Review: *Fjäskern*, *Djurdjevka Kolo*

• New: *Alley Cat* (follows TOUCH, TOUCH, TOUCH, STEP movement sequence used in *Djurdjevka Kolo*)

• Review: *Te Ve Orez*

• New: *Close Encounters*, *Işte Hendek*

Lesson 4

• Rhythmic warm-up: Requests (2) from a list of the dances that have been taught and reviewed

• Review: *Alley Cat*

• New: Introduce sideward movement, *Bannielou Lambaol*, *Hora Medura* (simplified)

• Review: *Close Encounters*, *Işte Hendek*

• New: *Cumberland Square*

Lesson 5

• Rhythmic warm-up: Use two-beat alternating arm sequences (see LEVEL V, Chapter 4); *Big Circle Dance*, include two-beat and alternating two-beat foot patterns (see Chapter 5, **Locomotor Movement I** dances)

• Requests (2)

• Review: *Bannielou Lambaol*, *Hora Medura*

• New: *Tipsy*, *Bele Kawe* (simplified), *Kendimé*, *Ugros*

• Request (1)

Lesson 6

• Rhythmic warm-up

• Requests (2)

• Review: *Tipsy*, *Bele Kawe*

• New: Introduce the rhythm pattern 1, 2, 3 &, 4 with *Limbo Rock*, *Plješkavac Kolo*

• Request (1)

Lesson 7

• Rhythmic warm-up

• Requests (2)

• Review: *Limbo Rock Plješkavac Kolo*

• New: *Twelfth St. Rag* (use simplified version in Part II), *Debka Daluna* (simplified)

• Request (1)

Lesson 8

• Rhythmic warm-up

• Requests (2)

• Review: *Twelfth St. Rag*, *Debka Daluna*

• New: *Popcorn*; *Hasapikos*

• Request (1)

Lesson 9

• Rhythmic warm-up

• Requests (2)

• Review: *Popcorn*; *Hasapikos* (do additional variations if the group is doing well with those presented in the preceding lesson)

• New: *Hora Pe Gheaţa*, (simplified version); teach without the arm pattern

Lesson 10

• Rhythmic warm-up

• Review: *Hora Pe Gheaţa*; *Pata Pata* (add the arms)

• Requests: Finish this last class with all requests that have been planned with the class in advance

How to Order Records and Related Publications

Phyllis S. Weikart has produced many movement and dance materials, including the following:

- *Rhythmically Moving 1–9 Series* (records or cassettes)
- *Teaching Movement & Dance: Intermediate Folk Dance* (manual) and accompanying *Changing Directions 1–4 Series* (records or cassettes)
- *Round the Circle: Key Experiences in Movement for Children* (manual)
- *Movement Plus Music: Activities for Children Ages 3–7* (booklet)

- *Music Plus Rhymes, Songs, and Singing Games* (booklet)
- *Beginning Folk Dances Illustrated 1–3 Series* (videos)
- *Fitness Over Fifty* (video)
- *Rhythmically Walking* (exercise cassette)

To order these and related publications, contact the High/Scope Press, 600 North River Street, Ypsilanti, MI 48198, (313) 485-2000, FAX (313) 485-0704.

Glossary of Terms
Rhythmic Movement and Folk Dance

Language-to-Movement Terms

Language Terms

BEAT The underlying steady pulse of the rhyme, song, or instrumental music.

RHYTHM Groupings of beats, divided beats, and rests.

TEMPO The speed of the movement in one's own beat or in the partner's or group's common beat.

Basic Locomotor Movements

HOP A transfer of weight from one foot to the *same* foot. Executed with an even beat. May be done in place or proceed in any direction. (If the hopping foot is changed, a step or leap is performed.)

JUMP A transfer of weight from one foot or both feet to *both* feet. Executed with an even beat. May be done in place or proceed in any direction.

LEAP A transfer of weight from one foot to the other foot. Both feet are off the floor in the transfer. Greater height or distance is used than in the run. Executed with an even beat. May proceed in any direction.

RUN A transfer of weight from one foot to the other foot. Both feet are off the floor momentarily before the transfer of weight. Executed with an even beat that often is faster than the beat used for the walk. May proceed in any direction.

WALK A transfer of weight from one foot to the other foot. One foot always is in contact with the floor. Executed with an even beat that allows the same amount of time between each step. May proceed in any direction.

Basic Locomotor Movement Combinations

GALLOP A forward or backward movement. One foot steps then the other foot closes; the step takes more time than the close (uneven rhythm). The same foot always leads. The easiest of the basic locomotor combinations.

SKIP A combination of a step and a hop executed in an uneven rhythm. Same rhythmic pattern as the gallop and slide. The time interval of the hop is shorter than the step. The skip may proceed in any direction. The leading foot changes with each skip.

SLIDE A sideward gallop. Same rhythmic pattern as the gallop. The same foot leads sideward followed by a close of the opposite foot. The side step takes more time than the close (uneven rhythm).

Other Movement Terms

BUZZ TURN A movement in which partners, using either the shoulder-waist or the social dance position, turn 360° in a forward direction with a series of turn and close steps using divided beats. The right foot leads.

CAMEL ROLL A movement from the forward foot to the backward foot to the forward foot again. The hips describe a movement in the shape of a "C."

CHARLESTON STEP (simplified) A step forward, a forward kick of the free leg, a step backward from the kick, and a touch of the free foot backward.

CORNER In partner formation, the person on the other side of you. Partner is on one side, corner is on the other side.

DO-SA-DO A partner movement in which partners move toward one another, pass back to back, and then move backward to place (usually begins with partners passing right shoulders).

ELBOW SWING A partner movement in which partners hook elbows and walk, run, or skip around in a forward direction, turning 360°.

FIGURE EIGHT A series of steps that describe the floor pattern of an "8."

GRAND RIGHT AND LEFT Partners face each other and begin to move around the circle in opposite directions giving right hands to each other, then alternating left and right hands with each person in turn.

HORSE TROT A "leaping" movement in which the legs bend and reach forward for each new step.

PARTNER BEAT Two persons move together with the same tempo.

RIGHT-HAND STAR Dancers move in a foward direction clockwise with right hands joined in the middle.

SCISSORS KICKS A forward or backward kicking movement of the legs in which the kicks occur in sequence.

SIDEWARD CAMEL ROLL Feet step from side to side and hips move in a "C" from side to side.

Language-to-Dance Vocabulary

Weight-Transfer Terms

ACCENT A forceful step on the designated foot.

BACK A step on the designated foot crossing in back of the other foot.

BACKWARD A step on the designated foot moving away from the facing direction (clockwise or counterclockwise) around a circle or one behind the other in a line.

CHANGE A step on the designated foot to begin a change of partners or change of places between two people.

CLOSE A step on the designated foot as it is brought next to the other foot. May occur in any direction.

CROSS A step on the designated foot crossing in front of the other foot.

FORWARD A step on the designated foot moving in the facing direction (clockwise or counterclockwise) around a circle or one behind the other in a line.

IN A step on the designated foot toward the center of a circle or straight ahead when standing side by side in a line.

OUT A step on the designated foot away from the center of a circle or away from the facing direction when standing side by side in a line.

SHUFFLE A step from one foot to the other while maintaining contact with the floor.

SIDE A step on the designated foot perpendicular to the facing direction. Dancers are facing center in a circle or side by side in a line.

STEP A weight transfer to the designated foot in place without moving in any direction (next to the other foot).

SWAY A step on the designated foot sideward with a movement of the upper body in the same direction.

SWIVEL The toes and heels move sideward either together (toes then heels) or toes of one foot and heels of the other in an alternating motion.

TOGETHER A step on the designated foot without lifting the other foot. Weight now is on both feet.

TURN A step on the designated foot that moves the body clockwise or counterclockwise 90° or 180° with a single weight transfer or a step that begins a multistep rotation (90°, 180° or 360°).

Nonweight-Transfer Terms

BEND A motion of the supporting leg toward the floor as the knee bends.

BOUNCE A movement of one or both heels that raises and lowers them to the floor. May be thought of as a jump or hop that does not leave the floor.

BRUSH A motion of the designated foot against the floor.

CHUG A movement of the supporting leg (generally backward) with the foot kept in contact with the floor.

CLICK, HEEL CLICK A forceful motion of the designated foot against the other foot while it is on the floor or in the air.

DIG A forceful motion of the designated foot to the floor with the front part of the foot contacting the floor.

DRAW A movement that slides the free foot along the floor up to the supporting foot.

HEEL A motion of the designated heel against the floor.

HIT A motion of one or two hands to the foot or to the partner's hands.

HOOK A motion of the designated foot against the back of the supporting knee causing the knee to bend. The hooking leg is bent with the knee turned out.

KICK A motion of the designated leg in front, back, or to the side of the body involving a straightening of the knee.

LIFT A motion of the designated leg in front of the body involving a bent knee. The lower leg is angled in front of the supporting leg.

PIVOT A motion of the designated foot against the floor that turns the body to face a new direction.

SLAP A forceful motion of the whole foot against the floor executed with the leg straight out from the body.

SNAP A snapping motion of the fingers of one hand or both hands.

STAMP A forceful heel motion of the designated foot against the floor.

SWING A motion of the designated leg from the hip, in which the knee is kept straight.

TOE A motion of the designated toes against the floor.

TOUCH A motion of the designated foot against the floor.

UP A motion of the designated leg in front of the body begun by raising the knee.

Dance Steps*

CHERKESSIYA IN, OUT, OUT, IN or IN, STEP, OUT, STEP

GRAPEVINE CROSS, SIDE, BACK, SIDE

GRAPEVINE PATTERN SIDE, CROSS, SIDE, BACK or SIDE, BACK, SIDE, CROSS

POLKA HOP, FORWARD,**/CLOSE, FORWARD/

SCHOTTISCHE FORWARD, FORWARD,** STEP, HOP

STEP HOP FORWARD,** HOP

THREE FORWARD,** 2, 3, REST

TWO-STEP FORWARD,** CLOSE, FORWARD, REST

YEMENITE SIDE, SIDE, CROSS, REST

Nonpartner Formations

BROKEN CIRCLE Dancers are arranged in a single circle with one place in which the hands are not joined, thus establishing a leader.

CIRCLE Dancers are arranged in a single circle with or without hands joined.

---

*The dance steps are illustrated in Chapter 5.
**BACKWARD, IN, OUT may be substituted.

FRONT BASKET   Dancers stand in a circle or line and spread their own arms sideward in front of the persons on either side. Hands are joined with persons one beyond the dancer on each side. The underneath arm corresponds to the travelling direction. (If the basket moves right, the right arm is underneath.)

REVERSE BASKET   Same as FRONT BASKET with hands joined in back of the dancer on each side. The arm on top corresponds to the travelling direction.

FREE FORMATION   Dancers are scattered around the dance space in a random pattern.

LINE   Dancers stand side by side. Line may be short with three to five dancers or long with one leader.

OPEN CIRCLE   Dancers are arranged in circle formation except no hands are joined during the dance.

Partner Formations

DOUBLE CIRCLE (PARTNERS FACING COUNTERCLOCKWISE OR CLOCKWISE)   Partners are arranged in a circle with both dancers facing in the same direction.

DOUBLE CIRCLE (PARTNERS FACING EACH OTHER)   Partners are arranged around a circle. Outside partner faces toward the center (IN) and inside partner faces away from the center of the circle (OUT).

HEADS   The two sets of partners in a square set who face each other across the set; one set of HEADS has their backs to the musical source. (See Square Set illustration.)

LONGWAYS SET, CONTRA LINE   Partners are in a double line facing each other or facing the head of the set.

SIDES   The two sets of partners in a square set who face each other and are not HEADS. (See Square Set illustration.)

SINGLE CIRCLE (PARTNERS SIDE BY SIDE FACING THE SAME DIRECTION)   Partners are arranged in a single circle with both dancers standing side by side facing the same direction.

SINGLE CIRCLE (PARTNERS FACING EACH OTHER)   Partners are in a single circle but they face each other.

SQUARE SET   Eight persons (four couples) are arranged so that one couple is on each side of a square facing the center.

STAR   Four or more persons all join right or left hands in the middle of their circle.

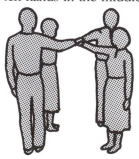

Group Formations and Handholds

ESCORT HOLD   Dancers are side by side or diagonally forward of one another. The hand in the moving direction hooks the bent elbow of the person ahead. The other hand is at the waist, elbow bent, with the back of the hand on the hip. Occasionally the escort hold requires dancers to be very close together, in which case the arm in the moving direction is underneath the neighbor's arm.

LINE AND CIRCLE "T" (SHOULDER HOLD)-
Arms are extended sideward at shoulder level to the near shoulders of the dancer on either side. Elbows are straight. Right arms are in back and left arms are in front.

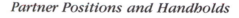

"V" (KOLO HOLD)   Hands are joined with arms down. The left palm faces to the rear (OUT) and the right palm faces to the front (IN). The left palm is on top.

"W"   Hands are joined at shoulder level with elbows bent. The right hand supports the neighbor's left hand. A convenient way to form this handhold is to take the "V" position as described and raise the arms.

Partner Positions and Handholds

DOUBLE SHOULDER   This modification of the shoulder-waist position is used when two males or two females are partners. Dancers hold each other's shoulders.

ELBOW SWING   Partners hook right or left elbows to walk, run, or skip.

ISRAELI TURN   Partners stand with right hips adjacent to each other. Right arms are extended in front of partner, holding the partner at the waist. Left arms are held high.

SHOULDER-WAIST   Partners face each other. Male holds the female at her waist. Female's hands are on the male's shoulders.

SKATER'S HOLD or CROSS-HAND HOLD   Partners are side by side with right hands joined in front of the right partner and left hands joined in front of the left partner. Right hands are joined on top and left hands are joined underneath. A promenade is sometimes danced in this position.

SOCIAL DANCE (CLOSED POSITION)   Partners face each other. Male holds the female's right hand in his left hand. Male's right hand holds the back of the female above the waist. The female's left hand is placed on the male's right shoulder.

VARSOVIENNE or PROMENADE   Partners are side by side with the male to the left of the female. Right hands are held at the female's right shoulder (male's right arm is straight across female's shoulders). Left hands are joined in front of the male with the female's left arm straight. (This position does not require a coed setting.)

Alphabetical Index
of Dances*

*See Appendix C for a list of dances by level of difficulty.

Subject Index